Apollo the Wolf-god

Daniel E. Gershenson

Journal of Indo-European Studies
Monograph Series, No. 8

Institute for the Study of Man
Washington D.C.

To Hama

———————

ISBN 0-941694-38-0

Copyright© 1991, Institute for the Study of Man, Inc.

P.O. Box 34143,
Washington D.C. 20043
Tel: (202) 266-9908 Fax: (202) 508-1018
iejournal@aol.com
www.jies.org

Table of Contents

PREFACE

This study is meant to be a contribution to the understanding both of ancient Indo-European thought and of the ancient Greeks and of their contribution to civilization. In linguistics today the Sapir-Whorf hypothesis of linguistic relativism is sufficiently accepted. It is generally understood that speakers of different languages see the world differently and divide reality into quite different groupings. The religious vocabulary of a people is perhaps the best testing ground for this hypothesis. Renato Poggioli, writing of the ambiguous phenomenon known under the Russian name of двоеверие, "double faith" or "doublethink," that is, on the persistence in the cultural life of Kievan Russia of pre-Christian traditions and beliefs side by side with the liturgy and doctrine of the new creed, has brought what may be viewed as its proof from the evidence of it in the Russian epic *Prince Igor*.[1] Even after the conversion to Christianity of the Prince of Kiev and his men, and in the presence of people who had themselves participated in the battle against the Polovetsians (Cumans) two years before, the bard sang of the interference in the battle of such Slavic deities as Dazhbog, Stribog and Veles. From this the conclusion is inescapable that although the ancient Slavic deities were no longer afforded belief by the listeners their functions were inseparable from their view of reality. For the Christianized people of Kievan Russia they remained as much an indispensable part of their vocabulary, and hence of reality, as they had been when they were actually afforded belief. Any polytheistic system, by its very nature, functions the same way.

The wider complex of the wolf-name in ancient Greek thought discussed below is of the same nature; it is a datum of ancient Greek and, even earlier, of ancient Indo-European thought. The same surely goes for many more of the gods and heroes of ancient Greece, and some day they too may be elucidated. Alex Wayman has written, "Deities are in some respects similar to words. One word will come to acquire much of the connotation of another word, not necessarily a synonym, and thereby cause that other to fall into disuse... a deity has his functions among the functions exhibited by the various deities of a given culture. One deity can replace another by acquiring the major characteristics of that other, and yet be of different character. Or, as sometimes happens, when one deity acquires certain characteristics of another, the latter may simply lose those and continue on with altered or diminished character."[2]

---

[1] Renato Poggioli, *The Spirit of the Letter, Essays in European Literature* (Cambridge, Mass., Harvard 1965) "The Igor Tale," pp. 3-49, an English version of the introduction to *Cantare della gesta di Igor; Epopea russa del XII secolo*, introduction, translation, and commentary by Renato Poggioli; annotated critical text by Roman Jakobson (Turin, Einaudi 1954).
[2] "Studies in Yama and Mara," *Indo-Iranian Journal* 2 (1959) 58.

CHAPTER I
THE WOLF AND APOLLO

We all meet the wolf when we are very young. Hardly a child grows up in a land reached by Western Civilization without hearing the tale of Little Red Riding Hood and shaking with fear when the wolf reveals himself in grandmother's bonnet lying in the bed. Even little tots of two and three learn to be afraid of the wolf and his big teeth. They listen with wide-eyed anxiety and deep sympathy to this story, or to the tale of the seven (or three) little geese (or goats) who are left alone by their mother, only to be outwitted by the clever wolf, gobbled up by him, and in the end, with the exception of the one who had hidden in the clock and was never eaten to begin with, happily extracted all alive by the hunter from the belly of the wolf he had killed. In English-speaking lands the story of The Three Little Pigs, two of whom also fell prey to the wolf is no less well-known.[1]

The wolf who eats little children and lies in wait at unexpected turns, or craftily misleads them into believing in his good intentions, is an ancient bugaboo.[2] In more recent times, as well as in antiquity, other animals have appeared in his place, but he still retains his primacy in frightening children. The tales told of all of them play on the very small child's fear of being devoured. As the child grows older the wolf is identified with the stranger of whom he must always beware, as the distinction between friend and foe becomes a meaningful, if not always a clear, one.

Yet not all the wolves we encounter in story are as easy to identify as the wolf in the story of Little Red Riding Hood. Children are likely to meet up with another facet of the hostile wolf in the English story of The Three Little Pigs, or The Three Little Geese.[3] The wolf's role here has been connected with the wolf's role in the story of the seven goslings,[4] but part of the story here is different. In these stories the wolf, in

---

[1] Cf. J. Bolte and G. Polivka, edd., *Anmerkungen zu den Kinder- und Hausmärchen der Brüder Grimm* I (Leipzig 1913) 37ff. Jakob Grimm No. 5 is *Wolf und die 7 jungen Geißlein*, "The Wolf and the Seven Little Geese."

[2] The horse that bites and Mormō (Theoc. 15.40) seem to have been the staple characters used to frighten children in ancient Greece. Mormō played the role in that culture of the "big, bad wolf" today (cf. the word μορμολυκεῖον in Arist. *Thesm.* 417, etc., used also for a scarecrow) and is closely connected with wolves.

[3] Cf. Bolte-Polivka (n. 1 *supra*.) 1.40-41, and Joseph Jacobs, *English Fairy Tales*[3] 250, XIV.

[4] On the story of the Three Little Pigs or Geese, or another variant of it, see Archer Taylor, "A Classification of Formula Tales," *Journal of American Folklore* 46 (1933) 78, where these stories are listed under "Blowing the house in." The outline of the story as he gives it is as follows: The wolf blows in the goose's house but can not blow down the hog's house. Instead he comes through the chimney, and falls into the fire or is boiled to death. Joseph Jacobs, *ibid.* (in the previous note), gives as a parallel Bernoni, *Trad. Pop. punt.* iii p. 65, "The Three Goslings," and a Negro tale in *Lippincott's Magazine*, Dec. 1877, p.753 ("Tiny Pig"). He suspects that the pigs were originally kids because of the hair on their chins, for the pigs refuse to let the wolf in with the words "No, no, by the hair of my chinny chin chin."

More references are found in A.A. Aarne and Stith Thompson (tr. and ed.),*The Types of the Folktale* (FF Communications No. 184, Helsinki 1961) 124 (p. 50). They refer to E.T. Kristensen, *Danske Dyrefabler og Kjaederemser* (Aarhus 1896) 48f., Nr. 68-70. Here it is a fox who attacks a lamb or a goose, and sow, but in one version (68) he tramples the houses down instead of blowing them in. In the Walloon version of this folktale in George Laport, *Les Contes populaires wallons* (FF Communications 101, Helsinki 1932) 124 (p. 30), the wolf destroys the huts of the first two pigs by breaking wind.

his attempt to get at his victims and devour them, "huffs, and he puffs, and he blows the house down." We accept him in this role naively, without questioning a wolf whose most prominent attribute is the strength of his lungs, or some other part of his body, and the force of the wind that issues from him. In fact, as soon as we reflect on it, it becomes apparent that this wolf is different from the wolves we hear about in nature. This wolf represents the wind. As soon as we know that for a fact, "wind-wolves," if we look for them, turn out not to be so rare as we might have supposed.

In this book I shall try to show that the wind-wolf has certain well-defined functions, some beneficial, connected with agriculture, and others destructive functions, and that many of the same functions belong to the god Apollo in ancient Greece, who bears the wolf-name as well. After all, both the wind-wolf and Apollo are mythological figures, and of another mythological figure, Achilleus, in the story of Tēlephos (cf. *CPG* ATW p. 2.16, Philostrat. *Heroic.* 687, Lucian *Nigrinus* 38, Ael. *H.A.* 1.56, and Charit. Aphrod. 6.3) the Greeks related that ὁ τρώσας ἰάσεται, "he who has wounded shall heal," meaning that destructive powers go hand in hand with beneficial ones. So the devouring wind-wolf of the folk-tale joins hands with the wolf that promotes the growth of the grain. The figure of the wolf in general has been much discussed in anthropological, social and historical studies in connection with adolescent bands termed youth confraternities (Männerbünde, Jünglingsbünde, Jungmannschaften),[5] where its destructive powers are much in evidence. That approach has concentrated on transformations between human and animal form, the theriomorphy discussed *infra*. Here our interest is in a wider field: the varied applications of the wolf-name; and our approach is somewhat different.

The method used in this study is to examine similarities between mythological figures, and more specifically between Apollo, an ancient Greek deity, and other figures. It would, however, be an insurmountable task and beyond the scope of this work to collect all parallels to or give an exhaustive account of the mythological figure in question here, as it is of any mythological figure. As is the case with most comparative studies in folklore and mythology, certain attributes are ascribed to the god or hero, and with them come an entire complement of affinite qualities and connections. Still, it is by no means the intent of this work to prove any direct correlation or correspondence between any one of the cases cited and any other. It should be quite apparent to the reader that within the scope of this study much that is not directly relevant to the case at hand will of necessity be omitted. The reader

---

[5] The earliest exponent of the data on youth confraternities seems to have been Heinrich Schurtz, *Altersklassen und Männerbünde* (Berlin 1902). Not long after, Gilbert Murray championed the idea that the wolf in Greek mythology stands for such werewolf confraternities on pp. 72ff. of "Anthropology in the Greek Epic Tradition outside Homer," in *Anthropology and the Classics*, ed. Robert Marett (Oxford 1908) 66-92, on the basis of the comparative evidence. His view is upheld by Louis Gernet, "Dolon le loup," *Annuaire de l'Institut de Philologie et d'Histoire orientales et slaves* 4 (Brussels 1936=*Mélanges Franz Cumont*) 189-208 (reprinted in Louis Gernet, *Anthropologie de la Grèce antique* [Paris, Maspéro 1968] 154-171) as well as by Henri Jeanmaire, *Couroi et Courètes* (Lille 1939) esp. p. 540ff., and by Martin Nilsson as well, "Grundlagen des spartanischen Lebens," *Opuscula Selecta* 2 (Lund 1952) 826ff. (first published *JRS* 12 [1912]). The comparative evidence has been elaborated upon by Bronislaw Malinowski, Myth in Primitive Psychology (London 1926); Lily Weiser, *Altgermanische Jünglingsweihen und Männerbünde* [=*Bausteine zur Volkskunde*, Heft 1] (Baden, Bühl, 1927); Otto Höfler, *Geheimbünde der Germanen* (1936); Stig Wikander, *Der arische Männerbund* (Lund 1938), Andreas Alföldi, *Die Struktur des voretruskischen Römerstaates* (Heidelberg, Winter, 1974), and many others.

should not automatically assume that what is not mentioned here has been overlooked, or is unknown; it may merely be the case that such material does not affect the argument either favorably or adversely.

There is another wolf who is almost as strange as the wolf who is the wind, when we think about it. That wolf is the kind she-wolf, like the one who adopted Romulus and Remus. Elsewhere we meet her cousins in the wolves who adopted Mowgli in Rudyard Kipling's *Jungle Book,* and took him into their pack. Other wolf children have actually been reported in recent times, as they have been for centuries. Are we then to change our opinion of the wolf's voracity and general ferocity? Wolves have really been shown to be less ferocious than they are often made out to be, but yet there is no sure report of a child's having been brought up by wolves. In recent times, the behavior of historical wolf-children has been related to infantile autism, a phenomenon no less alarming than the nursery wolf.[6] Where then do these stories come from? On the face of it the nurturing wolf is no more real than the huffing, puffing one, and needs explaining just as much.

If we follow the wolf further we find Apollo. At least, we learn that Aristotle's school of philosophy was called the Lyceum, that is the "wolf-place," because it was located in a district in the valley of the Ilissos close to Athens in a gymnasium attached to a temple of Apollo and called after the wolf (Greek λύκος), because that animal was closely associated with Apollo. Pausanias[7] relates that the Lykeion was named after a certain Lykos son of Pandion, and the god Apollo was first named Lykeios on this spot, that is, was first given this epithet here. At first sight the whole thing seems strange. Apollo's attributes, as they are generally presented, are not wolf-like in any significant respect. His aspect is mild,[8] especially as compared with that of Dionysos, and thus his wolf-nature too of necessity falls into the category of "mythical wolves," that is, wolves whose behavior is not at once comprehensible in terms of what is known of Canis lupus or Canis niger.

Hence we are concerned here with elucidating this side of Apollo's being in terms of a complex of ideas from the Indo-European linguistic area along the lines laid out by Joshua Whatmough. In a discussion of the correspondences between Indo-European languages[9] Whatmough wrote:

> As an illustration [of correspondences between Indo-European languages] it will be enough to take one word, the name of the "wolf" (perhaps not always clearly distinguished from "fox") that is widely enough distributed in regularly developed forms to suggest that the speakers of proto-Indo-European were familiar with the animal itself, and therefore must have lived in an area which was also its habitat. Thus there is a Sanskrit *vṛka-*, Greek λύκος, Latin (Sabine?) *lupus*, Gothic *wulfs*, Old Church Slavonic *vlъkъ*, Lithuanian *vilkas*. Greek ἀλώπηξ "fox" is probably, Italic (Latin)

---

[6] See the discussion of wolf-children and the weighing of the evidence in B. Bettelheim, *The Empty Fortress* (New York 1967). He concludes that the children thought to have been brought up by wolves in India were actually autistic.

[7] 1.19.3.

[8] In the interpretation of M. Nilsson, *Gesch. d. gr. Rel.*[2] (München 1961) I 536ff., and of C. Wernicke *PWRE* 2 (Stuttgart 1895) cols. 59-60. (to be discussed p.14f. *infra*) *e. g.*, he is primarily a pastoral god, guardian of the flocks. Older views would have him be a sun-god, certainly not wolvish. Nevertheless, his connections with death, with youthful clubs, or confraternities, and with the stranger, are not so cheerful.

[9] *S. v.* Indo-European, *Encyclopedia Britannica* (1968) Vol. 12, p. 171f.

vulpes "fox," certainly related. But there are some curious divergences: Swedish and Norwegian use *varg* "the villain, criminal" for wolf, Irish has *fáel* and (modern Irish) *fáel chú*; compare *cū allaid* ("wild dog") in the sense of "wolf" (the etymology of *fáel* is unknown[10]), and also modern Irish *mactire* (literally "son of the land"). It was common to use names of animals to designate human beings (much as in Uncle Remus): thus we have Sanskrit *Vṛka-karman* and *Vṛka-bandhu*, Greek *Lykourgos*, *Lykophrōn*, *Lykos*, Serbian *Vûk* and *Vukovoj*, Old High German *Wolf-arn*, *Wolf-bado*, *Wolfo*, Gothic *Wulfila*, Modern German *Wölfflin* and English *Wolf(e)* as a surname. This hardly looks as if the wolf were a beast of prey, but rather was thought of as a leader or totem. In the same way the Italic tribe Hirpini derived their name from *hirpus*"wolf," which will recall the legend that Romulus and Remus were suckled by a she-wolf, a story to which modern India constantly furnishes parallels. The notion of the werewolf (Gothic *wáir* "man") is that of a being which has the capacity to convert itself from man to wolf and back again at will. Evidently it is a mistake to draw conclusions from a mere list of names of animals or of plants and trees; it is necessary to know what these names connoted in a wider context than a merely zoological or agricultural catalogue.

It is precisely the wider context of the wolf-name that forms the subject of this study; the animal is not in question, but rather its symbolism and that of its name. The leading thread in our investigation is the question of Apollo as a wolf-god. The reader who has the patience to follow will discover that the clews that deity provides lead directly to the elucidation of the wider context of the wolf-name in the Indo-European linguistic area (and even beyond), and that that wider context reveals, in the last analysis, the ideology of the ancient Indo-European wolf-confraternities. It should be clear from what follows that Apollo was a thoroughly Indo-European god, the majority of whose cult-forms are directly associated with Indo-European traditions. In the context of modern classical scholarship, where Martin Nilsson's view that Apollo was actually a Hittite "god of gates" of Semitic (Babylonian) origin[11] is still widely held, this is an innovation.

All told, the Greek Apollo Lykeios, "Apollo the Wolf-god," has given rise to a large number of theories, both ancient and modern. So varied have the answers been to the questions, "Who was Apollo Lykeios?" and "What does his wolf-nature represent?" that they bear witness, taken all together, to the fundamental confusion that prevails concerning the subject. It comes as no surprise, then, to learn that the doyen of modern classical scholars, Wilamowitz, denied any validity at all to the problem, insisting as he did on an ancient tradition that Apollo's wolf-nature was a late misunderstanding.[12] Despite his dissent the validity of the ancient evidence for Apollo's association with the wolf is undeniable.

Our path will lead us to direct ancient Greek evidence, non-literary and literary, showing the non-derivative nature of the Greek wolf-complex, as well as to indirect, comparative evidence, largely from the Indo-European sphere. The traditions of the Indo-European linguistic area elucidate the question about Apollo's wolf-nature,

---

[10] But see note 20 *infra*, on this question.

[11] *Ibid.* (note 8 *supra*).

[12] U. v. Wilamowitz-Moellendorff, *Die Glaube der Hellenen* (Darmstadt 1959[3] originally published 1932) 1.

illuminating many facets of Whatmough's examples from the wolf-name; for the wider context of the wolf-name is a complex of active forces in the world. All these forces pertain to two things which are essentially one: agriculture, and influences from beneath the earth's surface. The same forces in other contexts are associated with other animal names that have similar connotations, namely "raven" and "dolphin," and their synonyms, in the first place, and "snake," "bear," "locust," etc. in the next. All of these once had a place in the purview of "the beyond."

The wolf's subjection to Apollo, the chief representative among the Olympian gods of the younger generation's strength in the Greek tradition, also appertains, at a further remove, to the context of Apollo's most celebrated feat, the slaying of the dragon, a context not usually connected with agriculture. Another of Apollo's chief functions, that of leader of the young confraternities, the group called the *ephēboi*, the young warriors who grew up to be the pillars of Greek society and defenders of its values, is firmly within the same sphere, inasmuch as the ephebes, like so many other associations of young and old in the Indo-European linguistic sphere, have been shown to be identical to the werewolves. We shall be able to close our argument when we discover, in the sequel, that werewolves appear to have strong agricultural connections in the Indo-European linguistic area.

To return to the wind-wolf we began with, we may now be more specific about the complex of active forces associated with the wolf-name; for the wind is one of its primary components: the wolf who stands for the wind is not uncommon in the Indo-European linguistic area. We have recognized him in the story of "The Three Little Pigs," and we find him again in ancient Greece. Most important for our investigations is his implied presence in one ancient etiology given for the epithet Λύκειος borne by Apollo. This is the version of the founding of the temple of Apollo Lykeios at Argos told by Servius,[13] in his list of explanations for Apollo's wolf epithet quoted below. Here a wolf appeared before Danaos doing battle with a bull and prevailing, to signify that the temple must be built. The story is connected with the drought which prevailed in Argos at the time Danaos and his daughters landed there. Danaos had sent his daughter Amymōnē to look for water. She came back with the report of a river gushing forth out of a spring, but flowing only a short way before it was swallowed up and disappeared, to her amazement, in a sinkhole in the ground. (According to Ps.-Apollod. 2.1.4 Amymōnē became the bride of Poseidon, after he rescued her from a licentious satyr at the site of a spring.) When Danaos came to view the wonder, the god Apollo appeared to him and told him he would see a wolf battling with a bull at the place: should the bull be victorious he must build a temple to Poseidon, but if the wolf carried off the spoils of victory, he must dedicate the temple to him, Apollo Lykeios, the wolf-Apollo.

Servius does not comment on this story nor does he derive any theory of the nature of Apollo Lykeios from it. Nevertheless, the meaning of the story is clear to anyone who knows the streams that dry up in the summer in the numerous limestone areas containing sinkholes around the Mediterranean. One famous stream that flows for only a short distance before it falls into a sinkhole is the river Meles near Smyrna in Asia Minor, famed as the river on whose banks the poet Homer was born, and even reputed to be Homer's father.[14] In an inscription from Smyrna[15] this river appears as a

---

[13] Servius-Danielis *ad Aen.* 4.377.

[14] Philostratus *Imagines* 2.8 describes how the Meles falls into a sinkhole, in his ecphrasis of the love of Homer's mother Kritheis for the river.

[15] *CIG* 3165.

divine savior from disease and sickness. The association of healing and poetry is Apollonian, and suggests a firmer association of this god with sinkholes than we might be able to assume from the Argive tale in Servius alone.

Many streams around the Mediterranean dry up in the heat of summer. Homer[16] tells how the stream Xanthos near Troy was dried up, bested by Hephaistos, the god of heat and fire, and in fact water does not "quench fire" in the summer in Greece and its environs, but rather vice versa. Where there is a sinkhole in the rainy season, often there is to be found only a subterranean passage with a cool wind issuing from it in the summer, if the stream is one that stops flowing. Danaos came to the sinkhole in a time of drought. The question to be decided by the battle of the wolf with the bull was whether or not he had found a permanent source of water, one belonging to Poseidon, whose symbol is the bull, which appears so often on the ancient coins of Sicily with a human head to represent a river-deity.[17] The wolf, on the other hand, the opponent of the bull at the sinkhole,[18] must represent the cold air issuing from the underground passage, just as *Wolf* is a name for the wind in German, as the studies of Wilhelm Mannhardt showed.[19]

The wind-wolf appears in many other linguistic contexts as well, most clearly in the Germanic-speaking area. For example, Mannhardt quotes a Norwegian riddle asking who the wolf is who sits on the blue vault of heaven and howls out to sea; the answer is "the wind."[20] (Mannhardt ranks as the true modern rediscoverer of the wind-wolf; for he collected a great deal of evidence,[21] concerning the "wind-wolf" from a questionnaire which he sent to village after village in Germany, France, and some Slavic-speaking areas also. See Chap. 2 *infra*.)

Now winds, as we shall see, in Greece and elsewhere, are often thought of as issuing from somewhere, usually from caverns or other subterranean passages. We shall discover in Chap. 3 *infra* that many places in Greece and elsewhere where gas issues from the earth are named after the wolf. Thus, along with the wolf, the wind is part of the realm of the beyond, the unseen area beyond the visible surface of the land,

---

[16] *Il.* 21.361ff.

[17] On these coins from Catana and Gela see *e.g.* Colin M. Kraay, *Greek Coins and History* (Methuen, London 1969) 37, 39. These are fifth-century types; earlier coins bore the bull.

[18] Κατα βόθρον is the modern Greek word for "sinkhole." Dindorf in Stephanus *TGL* assumes it to have been the ancient word as well. According to *LSJ s. v.* Βέρεθρον, that is the ancient name for the underground course of a river in Theophr. *H. P.* 3.1.2, 5.4.6, and in Posidonius 55 (Muller); but in *Il.* 8.14 and *Od.* 12.94 the word refers to the realms of Tartaros and the cave of Skylla. It appears to be the Ionic form of βάραθρον, "pit," and that is the meaning it has in Pherekydes' account of the story of Ixion (*FGrH* 3F51b). Cf. also *Archiv für Papyruskunde* 7 (1924) for the same meaning. Ζέρεθρον is the Arkadian form of the same word, according to Strabo 8.8.4, where he uses this form of the word to refer to an Arkadian sinkhole. He uses the word ἠθμός, "strainer," in the plural, to refer to the Boiotian sinkholes at Lake Kopais.

[19] W.Mannhardt, *Roggenwolf und Roggenhund: Beitrag zur germanischen Sittenkunde* (Danzig 1866²).

[20] *Ibid.* 5. There seems to be a Celtic parallel to the lore embodied in this Norwegian riddle in a word found in the second book of the Mabinogi, *Branwen verch Lyr.* Derick S. Thomson, ed., *Branwen verch Lyr* (Dublin Institute of Advanced Studies 1961) note 4, on "ac yr eisted yd oedynt ar garrec Harlech, uch penn y weilgi," "and they were sitting on the rock of Harlech, above the sea," writes: "weilgi: mut. of gweilgi (1) 'the sea,' 'the deep sea,' (2) 'a strong sea,' 'heavy sea.' The word seems to be cognate with Ir. *fáelchu* 'wolf,' and it is a metaphorical term, or kenning, for the sea. A further possibility is that the first element is *gwael* in the sense of 'wild.'"

[21] *Op. cit.*

sea, and sky, properly identified by M. Eliade, *inter alia*, as "chaos," in contradistinction to "cosmos," the ordered world.[22] In fact, the hidden world, so well expressed by the Greek plura τα ἄδηλα, "those things that are not manifest," exists inside as well as outside; for whatever lies beneath the surface appearances of the visible, ordered cosmos, Greek τὰ φαινόμενα, is outside, but what lies beneath the surface appearances of the human person is termed "inside," or "one's insides," Greek τὰ ἔντερα.

If the hidden world inside the human body is parallel to the hidden world beyond the earth, the sea, and the sky, another dimension of the old theory of the macrocosm and the microcosm now stands revealed; for the wind inside man is of two sorts, wind, as in "breaking wind," and spirit, although in many languages they are referred to by the same name, and hence may have been considered identical. If the wolf-name is applied to the wind, then by extension we should be able to understand its application to spirited young men and women in a social context. Here we find the werewolves and the ἔφηβοι (ephebes) who stood under Apollo's tutelage, as well as numerous nations and tribes that bear the name of the wolf. We shall discover that many of these peoples were settled in or near localities bearing the name of the wolf by reason of some natural phenomenon. The "high spirits" Homer and Plato talk of, θυμός and μένος, belong in the context of spirit as well.

The wolf, like the wind, is a messenger from outside, from the chaotic world, to the world of order. Eliade gives these two realms other names as well, and using his terminology we may term the wolf a messenger between the "sacred" and the "profane," in many cases, although far from universally. Despite his affinity to the wind the wolf is basically earthbound in mythic thought, although he may sometimes fly; his celestial and marine counterparts are the raven and the dolphin.

Apollo Lykeios is widely attested. In fact, just as the name of the wolf appears widely as an element in nomenclature in the rest of the Indo-European linguistic area, so it does in Greece too, especially in the sphere of Greek myth and religion.[23] This

---

[22] *The Sacred and the Profane* (New York, Harper, 1961).

[23] The *lyk*- element is found, *e. g.*, in the names Lykos, Lykoreus, Lykaon, Lykurgos, Lykortas, Lykomedes, Autolykos, and Harpalykos, from myth, and in the divine epithets Lykaios, Lykeios, Lykēgenēs, Lykoreus, and Lukios, all epithets of Apollo, as it is in λύκος, "wolf."

Greek personal names borne by individuals of the historic period with the *lyk*- root include Lykeas, Lykēs, Lykidēs, Lykinidēs, Lykinos, Lykiskos, Lykoleōn (the wolf-lion), Lykomēdēs, Lykos, Lykurgos, Lykophrōn, Lykōn, according to J. Kirchner, *Prosopographia Attica*[2] (Berlin 1966) 2.20ff., who lists those where the wolf-name is the first element in the name, but not those having it as the second element, *e. g.*, Aristolykos, Polylykos, Philolykos, Mnēsilykos, etc., with the exception of Autolykos (Kirchner 1.183) and Epilykos (*ibid.* 325). F. Bechtel, *Die Personennamen des Griechischen bis zur Kaiserzeit* (Halle 1917) 289, adds a number of names of this last sort with the place each is attested, as follows: Halkolyka, Thyphrestos; Harkolyka, Tainaron; Hermolykos, Kalymna; Timolykos, Kos (*CGC Caria* 197 42 [300-190]; and gives the following additional names from the *lyk*- root: Lykeas, Troizen *IG* IV 764 I_8 Lykeus in Lykeidas, Sparta, Ditt. *Syll.*[3] 84; Lykēn Dyrrhachion *CGC Thessaly* 71, 93 (229-100); Lykēs Perithoidēs *IG* II 5 no. 834 II_{89}; Lykias, Pharsalos, *IG* IX_2 no. 234$_{160}$; Lykiadas (Lykomēdēs Kasareus) *IG* xii 3 suppl. no. 1269$_4$; Lykon (Autolykos Krēs) *IG* V2 no. 293$_3$; Lykōnidē, Eretria *IG* xii9 no. 249B_{406}; Lykaithos, Athen.; Lykormas Larisaios, Paus. 10.78; Lykortas Megalopolitas, Ditt. *Syll.*[3] 626; Lykōpēs, Sparta, Herod. 3.55; Lykōtadas, Argos, Ditt. *Syll.*[3] 564$_4$; Lykodorkas, Argos; Lykolas Trichonios; Lykoleōn, Athen.; Lykomēdē, Iulis *IG* xii 5 no. 609$_{82}$; Lykomos, ancestor of the Lykomidai of Phlya, Plut. *Them.* 1; Lykophrōn, Corinth, Herod. 3.50; on p. 584 Bechtel adds other names such as Loukidas, Tanagra; Lykideus, Priene; Lykinos; and Lykiskos.

name is associated with Apollo in the majority of cases, as it is with the name of no other deity.[24]

Numismatic evidence tends to show that in the early fifth century Apollo had been brought into direct association with the wolf at Argos. The wolf characteristically figures on Argive coins. During the Persian wars, Argos "issued drachms, half-drachms, and obols with the whole, the half..., or the head of a wolf, the square punch-mark on the obverse being filled with a large A,"[25] while copper coins (half-drachms minted down to about 370[26]) long showed the forequarters of a wolf with rays extending from his head on their verso, while Apollo was pictured on their recto.[27] Silver coins of the same city almost invariably showed the half-wolf.[28]

The clearest numismatic indication, however, of Apollo's connection with the wolf is found on Imperial coins of Tarsos in Lykaonia minted during the reigns of Severus Alexander and Maximinus. A naked Apollo Lykeios is shown grasping the forepaws of two wolves while standing on the omphalos at Delphi.[29]

We know of Apollo Lykeios from a number of ancient written sources. His cult

---

[24] Other gods who have wolf-epithets, or at least epithets containing the *lyk-* root, are Zeus, Artemis, and Pan; for Lykaios appears as an epithet of Zeus (*v.* Cap. 6 *infra*), and also of Pan (*Anth. Pal.* 6.188 [Leonidas of Tarentum], Verg. *Aen.* 8.344, Dion. Hal. 1.32, and Calp. Sic. 4.132). On an inscription from Tegea (*I. Lac. Mess. Arc.* 2 *IG* v2.93) Pan has the epithet Lykeios, probably his original epithet there (cf. Paus. 8.53.11), where Pan Nomios, *i. e.* Pan of the flocks, had a sanctuary in the Nomian Mountains, a little beyond the Lykaian mountain in Arkadia, according to Paus. 8.38.11., and in Theoc. 1.123 he is said to wander about on Mount Lykaion. (For a probable connection between the epithet Lykeios and the epithet Nomios *cf.* p. 16 *infra*.)

Artemis had the epithet Lykeia in Miletus, along with Apollo Lykēos there (*v.* n. 60 *infra s. v.* Miletus), and at Troizen, according to Paus. 2.31.4, who reports that Hippolytos built her a temple there. He guesses at the origin of the name: "either Hippolytos got rid of wolves who were ravaging the area of Troizen, or else the Amazons, one of whom was Hippolytos' mother, gave Artemis the name." Artemis had a wolf-epithet in Arkadia as well; at Lykoa, at the foot of Mount Mainalon, there was a shrine of Artemis Lykoatis (Artemis of Lykoa) containing a bronze statue (Paus. 8.36.7). Artemis is more closely associated with the bear, however, in her cult as a goddess of motherhood and childbirth at Brauron in Attika, where she bore the epithet Iphigeneia, and especially in Arkadia, in the story of Kallisto, mother of the Arkadians. This is an important link in establishing the wider significance of the wolf-name.

Lykeios, found in the manuscripts of Paus. 8.38.6-7 as an epithet of Zeus, has long since been emended to Lykaios. Otherwise Apollo and Pan are the only gods to bear this epithet in the masculine gender.

[25] Charles Seltman, *Greek Coins* (London 1933) 95.

[26] *Ibid.* 169.

[27] Cf. T.E. Mionnet, *Description des médaillles antiques grecques et romaines* (Paris 1807) II 233, nn. 31, 32, 36; Müller-Wieseler, *Denkmäler der alten Kunst* 1, 41, 177; Fr. Imhoof Blumer, "Anaktorion, Argos, Lepsimandos; Tempelschlüssel auf Münzen," *Numismatische Zeitschrift* 3 (1871) 404 n.6, and *Boeotien und Argos* 55 n.17. Six coins of Argos showing the wolf with rays extending from his head on their verso are found in Havercamp *ad Orosium* p. 20. The recto shows a bearded figure which might be Apollo (cf. the bearded Apollo on the coins of Miletus).

[28] Cf. Mionnet, *ibid.* 229ff., 4-30.

[29] Maximinus' bust is pictured on the obverse: G.F. Hill, *Brit. Mus. Cat. of the Greek Coins of Lykaonia, etc.* 202ff., XXVI.4; XXVII.10; G. MacDonald, *Greek Coins in the Hunterian Collection*, II 551, 34 Tab. LX 15. Cf. also Fr. Imhoof-Blumer, "Coin types of some Kilikian Cities," *J. H. S.* 18 (1898) 171, 173.

The earlier coins of Tarsos shown in Colin M. Kraay, *Greek Coins* (London 1966) Pl. 673 (with an Aramaic inscription) and 674, are different types The city's connection with Lykaonia, established only later, is, no doubt, the reason the wolf appears on the later coins.

at Argos was particularly celebrated. It would seem to have been an oracular cult, like the cult of Apollo at Delphi, or at Klaros. A "prophetess," Gr. προφῆτις, of Apollo Lykeios at Argos is mentioned by Plut. *Pyrrhus* 31.[30]

Paus. 2.19.3, in his discussion of the temple of Apollo Lykios (as he calls him here, and again at 8.40.5) at Argos, calls it the chief building of note in the town. He relates that it was built by Danaos shortly after his invasion of Argos. A wolf, identified by the earlier inhabitants of the place with Danaos, the invader, attacked a bull belonging to them outside the walls of the city, and felled it. Danaos, Pausanias tells us, believed the wolf had been sent by Apollo. According to the people of Argos the wolf had been despatched by the god precisely because the invader had been living among his victims as much, or as little, as the wolf lived among men. This is the earliest theory we have concerning the nature of Apollo Lykeios (or Lykios). The god would clearly be a wolf-god, but his patronage of the wolf is here set in a social frame of reference; he is the patron of the outcast from society, the enemy or the outlaw. This is the aspect of the wolf-nature that belongs to the "lone wolf" we are familiar with.[31]

In Plut. *Pyrrhus* 32.9 the same story recurs, with the added detail that it was when Danaos first landed near the Pyramia in Thyreatis on his way to Argos that he saw the fight between the wolf, which he imagined represented himself inasmuch as it was a "stranger" attacking a native, just as he intended to do, and the bull. He did not attack Argos as he had planned because the king there, Gelanor, was overthrown in a revolution.

Another version of the founding of the temple of Apollo Lykeios at Argos is that told by Servius,[32] in his list of explanations for Apollo's wolf-epithet quoted *infra*. Servius' version of the omen that led to the building of Apollo Lykeios' temple at Argos may be as old or older than the one Pausanias and Plutarch give. According to Paus. 2.19.4., and Plut. *Pyrrhus* 32.9, a βόθρος, or artificial pit,[33] was dug in front of the temple at Argos. Perhaps this pit was meant to represent the sinkhole of Servius' narrative. Also, in front of the temple there stood a relief supposed to have been dedicated by Danaos himself, showing a wolf and an ox battling, with a girl, identified as Artemis, throwing a rock at the ox, according to Pausanias. In his account he also relates that inside the temple, next to the image of Biton, there burned an undying fire, said to have been lit by Phorōneus, at Argos reputed to have been the first man.[34]

---

[30] Cf. also Σ Aesch. *Suppl.* 686 (from *PWRE* 13,2 col. 2268), *I. Arg.* (*IG* 4) 1119, a proxenic decree for deposit in the temple, published by N. Novosatzky, *Ephem. Arch.* (1885) 57. Following Soph. *El.* 6, the earliest literary evidence for the wolf-Apollo, Eustathius *ad Il.* 4.101 (449.1), repeats that the marketplace of Argos was called Lykeios (cf. also Hesychius *s. v.* Λύκειος ἀγορά).

[31] Otto Gruppe was the last to make this feature of the wolf-Apollo basic to a purely mythological approach to the problem. It appears to have first been emphasized in modern times by Otto Jahn, "über Lykoros" *Ber. d. sächs. Ges. d. W.* (1847) 423 (cf. H. Immerwahr, *Die Kulte und Mythe Arkadiens* I [1891] 21ff.). It has been basic to the interpretation of the wolf-context in the Germanic linguistic area, and in the last decades it has found its place in classical scholarship as well, in the work of the "sociological" school. *V.* Cap. 6 *infra, et passim*.

[32] Cf. p. 5 and n. 13 *supra*.

[33] Βόθρος is a synonym of βάραθρος, and can easily stand for the Arkadian ζέρεθρον in the story told by Servius of the battle of the wolf and the bull at Argos.

[34] This account is also found in Σ Soph. *El.* 6. If the girl is Artemis the connection with Apollo is corroborated; for she aided him in many of his dragon-slaying exploits, and here the bull would be a common enemy.

Thus there can be no doubt that in ancient Argive tradition the epithet Lykeios was associated with the wolf. The connection is found in literature as well. The Lykeian marketplace in Soph. *El.* 6-7 is identified as belonging to the "wolf-slaying god." Elsewhere too the god is pictured so: Paus. 2.9.6 tells of aid proffered to the people of Sikyon by Apollo Lykios when their cattle was being stolen away by wolves. He told them of a kind of poisonous bark that drove wolves away. This story and the epithet, or rather gloss, on Lykeios, λυκόκτονος "wolf-slaying,"[35] have given rise to one of the more popular, and simplistic, explanations of the wolf-epithet applied to Apollo, one that demands no investigation into the wider context of the wolf-name, outside the zoological identification, as demanded by Whatmough. This explanation, championed by M. Nilsson and H.J. Rose, among others,[36] makes the epithet Lykeios and the cult attached to it part of Apollo's role as "protector of the flocks," attested to by his rare epithet Nomios, applied by Kallimachos[37] to Apollo tending cattle in the service of King Admetos, and conceivably lent support to by his epithet ἀλεξίκακος, "warding off evil."[38]

In fact, Nomios ("protector of flocks," or else "god of law") is by no means so widely attested as a cult epithet of Apollo as are Lykeios and Agyiētēs.[39] There are only two localities where Apollo Nomios occurs without doubt, Arkadia and Epeiros, both attested in literary sources, and in one place an inscription has the word Nomios, and "Apollo" has to be supplied. Both Clement of Alexandria[40] and Cicero[41] tell of a cult of Apollo Nomios in Arkadia, while a sanctuary of his at Orikos in Epirus is mentioned by Ap. Rhod. 4.1216. He is mentioned in Theoc. 25.21, as well. In a dedication from Epidauros made by a pyrphoros, in IG 1² 447, the god's name has to be supplied. The meaning of the word νόμιος is by no means certain. It might just as well apply to Apollo's legal functions as to his pastoral role in the story of his servitude at the court of Admetos. For example, there is no unequivocal indication that Apollo was a god of herdsmen. In fact, to judge from bucolic poetry, whose main subject is the life of herdsmen, Apollo and the Muses are present to the herdsmen as gods of song and music, whereas Pan and the Nymphs have to do with the animals and their care. As far as Kallimachos' reference to Nomios in the context of Apollo's servitude at the court of Admetos is concerned, it is conceivable that his intent was to emphasize that Nomios referred to a pastoral, rather than a legal, aspect of the god's functions.

However, there is room to consider another possibility: that Apollo's role of "protector of flocks," attested in Kallimachos' reference, and perhaps inherent in the other occurrences of his epithet Nomios, belongs to the wolf-nature inherent in his wolf-name. His wolf-epithet will, in that case, not be equivalent to "warding off" or "killing wolves," Sophokles' testimony in *El.* 6-7 notwithstanding. What must be an ancient conception of the wolf found among the Estonians and the Latvians, as well as

---

[35] This epithet is restored in an epigram from Lerna, in the Argive plain, by Kaibel, *Epigrammata Graeca* (Berlin 1878) 821.6. If the restoration is correct, it may represent a rationalization of the epithet Lykeios, as it is in Sophocles as well. On the other hand, we shall see below that Apollo was the slayer of Lykos in Delphic story.

[36] This theory is adopted by Eckels, *Greek Wolf-Lore*, (Philadelphia 1937) as well.

[37] Kall. *Hymn. Ap.* 47.

[38] Paus. 1.3.4, 6.24.6, and 8.41.8.

[39] "Leader," or "God of Roads." As such this epithet comes close in meaning to Apollo's wolf-name, both in a physical and a social context.

[40] *Protr.* 2.28 P. 24 P.

[41] *De natura deor.* 3.57.

the Chukchees, calls the wolf a shepherd, while among Bulgarians and Vlachs he used to be known as a sheep-dog. It is told of this sheep-dog in Bulgaria that he was cheated of his wages and consequently began to maul the sheep.[42] Hence Nomios, if indeed it means "shepherding," and ἀλεξίκακος, "warding off evil," may once have served as epithets of the wolf-god himself. It is surely significant in this context that the epithet Lykeios was applied to the herdsmen's god Pan in Arkadia.[43]

There is little doubt that the epithet Lykeios was connected with the wolf at Athens as well. It is more than likely that a statue of a wolf stood near the temple of Apollo Lykeios at Athens; for the temple served as a court of law in early times, and courts at Athens were under the protection of the hero Lykos in the form of a wolf. According to Pausanias[44] this Lykos was reputed to have been the founder of the cult of Apollo Lykeios and the builder of his temple, the famous Λύκειον (Lyceum), and erector of the statue of the wolf that stood before it at Athens.[45] The same source[46] tells us both Apollo Lykeios and the people called the Lykians (who were originally called the Termilai, if they are from southern Anatolia) were named after the Athenian hero.[47] The Athenian cult of Apollo Lykeios seems to have been old and well-established; for we find that there were burial rites for murdered wolves (werewolves?) at Athens.[48]

A statue of a wolf stood at Delphi, the center of Apollo-worship in Greece, as well, a gift of the people of Delphi,[49] of whom Pausanias[50] tells the following story: A temple robber used to plague Apollo at Delphi. He used to hide out, with the treasure he had made off with, high above the town on the slopes of Mt. Parnassos, until he was killed by a wolf, who subsequently came down into the town howling. The people understood that the wolf had been sent by Apollo, and following him up

---

[42] *Handwörterbuch des deutschen Aberglaubens*, s. v. Wolf 3b. There is a Greek proverb λύκος ποίμην, "a wolf [as] shepherd," interpreted as meaning "a false friend," in *CPG* 2.513, Apostol. 10.96b.

[43] Cf. n. 24 *supra*.

[44] 1.19.3.

[45] The Lykeion was a holy precinct in the northeastern part of the city of Athens, perhaps including a temple of Apollo Lykeios. It was the place where the Archon Polemarchos held his court before the time of Solon (v. Suidas s. v. ἄρχων; Bekker, Anecdota 1.449, s. v. ἄρχοντες; Hesychius s. v. 'Επιλύκε<ι>ον, λυκαμβὶς ἀρχή.) For another explanation cf. Aristotle *Ath. Pol.* 3.5, who maintains the site is named 'Επιλύκειον after a certain Epilykos, who improved the building.

For the wolf's statue in law courts at Athens cf. Eratosthenes in Harpokration s. v. δεκάζων; Et. Magn. s. v. δέκασα; Hesychius s.v. λύκου δέκας; and Leutsch-Schneidewin, *CPG* 1.115 (Zenobius 5.2, also Diogenianus C100 and 320).

[46] *Ibid.*

[47] Cf. also *CIA* 3.89 and 292 for the temple of Apollo Lykeios at Athens. The second of these is the inscription on the seat of the priest of Dionysos at the theater of Dionysos. Other ancient texts where the Lykeion is mentioned in connection with the Polemarchos and military exercises have been cited in the last note. We may add for the gymnasium Harpokration s. v. Λύκειον and Lucian *Anacharsis* 7, where there is a description of the statue of Apollo Lykeios that stood in the gymnasium at the temple. Cf. P. Gardiner and Imhoof-Blumer, *op. cit.* for this statue on coins, and Σ Demosth. 24.114, Aristoph. *Peace* 356, and Xen. *Hipp.* 3.6 for cavalry exercises there. Thirty girls called Lykiades, according to Hesychius s. v., brought water to the temple. V. also Porph. *de Abst.* 3.18.

[48] Philostephanos of Kyrene (third cent. B.C.E.), quoted in Σ Ap. Rhod. 2.124 Wellauer.

[49] Paus. 10.14.7.

[50] *Ibid.*

the mountain they found the stolen gold. Apollo worshipped under the name Lykeios at Delphi is evidenced in a fifth-century inscription,[51] where we find δάρματα, "skins," dedicated to Apollo Lykeios by the local phratry of the Labyadai.

There is additional evidence of the wolf's association with the god of Delphi: In the amazing story cited by Phlegon of Tralles[52] from the historian Antisthenes of Rhodes, concerning the Romans' invasion of Aitolia in their campaign against Antiochus the Great (189-188 B.C.E.), a red wolf appears as the messenger of Apollo Pythios, the oracular god of Delphi come to the Greeks' aid. Antisthenes was alive, it seems, at the time of the campaign. On the shore a certain Publius, who had been uttering oracles, prophesied that a great red wolf would come to devour him; the wolf did so, but left his head, which continued to speak oracles and prophesy. This wonder was seen by an entire army on the beach, no doubt in a sort of trance.[53]

Moreover, a Delphian hymn to Lykōreus, there identified with the oracular Phoebus (i. e. Apollo), has survived.[54] The name Lykōreus is connected to the area of Delphi and Mt. Parnassos exclusively, as is Lykōros, and appears in a number of other literary sources besides this hymn.[55] In one source[56] it is connected with the pedigree of Kaphauros, the grandson of Apollo, called Lykōreus here, and Akakallis. The god may be given the epithet Lykōreus here because he and Akakallis were parents of Milētos, as well, the founder of the renowned city of the same name, who as a child was exposed to die but was fed by wolves until he was rescued by herdsmen.[57]

The epithet Lykōreus is surely related to the name of the town Lykōreia on Mt. Parnassos. The wolf's association with the region of Delphi at that spot may antedate the stories cited so far. According to one version of the story of Deukalion and the flood,[58] the remnant saved from the floodwaters were led to safety on the peak of Mt. Parnassos by howling wolves, and so called the town they founded there Lykōreia (a popular etymology from λύκος, "wolf," and ὠρύω "to howl"). Another possible etymology of the name, Pausanias notes,[59] is the name of the hero Lykōros, the son of Apollo and the nymph Korykia the patroness of the Korykian Cave on Mt. Parnassos. At any rate, Lykōreia, as an oracular site sacred to Apollo, was of greater antiquity than Delphi itself, and shows, through its mythology, that Apollo was long associated with the wolf in the region of Delphi.

Aside from Argos, Athens, Delphi, and Sikyon, epigraphic or literary evidence

---

[51] C. Homolle, "Inscriptions de Delphes," *BCH* (1895) p. 12, 1.37.

[52] Phlegon 3 *FGrH* 257F36.

[53] Cf. Schwartz in *PWRE* 1 cols. 2537-2538 (Stuttgart 1894).

[54] Eusebius *Praep. Ev.* 3.14.5, from the lost treatise of Porphyry *On the philosophy contained in oracles.*

[55] Kall. *hymn. Ap.* 19; Euphorion fr. 53 (Meineke); and the invocation to the Orphic hymn to Apollo (*Orph. Hymn.* 34[33].1).

[56] Ap. Rhod. 4.1490.

[57] Apollo and Akakallis were the parents of Amphithemis and Garamas, as well as Milētos, according to Apollonios of Rhodes *ibid.* and Σ *ad loc.*, and Ant. Lib. 30. Akakallis bore a son to Hermes, as well, however. This makes her case parallel to the birth of the twins Philammon and Autolykos ("the very wolf"), the former the son of Apollo and the latter of Hermes; moreover, according to another tradition Akakallis also bore the twins Phylakides and Phylandros to Apollo, and these children, like Miletos, were exposed, and were nurtured by an animal, this time a goat (Paus. 2.77, 10.16.5), a statue of which was sent to Delphi by the people of the city Elyros on Krete. Here we encounter the alternation of goat and she-wolf among the Greeks.

[58] Paus. 10.6.2f.;St. Byz. 279 Holst; Etym. Magn. 571.

[59] *Ibid.*

shows that the cult of Apollo Lykeios flourished, or was known, at least, in many other places in and around the ancient Greek-speaking world as well.[60] The month Lykios, corresponding to February-March, or to May, is attested from a number of other places.[61] It has been argued on the analogy of names of months like Karneios and Sminthios that the name implies the existence of a cult.

Aside from Lykeios and Lykios, not always clearly distinguished in the sources, Lykaios, reported by Hesychius[62] as an epithet of Apollo at Chryse on Lemnos, is, as we have seen, directly associated with the cult of Apollo at Delphi, and the name

---

[60] Megara, Epidauros, Lerna, Sparta, Eresos on Lesbos, Erythrai, Metapontium, Lemnos, Kalymna, Paros, Miletos, Jader (Zadar) in Illyria, and Xanthos and the Milyas in Lykia (in these last places under the name Lykios): Megara: *I.M.B.* (*IG* 7) 35, with just the name of the god in the genitive. Epidauros: Kavvadias, "Inscriptions from Epidauros," *Eph. Arch.* (1883) 89, Nos. 25-26. Lerna: a dedication to Apollo Lykeios, the Lernaean Nymphs, and Dionysos, in Kaibel, *Epigr.* 821. Sparta: Alkman, fr. 49 and 50 (*Poetae Melici Graeci*, ed. D.L. Page). Eresos: *I. Ins. M. Aeg.* 2 (*IG* 12.2) 526b31, where the name of the god appears in an oath. Erythrai: In a law concerning priesthoods from ca. 250 B.C.E. in Ditt. *Syll.* 1014.20. Metapontium: *I.G.I.S.* (*IG* 14) 647. Kalymna: R. Dareste, *BCH* 10 (1886) 240. Paros: an inscription published by Rhangabe in *Ant. Hell.* 2.896 (where "...ΥΚΕΙΟΣ" is read "'Απόλλωνος Λυκείου"). Lemnos: the references are found under Λύκιον ποτόν, Σ Soph. *Phil.* 1461, Zenobius 4.99, Hesychius and Suidas *s. v.* Miletus: *Siebenter vorläufiger Bericht von dem königlichen Museen über die Ausgrabungen in Milet und Didyma*: *Abh. Akad. Berlin, Anhang* (1811) 18. Jader (Yugoslav Zadar, Ital. Zara): *C.I.L.* 3.2902 ("Apollini Lycio," which may represent either Lykeios or Lykios). Xanthos and the Milyas: The Lykian temple at Xanthos, attested by Diodoros 5.56.1, who tells of its having been founded by Lykos the Telchin, and another Lykian oracular temple of the Milyas were dedicated to Lykios. For the latter temple see B. Keil, "Apollo in der Milyas," *Hermes* 25 (1890) 313-317, who restored [Λ]υ[κ]ίου in an inscription. Lykios may also appear on coins of Themisonion in Phrygia; it is restored there by Loebbecke: Λύκ[ιος] Σῷζων, a reading opposed by Ramsay in *AJA* (1887) 362.

Lykios, not Lykeios, is clearly the epithet applied to Apollo in Asia Minor, in historic Lykia and in Themisonion, if it does indeed occur there. In fact there were two countries named Lykia in ancient tradition: one near Zelea on the river Aisēpos in northern Asia Minor, and the other the historic Lykia in southwest Anatolia. Elsewhere there is confusion between Lykios and Lykeios, which sounded exactly alike by the end of the Fifth Century B.C.E., especially at Argos. Pausanias cites Lykios consistently when he speaks of Argos, and also when he speaks of Sikyon. Older sources give Lykeios for Argos, certainly. Nevertheless, Argos and Lykia are associated: the Kyklōpes who built the Cyclopean walls of Argos seem to have been of Lykian origin, and Proitos, for whom the walls of Tiryns were built by the Kyklōpes in order to allow him to wrest the throne from his twin brother Akrisios, was married to a Lykian princess, and Lynkeus, the Argive hero, also has Lykian connections. Both ancient and modern theories have had to account for the discrepancy in names and for the Anatolian connection.

[61] These are (1) Lamia, (2) Chaleion in Ozolian Lokris, (3) Epidauros Limera in Lakonia (near Sparta), (4) Byzantion, and (5) Chersonnesos. See for (1) *I. Gr. Sept.* 2, *I. Thess.* (*IG* 9.2) 75.18; for (2) H. Collitz, F. Bechtel, O. Hoffmann, *Sammlung der griechischen Dialekt-Inschriften* 2144, and also Haussoullier in *BCH* 5 (1881) 429; for (3) *I. Lac. Mess. Arc.* 1 (*IG* 5.1) 932.12 and cf. Mylonas in *Eph. Arch.* (1884) 86; for (4) Corpus gloss. lat. 5.218 (the Vocabularium of Papias); and for (5) Vassily Latyschev, *Inscriptiones Antiquae Orae Septentrionalis Ponti Euxini Graecae et Latinae* 4 (1901) 70. The month at Byzantion is identified with May in the source, that at Chaleion with the Delphic month Bysios, or February-March. According to Bischoff, *Leipziger Studien zur classischen Philologie* 7 (1885) 340, and Hiller von Gärtringen *IG* 9.2 p. 320, the month Lykeios at Lamia corresponded to March-April. Bischoff, in *PWRE* 13.2 (1927) 2270 suggests a festival called Lykeia in February-March; for he imagines that this was the season of the month Lykeios at Epidauros Limera and at Byzantion, as it was at Lokroi.

[62] *S. v.* Λύκειον ποτόν.

Lykēgenēs appears in the prayer of Pandaros the Lykian on Zeleia to Apollo.[63] Because of the stem *gen-*, "born of," in this word, it has been taken to refer to the context of a story told by Aelian,[64] to the effect that Apollo takes especial joy in the wolf because he was born to Leto when she was in the shape of a she-wolf. (This is an etiological tale to explain the epithet Lykēgenēs.) Aelian also surmises that the statue of the wolf set up at Delphi served as a reminder of Apollo's birth. There is further evidence for the myth of Apollo's birth from Leto in wolf's shape in the *Etymologicum Magnum*[65] which tells how Leto was turned into a wolf for the same twelve days in the year when she-wolves whelp. The same entry contains the notice that wolves had a special position at Athens: an Athenian who killed a wolf had to pay the bill for the funeral, ἐγείρει αὐτῷ τὰ πρὸς τάφον. The same information is found in Σ Ap. Rhod.,[66] with the added note that it derived from the *Commentaries* of Philostephanos of Kyrene who, as we have noted *supra*, may be speaking of werewolves. Hence it is likely that the story of Apollo's birth from a she-wolf is no more than an etiological explanation for the epithet Lykēgenēs, and in fact Aristotle[67] mentions, in the context of the twelve days in the year when she-wolves whelp, that Leto metamorphosed herself into wolf's shape out of fear of Hera, in an attempt to escape her wrath. The same tale is told by Antigonus of Carystus,[68] who adds that Leto had come to Delos for those twelve days, after sojourning among the Hyperboreans. This story may be Delian, as a matter of fact, but it could derive from Lykia, as well, where the local story, in one version, at least, told of Apollo's birth from Leto in wolf's shape on the banks of the river Xanthos.

As noted above (n. 60), the name Lykia signified one of two localities in antiquity. Eustathius, in his comments on the Lykian Pandaros and Apollo Lykēgenēs,[69] identifies "Zeleates," "Trojans," and "Lykians" as three names for one and the same people, and goes on to infer that Apollo Lykios had his name from that people, in northwest Asia Minor. This accords with the remark of Strabo[70] and with Arrian. These sources derive Apollo's epithet Lykios from the Lykia in northwestern Anatolia, and not from the more familiar historic Lykia. However, Eustathius[71] declares that either one of these two lands might be the origin of the epithet Lykēgenēs, and goes so far as to write:[72]

> Strabo (14.3.5) claims, however, that the Pandaros honored in Pinara, the great city of "Karian" Lykia, shared his name with the Pandaros of the *Iliad* only by chance, and that this latter is identical with Pandaros the son of Lykaon reported from Boiotia, whence Lykaon derived his name; for that was where Leto came, to escape Hera's envy, after she had borne Apollo.[73]

---

[63] *Il.* 4.101,119.
[64] *N.A.* 10,26.
[65] Ed. Gaisford, 680.21, *s. v.* πόλιοι λύκοι.
[66] 2.124 Wellauer.
[67] *Hist. An.* 6.35 (580a14).
[68] *Hist. Mir.* 56(61).
[69] *ad Il.* 2.284 (354).
[70] 12.4.6 following *Il.* 2.824.
[71] *ad Il.* 4.101 (449).
[72] *ad Il.* 4.88 (448).
[73] Boiotia seems to come into the picture here because of the town of Tegyra, which was one of the places that claimed to be Apollo's birthplace. Cf. Plut. *de defectu oraculorum* 5 [412c], *Pelopidas* 16; and St. Byz. *s. v.* Tegyra. Eustathius' syncretistic way of thinking will have

Hence, according to Eustathius in these passages, Apollo's epithet Lykios derived from the land of Lykia in "Karia" and the wolf-epithet Lykēgenēs also derives from that country. This is the source of one of the influential modern theories of the wolf-god's identity: Lykēgenēs, along with Lykios, and Lykeios, were thought to mean "the Lykian god." This is a solution that begs the question; for as we shall see, it is more than likely that the name "Lykia," like a number of other geographical names, means "wolf-country." Let us review the ancient theories of the origin of Apollo's epithets from the root *lyk-*: Three interpretations prevailed in antiquity as to the ultimate origin of these epithets. (1) Either they were thought to derive from the wolf, or else (2) from some root meaning "light," or (3) they were referred to some hero or giant named Lykos.

In traditional stories brought above from Delphi, Sikyon, and Argos the wolf was connected directly to these epithets. However, the meaning and the origin of the god's connection with the wolf appeared no less equivocal in antiquity than today. At Sikyon, as we have seen, he was said to have rid the area of wolves. The same origin of the epithet Lykeios is suggested by Σ Soph. *El.* 6 Elmsley, where, as we have seen, Apollo is termed Lykoktonos, "wolf-slayer" (and a similar theory was presumably held be all those who used the name). The Scholiast remarks:

> Some say Apollo is Lykoktonos because in his role as a divinity of flocks he kills his depredators, and that is why, they say, wolves are sacrificed to him at Argos; but others explain that the animal is holy to him in the same way as deer are to Artemis, saying that this is the reason the wolf appears on the Argive coinage.

This last theory, wherein Apollo was the patron of the wolf, and not its persecutor, is the one upheld by Plutarch also,[74] but it too begs the question: "Why was the wolf holy to Apollo?"

Hesychius,[75] remarking on the passage in Sophocles, refers the connection of the epithet "wolf-slayer" with Apollo's role as god of herds and keeper of the cattle to Aristarchus; but Hesychius goes on to remark that Aristarchus is wrong on this point because the wolf is holy to Apollo. Hence it appears that the attempt to explain Apollo's wolf-epithet in terms of the god's pastoral functions is as old as the third century B.C.E. Festus too[76] derives the epithet Lykeios from slaying wolves, and the same derivation is found in Servius-Danielis' *ad hoc* interpretation of the origin of the name Lykeia applied to Artemis at her temple in Troizen; he guesses it might refer to Hippolytos having rid the land of a plague of wolves.[77] Hence it seems that the protection of the flocks was the primary and most natural association a wolf-epithet evoked in later antiquity. Nevertheless it is unlikely that Apollo's epithet Lykoktonos is original. Just in the same way that Dionysos, one of whose sacred animals is the goat, had the epithet Aigobolos, "goat-striker,"[78] Apollo, it seems, assumed the wolf-slaying epithet in a pastoral context.[79] In the modern period, as we have noted, this

---

modified that claim to make it a place of refuge for Leto after Apollo's birth on Delos.

[74] *Pyth. oracl.* 12.

[75] *S. v.* λυκόκτονος θεός.

[76] P. 106 Lindsay.

[77] For a temple and a divine epithet called after a hero's experience cf. the temple of Athena Optiletis founded at Sparta by Lykurgos when his eye was put out, according to Paus. 3.18.2.

[78] Paus. 9.8.1. and cf. also p. 16 *supra*.

[79] With Apollo Lykoktonos and Dionysos Aigobolos we may compare Apollo Smintheus, who seems to have been first a mouse-god and only later a mouse-killer, on the evidence presented by

old explanation has enjoyed a great vogue, adopted as it was by Nilsson and Wernicke.[80] Nevertheless, from the beginning it encountered opposition from those who have preferred to view the wolf as the emblem of the loner, or who have found some other reason for Apollo's association with the wolf-name.[81]

Perhaps there is a hint of an older theory in the prayer of the chorus in Aesch. *Seven* 145-146: "Lykeios, lord, be wolvish toward the enemy's army." Here the implication is that the wolf will be fierce and destructive. This paronomasia is natural, and though it surely belongs to the sphere of the wolf, does not define the epithet, and, like the epithet Lykoktonos, is not likely to be original. These epithets may , however, indeed be ancient; and they are not directly part of any pastoral function. Apollo Lykeios and Lykoktonos both appear to have an ambiguous relation to their emblematic animal, and to the complex implied by its name. In the sway Apollo wields over the animal and the realm it represents he seems to possess the power of life and death; he appears as the wolf's patron and as its enemy at the same time.. In the same way, to quote a much better known case, Artemis is at once the protectress and the huntress of small animals. This should come as no surprise, however; for we have already encountered the Greek saying, ὁ τρώσας ἰάσεται, "he who has wounded shall heal," which illustrates how destructive powers go hand in hand with beneficial ones.

The most complete list of ancient theories concerning the meaning of Apollo's wolf-epithet to have come down to us is given by Servius-Danielis on *Aen.* 4.377. Of the eight hypotheses presented there six identify the *lyk-* root with actual wolves. The first tells that Apollo had the epithet Lycius (*sic!*) because he assumed the shape of a wolf when he slept with the nymph Kyrēnē. Kyrēnē is the eponymous nymph of the North African city of the same name, the capital of Cyrenaica, and the mother of Aristaios by Apollo. This report of Servius is unique. It may be connected with the worship of Zeus Lykaios in Kyrēne reported by Herodotos.[82] Then Servius suggests, in another unique communication, that Apollo is called Lykeios because he was in wolf-shape when he slew the Telchines.

Servius' third explanation tells us the wolf was the first to bring Apollo the laurel-branch from Tempē after the god's victory over the Python. This is the laurel

---

I. Trencsényi-Waldapfel, "Apollo Smintheus in Innerasien," *Acta Orientalia Academiae Scientiarum Hungaricae* 15 (1962) 351. We shall have occasion to speak of Apollo Smintheus at greater length below.

[80] Cf. n. 8 , and p. 11, *supra* .

[81] Aristarchus' theory of the meaning of the epithet Lykeios is the oldest extant *expressis verbis*, unless we follow D. Bassi in attributing Aristotle's account of Leto's wolf's-form to the speculations of earlier Homeric scholars concerning the origin of the epithet Lykēgenēs. Aristarchus' theory has appeared "conservative" and safe, connected, as it was later, with Apollo's epithet Nomios, and bolstered by a much-disputed interpretation of his epithet Karneios, deriving it from the pastoral sphere. Still, its only ancient support is from the story in Paus. 2.9.6 of the poisonous bark provided by Apollo to the Sikyonians to allow them get rid of a plague of wolves. Pausanias, however, goes on to remark that when he came to Sikyon he found Apollo Lykeios' temple there abandoned and his cult neglected, and this at a time it was still flourishing at Argos and at Athens, and no doubt elsewhere as well. The wolf's patronage of law-courts at Athens, and his battle with the bull as Argos certainly do not suggest that Apollo had him as his emblem because he wished to turn him away from the cattle and protect the flocks; from the Argive story, at least, rather the opposite would seem to be the case. The persistent opposition to the Aristarchus-Nilsson theory in antiquity is expressed aptly in Σ Soph. and in Hesychius.

[82] 4.203. The connection is suggested by Broholm "Kyrene," *PWRE* 12.1 (1924) col. 153.

with which Apollo crowned himself after his victory, and the usual version of the story is that Apollo brought it himself.[83] The next theory Servius propounds is the one adopted by Aristarchus and Nilsson, namely, that Apollo, as god of the flocks, destroyed the wolves at Sikyon. There then follow two other theories that appear nowhere else:

(1) "There is another story told to explain why the region is called Lykia. Diana used to enjoy hunting in the area, but once upon a time wolves penetrated those places in such force that they did away with all the game there in their approach. So the goddess was deprived of all the pleasure she had from hunting; for no animals but wolves remained. Apollo.... because of this (a temple) was dedicated." Because of a lacuna in the text here we can not quite make sense of this story, but the best conjecture is that it is an expanded version of Apollo's role as wolf-slayer, a role he appears in in Lykia as well.[84] Lykia would then be a land freed of wolves by Apollo, in an attempt to restore the game population of the area and so to please Artemis by restoring the hunt.

(2) The last theory is the one we have come to know that tells of the sinkhole. "When Danaos came [to Argos] from Egypt, he found the ground parched because of Neptune's anger at the River Inachus for having sided with Minerva against him when the honors for the foundation of Athens were assigned. So he sent his daughter Amymōnē out to look for water. She found a spring, noticed that it fell into a cleft in the ground, and all was then completely dry, and went back to tell her father. He was moved by her account of the amazing sight, and so he consulted the oracle of Apollo, who told him to go to the place where he would find a bull and a wolf fighting, and there to watch the outcome of the struggle. If the bull won, he was to build a temple to Neptune, but if the wolf was victorious he should consecrate a shrine to Apollo. Danaos saw the wolf win, and dedicated a temple to Apollo Lycius."

This version of the Danaos story assigns divine patrons to the wolf and the bull, namely, Apollo and Poseidon respectively,[85] and gives as the background of the struggle between them a drought and the discovery of a spring that disappeared into a sinkhole in the ground, appearing to dry up completely. It is noteworthy in this context that Hyginus[86] related that Amymōnē rode to Lerna on the back of a dolphin; although she is known as the bride of Poseidon, this may indicate some relation to Apollo Delphinios, also a patron of the dolphin and especially of dolphin-riders. Amymōnē is surely connected with water, as are all the daughters of Danaos. In any case, this story is of paramount importance for the argument that the wider context of the wolf-name includes the wind, because an empty sinkhole in the Mediterranean area will become a wind-tunnel, as we have noted.

Thus ancient sources which associate Apollo's epithets derived from the *lyk*-root with the wolf present no consensus on the reason for the association of the animal with the divinity. On the other hand, in those ancient interpretations that derive these epithets from a root meaning "light" we find a praiseworthy concern to discover whether a single conception lies behind all the different manifestations of Apollo's *lyk*-epithets. In fact, these are the only ancient interpretations that can be termed

---

[83] This is the version implied in Plut. *Quaest. Gr.* 12.293c, and in Ael. *V. H.* 3.1.

[84] Festus p. 6 Lindsay.

[85] The bull is as often identified with Dionysos as with Poseidon (Neptune). *V. infra* for further discussion of the roles of these two gods in connection with Apollo Lykeios and his struggle with the wolf.

[86] 2 (Erat. *Katast.* 31).

"scientific." They are the Stoic rationalistic counterparts of nineteenth century naturalistic interpretations, and they all connect the epithets from the *lyk-* root with Apollo's rôle as sun-god, and hence are controversial in the light of modern-day views of Apollo in this rôle.[87] Unlike the nineteenth-century proponents of the view that the wolf-epithets of Apollo are essentially light or sun-epithets,[88] the ancients who held this view mostly tried to explain why the wolf is associated with the sun or light. Macrobius *Saturnalia* 1.17.36ff. is worth citing in its entirety in this connection. He quotes a number of earlier authors, all of them Stoics, in support of this view; none of them are earlier than the third century B.C.E., while Macrobius fl. c. 400 C.E.:

> We have heard many explanations of Apollo's epithet Lycius. Antipater the Stoic [of Tarsos, second century B.C.E.] writes that Apollo is called Lycius "because all things in the world grow bright (or white, λευκαίνεσθαι) when the sun shines on them." Kleanthes [331-232 B.C.E.) remarks that Apollo is called Lycius because he eats away moisture with his rays just as wolves eat up flocks. The ancient Greeks called the first light that appears before sunrise λύκη from "brightness" [τὸ λευκόν]. Today too that time of day is called λυκόφως. The poet writes of it (*Il.* 7.433): "when dawn has not yet come and it still was ἀμφιλύκη," night, and again (*Il.* 4.101): "Pray to Apollo Lykēgenēs, famed for the bow," and Lykēgenēs means "he who gives birth to the λύκη," i. e., "he who created light with his rising." The refulgence of his rays precede the sun far and wide; little by little they thin out the mist of darkness and give birth to light.
>
> The Romans seem to have formed their word "lux" ("light") from λύκη, no less, just as they have taken so many other things from Greece. And the most ancient Greeks called the year λυκάβας, i. e. "the one who comes (βαινόμενον) and is measured out by the wolf."[89] The city of Lycopolis in the Thebaid also furnishes evidence that the sun was called λύκος. It worships Apollo and the wolf, λύκος, with equal reverence, honoring the sun in both cults, because this animal snatches up and consumes everything just like the sun, and, most of all, with its sharp eyesight it overcomes, and sees through, the night. Some people think that λύκοι have their name from λύκη, i. e. from the dawn, because these animals limit themselves to that part of the day, for the most part, to make their forays against the flocks, because after their nightlong fast the cattle are let out of their pens to pasture just before dawn.

Accordingly, Macrobius' identification of the wolf with the sun and light derives

---

[87] Cf. C. Wernicke *PWRE* 2 (Stuttgart 1895) cols. 59-60. Apollo as the god of the sun is not attested earlier than (a fragment of) Euripides *Cretans*, and he attained popularity in this rôle due to the scientific explanations of religious phenomena current in the Stoic school of philosophy. Joseph Fontenrose was the leading proponent of the view that Apollo the sun-god was a late invention. Cf. his "The Gods invoked in Epic Oaths," *AJP* 1968. His view prevails in scholarship today. On the other hand, Walter F. Otto, "Apollon," *Paideuma* 7 (1959-1961) 19-34, sees in Smintheus and Karneios (although not in Lykeios) old cult-epithets with solar implications.

[88] For a review of these modern theories v. Appendix A.

[89] Up to this point Macrobius is quoting Kleanthes, or at least paraphrasing him. What follows appears to be meant as support for Kleanthes' use of the word "wolf" as a synonym for "sun," with no further elucidation. On the word λυκάβας cf. D.J.N. Lee, "Lykabas," *Glotta* 40 (1962) 168ff. and Chap. 2 n. 46 *infra*.

from the learned circles of the Stoic school; for he cites Kleanthes and Antipater of Tarsos, and the Stoic origin of this doctrine is corroborated by Plutarch.[90] We can easily understand the great interest in fire and in the sun among the Stoics. They believed, along with Herakleitos and Zeno of Citium, their founder, that the world-soul, the *logos*, manifests itself in fire. Both Kleanthes and Antipater were younger than Aristarchus, who, as we have seen, held that Apollo's wolf-nature adheres to him by virtue of his role as god of flocks and shepherds, and does not seem to have known of a theory connecting the *lyk-* epithets with light. In any case, an early date for such an identification would be precluded, and the fact that Kleanthes must take pains to justify the use of the wolf-name to refer to the sun implies that "wolf" was not synonymous with "sun." (In the case of the wind, we see from Mannhardt's results that the word "Wolf" did indeed serve as a name for the wind in the Germanic linguistic area.)

The identification of the wolf with the stranger has survived from antiquity as well, and in recent times has secured confirmation, especially in France and Germany,[91] from the finding that in many societies "stranger-wolf" is the appellation of adolescent bands, estranged to some extent from the entire community and preying upon it. Today it is accepted that the wolf associated with such prehistoric and historic werewolf confraternities was not a totem, whatever that may be.[92] We shall see that one of its functions, at least, was to symbolize the wind, part and parcel of the wider context of the wolf-name. With this in mind, we hope to be able to clarify the ideology of these adolescent bands in Greece and elsewhere, and to gain a new insight into the way they justified their behavior.

The idea that Apollo Lykeios is connected with the fugitive or lone stranger, which occurs in Otto Gruppe's discussion[93] and in that of other modern scholars, like Immerwahr, seems to have originated in the version of the Danaos story found in Plut. *Pyrrhos* 31, and in Paus. 2.19, cited above These scholars have held that the epithet Phyxios applied to Apollo refers to the fugitive (from Gr. φεύγω "to flee" or "escape," Lat. *fugio*). This can not be, however; for such an interpretation has no basis in the primary source of the epithet, Philostratos *Her.* 10.4 p. 710f.[94] Philostratos tells how, when wolves came down from Mt. Ida in the ninth year of the siege of Troy, Palamedes understood the circumstance as a sign from Apollo that a plague was in the offing; his advice to the Achaians was to supplicate Apollo Lykios and Phyxios, for safety. "Phyxios" here refers to escaping the plague, not to the lone wolf, and moreover it is in hendiadys with Lykios, so that Philostratos means to say "Apollo Lykios, who can insure our escaping the plague" and hence has the function of a healer; still modern scholars have juxtaposed "Phyxios," understanding by it "of fugitives," with Danaos, the lone-wolf fugitive, and concluded that Lykios was the god of the outcast.[95]

---

[90] *De pyth. or.* 12 (400C-D).

[91] Cf. M. Eliade, "Les Daces et les Loups," *Numen* 5-6 (1956) 15-31, esp. p. 20ff. This article appears in English as Chap. 1 of M. Eliade, *Zalmoxis, the Vanishing God* tr. W.R. Trask (Chicago 1972) 1-20.

[92] See Claude Lévi-Strauss, *Totemism* tr. Roger Needham (Boston 1963), Chap. 1 "The Totemic Illusion," where "totem" has been shown to be a meaningless category; for "totems" are by the nature of things symbols bearing pertinent meanings.

[93] *V.* n. 31 *supra*.

[94] Cf. also Tzetzes *ad Hesiodi Theogonian* 326ff. in Gaisford *P. G. Min.* v. 2.

[95] Phyxios is better attested as an epithet of Zeus, although here too the meaning "of fugitives" appears to be late and conjectural. Cf Apollod. 1.7.2, and Σ Ap. Rhod. 2.1147, where the epithet

The epithet Phyxios applied to Apollo occurs only in the passage from Philostratos. Today the "lone wolf" explanation has few, if any, adherents among classicists. The reason it became so popular a century ago is that the word "warg," meaning "wolf," occurs in Middle High German as a name for the fugitive criminal destined to be hanged (and hence killed by strangling "gewürgt"). Such a person was understood to have been called a "wolf" because he was a fugitive, an outlaw, a "lone wolf." The German scholars who favored this explanation of the "warg," were sure the word meant "wolf"; the idea that the word can mean "wolf" later fell into discredit, although it has its champions today again.[96] It is likely that Phyxios is Philostratos' own addition to the story of Palamedes and the plague, in an attempt to explain, through a hendiadys, how Lykios came to be the averter of a plague (a function of Apollo Smintheus, as we shall see in the next chapter, but not of Apollo Lykeios or Lykios elsewhere). Philostratos can not be adduced as evidence for a connection between Lykios and averting a plague either; he seems to be insisting on just such a connection, or even inventing it, and the only importance the passage may have is the attempt to see beyond the wolf to some wider context of its name.

The view of Apollo as a sun-god and of the wolf as a sun-animal so overshadowed the study of mythology in the nineteenth century that even when the wolf *was* identified with the wind, and the wind-wolf identified with Apollo, the very suggestion caused consternation in learned circles. Kelly's suggestion that Apollo had not yet become a sun-god in Homeric times, but was a god of summer-storms (*sic!*) and as such associated with the Telchines, and his rationalization Apollo:Zeus::Rudra:Indra, fell on deaf ears.[97] F.L.W. Schwartz had proposed the same theory earlier,[98] but had not carried it through. Wilhelm Mannhardt, who relied largely on Schwartz in his *Roggenhund und Roggenwolf* the early results of his questionnaire, ignored any connection of the wind-wolf with Apollo, although he marshals the Greek evidence for the identification of the wolf with the wind. This is so despite the fact that the evidence he collected in the field concerning the range of the Teutonic wolf-name provided a striking parallel to Apollo's epithets, a parallel we shall examine in the next chapter. Mannhardt goes so far as to deny that his wolves are in any way related to the wolves of Wotan, and he seems to have seen them as purely agricultural constructs. Joseph V. Grohmann considered Apollo to be a storm-

---

refers to Deukalion's having escaped the flood, or else to Phrixos' having escaped sacrifice at the hands of his father Athamas. Σ Ap. Rhod. 4.699 stands alone in referring this epithet to Zeus as the guardian of fugitives. Cf. Paus. 2.21.2 and 3.17.8.

[96] Mary R. Gerstein, "Germanic *Warg*: The Outlaw as Werwolf" in Gerald J. Larson (ed.) *Myth in Indo-European Antiquity* (Berkeley/Los Angeles 1974) 131-156.

[97] Walter W. Kelly, *Curiosities of Indo-European Tradition and Folklore* (London, Chapman & Hall, 1863) 244-245, in his chapter "The Wolf." The Mediterranean area does not know summer-storms.

[98] *Der Ursprung der Mythologie, dargelegt am griechischen und deutschen Sage* (Berlin, Wittertz, 1860) written in collaboration with Adalbert Kuhn, who, a year earlier, had published his *Herabkunft des Feuers und des Göttertranks* (Berlin, P. Dümmler, 1859), in which he substituted weather phenomena, in particular thunder and lightning, for the solar hypothesis of Max Müller. Kuhn's was the second great naturalistic hypothesis of the nineteenth century, and it must have been gratifying to Mannhardt that his data were in accord with it. F.L.W. Schwartz' great work on clouds and wind in mythology, *Wolken und Wind, Blitz und Donner* (Berlin, Wittertz 1879) appeared thirteen years after Mannhardt's *Roggenwolf und Roggenhund* (Danzig 1866) and yet is totally ignorant of it.

god but made no mention of Apollo Lykeios at all.[99]

Just as the chthonic and "totemistic" aspects of the Greek gods were being discovered, in the last years of the last century and the early part of this one, the naturalistic approach to myth, and the solar hypothesis, were abandoned. With them, there disappeared from scholarly works any mention of a possible association of Apollo and the wind. Indeed, the whole idea seemed more and more far-fetched in view of more modern conceptions. To put it another way, with the rise of sociological modes of explanation, and later of racial and psychological ones, disfavor attached to any explanation that smacked of a solar, heavenly, or naturalistic hypothesis. And so, another controversy occupied the foreground of scholarly concern regarding Apollo Lykeios; in place of the argument over the nature of the "wolf," scholars began to argue over whether the epithet derived from the land of Lykia, and over whether or not Apollo was a native Greek god.

The claim that Apollo Lykeios was the "Lykian god" begs the question, as we have noted; for the name "Lykia," like a number of other geographical names, originally meant "wolf-land." Still, as we have seen, Eustathius in ad Il. 4.101 (449) declared that either of the two countries named Lykia might have been the source of the epithet Lykēgenēs and in ad Il. 4.88 (448) implied that Apollo's epithet Lykios is derived from the land of Lykia in "Karia," i. e. in southwestern Anatolia, and that the wolf-epithet Lykēgenēs also derives from that country. This is the ultimate source of the theory made famous by Wilamowitz. In 1903, in an article entitled "Apollon,"[100] he suggested that the Lykian epithet is exceedingly ancient and must be interpreted quite separately from the wolf-epithet. His earlier view had its effect despite the fact that in his Glaube der Hellenen[101] he retreated somewhat from this position, and held that the derivation of the epithet from Lykia is uncertain, that the conception of Apollo as a wolf-slayer is certainly wrong, and, following Farnell,[102] that the wolf is indeed the animal of Apollo.

If Wilamowitz felt unsure, in his later years, about the relation between the wolf and Lykia, still he was convinced that Apollo was an Asiatic deity imported into Greece about the time of Homer, and no later. This theory has its roots not in Eustathius in the eleventh century, but in a remark of Welcker's in the nineteenth![103] His assumption was that since Lykians had come to Argos the Lykian Apollo probably came by the same route to Greece. In Wilamowitz' earlier view the "Lykian" epithet of Apollo confirmed Apollo's Asiatic origins, and this has meant that the meaning and origin of the epithet Lykios, and by extension of Apollo's other epithets from the root lyk- have become inextricably involved in the controversy over the origin of the god, whether Asiatic, i.e. Lykian, Northern, or Hellenic.

To most minds this controversy turned on the origin, and hence the nature of Apollo's godhead; and the interpretation of Apollo's wolf-epithets was crucial for the argument. In fact, however, the origin of a deity like Apollo is of little importance for an understanding of his nature and role in Greek thought.[104] It cannot be denied that

---

[99] Apollo Smintheus, etc. (Prague 1862).
[100] Hermes 38 (575-586).
[101] Darmstadt 1959[3] originally published 1932, p. 1.
[102] L.R Farnell, TheCults of the Greek States I (Oxford 1907) 112ff.
[103] F.G. Welcker, Griechische Götterlehre (Göttingen 1857) 477 wrote:
> Wahrscheinlicher ist daß Apollo Lykios nach Athen, wie Lykier nach Argos, von Asien aus gekommen ist.
[104] For the definition of the polytheistic world-view as a unified conception of reality, v. Renato

as far back as Homer, and in the classical period certainly, no god is more Greek than Apollo, unless maybe Zeus. Whatever Apollo's origins, his position among the gods of Greece, in the organic thought about the world they represent, is secure, and he can never be thought of as in any way a foreign implant in Greek soil, at least in any period where the term "Greek" ("Hellenic") had any meaning. The most pertinent remark on Apollo Lykeios and his origins is still that of Farnell,[105] "Apollo Lykeios who gave his name to Lycia belonged to the oldest stratum of the religion and his cult was the common heritage of many races," with the stricture that the "many races" are basically Greek, and that both Lykia and Lykeios have their names from the wider context of the wolf-name. The country is not named after the god.

An interest in origins, however, was part and parcel of the racial theory popular in the early years of the twentieth century, which has left traces hard to erase in present-day descriptions of Greek religion. For example, some still believe that the "chthonic" deities of Greece were not native (Indo-European), because according to the popular racial theories of the first half of the twentieth century Nordic invaders, worshippers of manly, warlike, Olympian gods, later to form the aristocracy of the Hellenes, came down from the North, found there and absorbed, a short, dark race worshipping chthonic mother-goddesses. The oracle at Delphi, with its priestess, and its "dark" rites, seemed to self-styled arbiters of what is Greek and what is not, like Wilamowitz, not to agree with the nature of the Olympians, who, to paraphrase Hölderlin's *Schicksalslied*, walked in luminous radiance, above everything dark and suspect.

From the very beginning there was trouble with Wilamowitz' hypothesis. He had assumed that the bulk of the evidence tended to show that the Greeks had adopted an Asiatic deity with his sanctuaries (oracles), but the possibility remained that the Greeks might have brought a god of their own to Asia. Eduard Meyer[106] held fast to the latter hypothesis, and presented substantial arguments to show, what is now proved from epigraphy, that the name Apollo was a Greek import to Lykia,where the name Apollonides, for example, appears as Pelunida. Erich Bethe[107] also argued that Apollo is a Greek god and quite indigenous to Greece.

Thus the best path to take among the vagaries of modern interpretations of Apollo's wolf-associations seemed to be that of Nilsson: to approve the weak argument that Apollo Lykeios is none other than a facet of Apollo Nomios, the protector of the flocks. As W.K.C. Guthrie wrote:[108]

> The alternative [to Lycia] is to interpret it as "wolf-god," which was the interpretation of the Greeks themselves. Rose [i. e. H.G. Rose] describes this as "falling back" on the meaning 'wolf-god,' which does not sound as if it expresses great satisfaction, and he accepts the theory according to which Apollo was originally a deity of shepherds. To shepherds one of the chief concerns of life is the presence or absence of wolves, and their god was one who could protect them from their depredations or bring them on if he were angry.

We can not make do with this, however, first because the evidence for Apollo Nomios is, as we have seen, scanty, and most important, because it takes the wolf to be

---

Poggioli, *op.cit.* (Pref. n. 1 *supra*).

[105] *Ibid.* n. 101 *supra*.

[106] *Geschichte des Altertums* I (Stuttgart-Berlin 1909) 639.

[107] "Apollon der Hellene," *ANTIΔΩPON Festschrift Jakob Wackernagel.*

[108] *The Greeks and their Gods* (London 1966) 82.

no more and no less than Canis lupus, and so ignores the pleas of J. Whatmough.[109] Ten years later van Groningen wrote, in full agreement with the sentiments expressed by R. Poggioli:[110] "The similarities we perceive among phenomena find their religious explanation in the identity of a given divine power. In this way Apollo is a figure that expresses the connection between related realities."

We may say the same of Apollo Lykeios. If he is a wolf, does that mean he is no more than the animal Canis lupus? Cannot the term "wolf" refer to a womanizer, and does not the Latin word *lupus* refer to a nasty disease? And what of the wolf who "huffs and he puffs" in the nursery story? Why should the situation ever have been different? Let us see where the wind-wolf can be found in Greece.

---

[109] Cf.p. 3 and n. 9 *supra*.

[110] *Apollo* (Haarlem 1956) 7."De gelijkheid die wij aan de verschijnselen waarnemen, vindt haar godsdienstige verklaring in de identiteit van een bepaalde goddelijke macht. Zo is ook Apollo een gestalte die den samenhang van verwante werkelijkheden uitdrukt." For Poggioli cf. Preface, and n. 2 there *supra*.

CHAPTER II
EVIDENCE FOR THE WIND-WOLF

Our hypothesis is that "wolf" is a name for the wind, and hence for a complex of ideas that played an important role in the ideology of werewolves, such as are attested by Philostephanos at Athens. This complex of ideas involves the supposed influence of the wind. That influence was perceived as an arcane extra-terrestrial force, manifesting itself as breath, which emanates from the earth and is also found hidden inside the human body. This force was thought to originate and sustain life and growth, as well as being responsible for blocking and annihilating life and growth; the same force reveals and conceals, and so brings to light those who recognize the relationship between the manifest and the hidden and those who do not. The prophetic role of Apollo is therefore not foreign to his wolf-name.

Borne by Apollo, the wolf-name can be connected with his rôle in relation to the crops. This rôle of Apollo has largely been played down in modern treatments of the god, but the Thargelia was one of his chief festivals at Athens. This was the festival of the first fruits of the grain, celebrating the end of the harvest of barley and the start of the harvest of wheat. A two day festival, it fell on the sixth and seventh of the month of Thargeliōn, and during the festival a scapegoat, the *pharmakos*, was led out of the city to a symbolic death. At Delos, the island sanctuary of Apollo, the same days were the birthdays, respectively, of Artemis and of Apollo, the divine twins.

At Delos too there is evidence of the firm connection Apollo had with agriculture. Rhoiō, named for the pomegranate, bore Anios the hero of the island, to Apollo (or else to Zarex the son of Karystos). Anios, the first king of Delos and first priest of Apollo there, was taught prophecy by Apollo himself and given divine honors as daimon. By Dorippē he was the father of Oinō, Spermō, and Elais, called the Oinotropoi, or "wine-growers," though their names denote "wine," "grain," and "olive oil."[1] The name Anios too comes from the agricultural sphere; for it seems to be from the verb ἀνύω "to bring to maturity, to speed, fulfill." Wine, grain, and oil are the three staples of the ancient Mediterranean world,[2] and mark out the sphere of agriculture as falling within the purview of Apollo.

In the Dorian areas of the Greek world one of the most important festivals of Apollo was the Karneia, which was, in one of its aspects, a feast of bringing in the grapes. One of the chief features of the festival was a race by the *staphylodromoi*, "grape-runners" who pursued a "willing victim."[3] It was celebrated some three months after the Thargelia, and so fell out in August-September, when the grapes are harvested in the Mediterranean area. Like the Karneia, the Thargelia seems to have been dedicated to Apollo in his aspect of god of prophecy for at Eleusis, the cult site of Demeter and Kore, the goddesses of the grain, Apollo Pythios, the oracular god of Delphi, was celebrated at that festival.[4] Similarly, the Karneia was in honor of a prophet who led the the family of Herakles returning from exile to the Peloponnesos, the seer Karnos the Akarnanian whom Hippōtēs murdered at Naupaktos, just before the crossing into the ancestral homeland. His death was the occasion for the festival of the Karneia, when the men of Sparta dwelt in groups of nine in huts of greenery, also a

---

[1] Tzetzes *ad Lyc.* 580ff. et al.
[2] Cf. Deut. 11.14.
[3] W. Burkert, tr. J. Raffan, *Greek Religion* (Harvard 1985) V. 2.3, 234-235.
[4] Suidas *s. v.* Pythion.

harvest symbol, in memory of the military formation under which the children of Herakles traveled. Karnos is called "an apparition of Apollo,"[5] so that here too a prophetic Apollo has lent his name to a festival with agricultural connections that included a mock human sacrifice.

When we examine the comparative evidence, we also find grounds for thinking that Apollo's agricultural significance is of no small importance. This evidence concerns a number of his epithets, chief among them Lykeios; for from ancient Greek sources alone, we shall be able to construct the syllogism whose conclusion is that Apollo the wolf-god was a weather deity: the wolf did really belong to Apollo in antiquity, and his wolf-epithets are old, well-known, and widely attested; and we shall demonstrate not only that Apollo appears as a weather-god in ancient texts and cult, but also that the wolf-name has manifold connections with wind and weather in antiquity.

First, let us review the comparative evidence.

The data Wilhelm Mannhardt collected in the last century among German, French, and Slavic peasants led him to identify various phenomena connected with the growth of the grain as part ot the wider context of the wolf-name. That data is published in *Roggenwolf und Roggenhund*,[6] a study unconnected with Apollo, except for one cursory mention of Leto in wolf-form on its last page. The phenomena, or forces, he pointed out were seen as both fostering and impeding, i.e. terminating aforetimes, the ripening of the grain. Mannhardt's main thesis is that "Wolf," and sometimes "Hund," "dog," are names for the fructifying wind or mist,[7] which can also sometimes bring destruction in its wake, but his work also shows that "Wolf" was a German popular appellation not only for the wind, the mist, and the weather, but also for certain animals and a fungus.

Today Mannhardt's wind-wolf is found much earlier, in the Indo-European chalcolithic Cucuteni (Tripolye) civilization, which flourished in the southwestern Ukraine, Bessarabia, Moldavia, and parts of Wallachia and Transylvania between c. 5000 and 3500 B.C.E.[8] In a Tripolye painted-ware decoration from Schipenitz (in the Bukovina), depicting rain falling on a seed hidden in a mound on the earth, there appears a theriomorphic figure who no doubt represents a wind-wolf in the month of March or April.[9] This flying wolf, described as bristling up for the attack in the literature, is of a type well-known from Petreni, in Bessarabia, and from Koshylovtsy, other sites belonging to the same civilization,[10] as well as from Schipenitz. In fact the Schipenitz portrayal of this animal in the sky is enough to identify it as a wolf, in view of the comparative Indo-European evidence. B.A. Rybakov[11] shows paintings from Petreni and Schipenitz portraying wolves (he calls them "dogs"), wafted aloft in the air, protecting heavenly plantings and, from a frieze from Valea Lupului (Wolf's

---

[5] Konon 26 *FGrH* 1.210.

[6] Chap. 1 p. 6 n. 19 *supra*.

[7] *Ibid*. p 7ff.

[8] Marija Gimbutas, *The Goddesses and Gods of Old Europe* (University of California, Berkeley and L.A. 1982) esp. pp. 33-34.

[9] B.A. Rybakov, "Cosmogony and Mythology of the Agriculturists of the Eneolithic [part I]," *Soviet Anthropology and Archaeology* vol. 4, no.3 [1965] fig. 18,2, p. 28. I am indebted to Prof. Marija Gimbutas for having kindly drawn my attention to the evidence from the Soviet Union.

[10] Radu Vulpe, "Figurine thériomorphe de la civilisation Cucuteni B," 59, *Ipek* 12 [1938] n. 3, and 60 figs. 5 and 6.

[11] *Ibid*. "[part II]" figs. 41 and 42 pp.46 and 47.

Valley), guarding new shoots. He compares the flying dogs to the Sassanian *Senmurw*, a great bird with a canine face that causes seeds of all plants to fall to earth from the world tree when she lands on her great nest in that tree (on which *v*. Chap. 3 *infra*).

If this is Indo-European work whose roots derive from before the separation of the tribes who entered Central and Southern Europe the wind-wolf would appear to be earlier than either his Greek or his Germanic avatars. In any case he reappears in the Middle Ages in the foundation story of the Flemish town of Tongeren, where Bavo the Wolf flew up high into the sky to protect the people who settled the place in a fierce battle.[12]

There is also evidence of a flying wolf from the Serbian Vuk Grgurović, known as Zmaj Ognjeni Vuk, the historical hero of Serbia, who opposed the Turks between 1459, when the Serbian kingdom fell, and 1485, the year of his death; for his names identify him as a wind-wolf. His epithets, along with his name Vuk, "wolf," mean "flying serpent, fiery wolf," and he has been assimilated to the ancient Indo-European figure of the flying wolf, in the same common Slavic werewolf tradition found also in the Russian Vseslav epos.[13]

Mannhardt's *Roggenwolf und Roggenhund* was his first publication containing results of the questionnaire he had sent out. To this day all his results have not been worked through in their entirety, and not all of the questionaires may still be accessible, or even certainly in existence; for they were carried away by the Soviets during the Second World War and only some of them returned to Germany. In his later works (notably his famous *Antike Wald- und Feldkulte* [14]) Mannhardt continued on the path he had first trodden when he made the selection he published in *Roggenwolf und Roggenhund*, and these works were based on the interpretations he had made of this selected material. Yet in *Roggenwolf und Roggenhund* there is little of the thesis formulated in *Antike Wald- und Feldkulte* for which Mannhardt is best known today: namely, that the business of early religion is to use sympathetic magic to work upon the wicked spirits of the grain and of the wood; for in his view the archaic religious spirit saw the world as the stage of an unceasing war between good and evil spirits. *Roggenwolf und Roggenhund* does, however, foreshadow Mannhardt's later, famous thesis in one respect: it claims the wolf in the rye is a Korndämon, or "grain-spirit," in a formulation for which Mannhardt has been taken to task often enough in this century. Yet that formulation is peripheral to the objective results presented in *Roggenwolf und Roggenhund*, and does not bear on their validity.

Among the phenomena termed "Wolf" in the area covered by Mannhardt's questionnaire several are especially striking in view of certain of Apollo's cult epithets. Since one of Apollo's important roles was to bring up the grain, his wolf-epithets, along with other epithets he bears, have reference to this side of his godhead, as well as to his relation to the ephebes, the youths between seventeen and twenty-one in training in the Greek *polis*.[15]

Dumézil[16] has denied the possibility of a significant contribution on the part of

---

[12] This story is related fully in Chap. 7 *infra*.

[13] R. Jakobson and G. Ružičić , "The Serbian Zmaj Ognjeni Vuk and the Russian Vseslav Epos," *Annuaire de l'Institut de Philologie et d'Histoire Orientales et Slaves* 10 [1950] (= *Mélanges Henri Grégoire*).

[14] Strassburg, H. Patzig, 1877.

[15] *V*. also Chap. 6 *infra*.

[16] Georges Dumézil, *L'idéologie tripartite des Indo-Européens* (Collection Latomus vol. 31, Bruxelles) 91.

Greek studies to the field of Indo-European ideology. He wrote:

> La Grèce—par rançon sans doute du "miracle grec," et aussi parce que les plus anciennes civilisations de la Mer Égée ont trop fortement marqué les invahisseurs venus du Nord—contribue peu à l'etude comparative: même les traits les plus considérables de l'héritage y ont été profondement modifiés.

This is a formulation we can not agree with; for our results show striking correspondences between general Indo-European ideology and Greek traditions. More pertinent to the investigation of Apollo the Wolf-god, in our view, are the words of von Kienle[17] to the effect that Apollo the Wolf-god exhibits no traits common to other Indo-European peoples, though they also are to be rejected; for, indeed, not too many years later Krappe[18] pointed out amazing parallels between a Greek myth from northwest Anatolia and a Northern European, i.e. German, myth.

In our study the contribution of the Greek material to a general understanding of an Indo-European phenomenon will be seen to be far from nugatory, we hope. In Greece a connection is found between all three of the "functions" of the tripartite Indo-European ideology Georges Dumézil discovered and elucidated. Such a connection recurs elsewhere as well. Its basis is in the area of agricultural work and cult, and so, perhaps, in the Greek material we may have a piece of "third function" ideology, which remained just that outside Greece, and which surfaces only by chance into written documentation in the Baltic lands.[19] The Baltic peoples, like the Greeks, seem to lack clear evidence of the tripartite system that is the heritage of the Indo-European peoples. Now, maybe we will be able to understand why exactly *les traits les plus considérables de l' héritage y ont été profondement modifiés.*

To return to Mannhardt's findings, he begins with the literary evidence of the second part of Snorri Sturluson's *Prose Edda*, the *Skáldskaparmál*, or *Poetic Diction*. There, among the kennings, is the expression, in c. 27, *hunðr eða vargr viðar*, "the dog or the wolf blows," as a metaphor for the wind.[20] In another old Norse poem the expression *fýrisgarmr*, literally "dog of the pine-forest" refers to the wind.[21] However, inasmuch as the wolf can also stand for fire and for weaponry in old Norse poetry, the existence of a wolf-metaphor for the wind outside poetry may be doubted; in this context Mannhardt introduces the modern Norwegian riddle quoted *supra*,[22] as well as two modern German cases of feeding the wind quoted in nineteenth century German antiquarian works on Teutonic survivals: An old woman in Munderkingen made black pap, set it out on the rafters outside, and said "The wind-dogs must be fed";[23] and an old woman of Bamberg shook her flour sack out of the window when a strong wind was blowing, saying "lege dich lieber Wind, bring das deinem Kind," "calm down, dear wind, bring this to your child," as if she were speaking to a hungry animal.[24] Mannhardt does not adduce the parallel story of The Three Little Pigs from

---

[17] Richard von Kienle "Tier-Völkernamen bei indogermanischen Stammen," *Wörter und Sachen* 14 (Heidelberg 1932) 39: *Apollo als Wolfsgott weist keinerlei Züge auf, die sich bei anderen indogermanischen Völkern wiederfinden ließen.*

[18] A.H. Krappe, "Cyzicus the Mysing," *AJP* (1936).

[19] *V.* Appendix C *infra.* for further discussion of this point.

[20] *Skáldskaparmál* c. 27.

[21] *Magnússaga hins Goða* 20.1

[22] Chap. 1 p. 6.

[23] Birlinger, *Volkstümliches aus Schwaben.*

[24] Prätorius, *Weltbeschreibung.*

England and Belgium, which we began with.

Most important for Mannhardt's thesis is the material he collected with his questionnaire from all over Germany and the neighboring countries (p. 5ff.) that shows that the wind blowing over the fields of grain was regularly described with the words, "The wolves [or dogs] are among the grain." Children were warned against going into the fields: "The wolf is in there, and he will eat you up!" This is the rye-wolf, German "Roggenwolf," who stands for various weather phenomena. Mannhardt strives to discover a real animal called "rye-wolf" (p. 13); his investigations show a living being in the fields, a wild animal, also thought of as the wind, was believed to devour grain and children, and to howl, to roar, and to leave footprints in the stands of wheat and rye. Such a living being plays in the fields, but also scares away anyone foolhardy enough to venture into the fields of growing grain. When reaping begins it flees before the fieldhands, and is forced into an ever diminishing area, until it is caught in the last sheaf of grain, but only after it has brought illness upon its pursuers and disgrace upon the girls among the reapers. The question he asks now is whether any one of the insects or small animals, also colloquially termed "wolf," that live among the grain is the original "rye-wolf." Mannhardt's conclusion is that none of them is, but he gives a list of animals called "wolf" in various sections of Germany: the mole cricket (Gryllotalpa vulgaris), the black weevil (Calandra granaria), the cornworm or the larva of the corn-moth (Tinea granella or Phalaena granella), the German marmot (or rather the hamster, Cricetus cricetus), the larva of the cockchafer or May bug (Melolantha vulgaris), and the cockchafer itself. In addition (p. 16), he found that ergot (Claviceps purpurea) and burls were named "wolf" in many places.

The mole cricket is a large cricket that lives underground like a mole, and possesses a pair of strong, spade-like front legs used to dig and push back dirt. As its name implies, it burrows through the soil like a mole, although it is in fact a cricket. Hence it partakes of the nature of both.

The cockchafer and the black weevil are beetles that live in the grain. The cockchafer is a large scarab-like beetle that causes considerable damage, while the black weevil is small and lives in a single grain of wheat or rye, devouring it from the inside. The larva of the cockchafer is a fat grub that lives in the ground for three years and eats away at the roots of the grain, while the cornworm is a small grub that inhabits a single grain of corn, like a weevil.

The hamster is a small, ratlike European rodent with a short tail and cheek pouches to store grain. It lives in the fields of grain. Ergot and burls, unlike the rest, are plant material. Ergot is a fungus, actually the sclerotium of a mushroom, that attacks a grain of rye, or wheat or barley, in wet areas, or in dry regions in rainy years, and turns it purplish-black and swollen, giving it a sweetish taste. When the swollen grain falls off numerous small purplish mushrooms grow up out of it. The nucleus common to most ergot alkaloids is lysergic acid. Lysergic acid diethylamide, produced naturally when damp grain contaminated with ergot is stored for long periods, is LSD, and simple lysergic amides occur in most varieties of ergot.[25]

Burls, which are more or less round bark-covered excrescences, are to trees as ergot is to cultivated grain crops. It is interesting in this connection to note that in ancient Greece grain and trees were pre-eminently the domain of the goddess Demeter (and of her daughter Kore). She is conventionally pictured holding ears of grain and

---

[25] Albert Hofmann, "A Challenging Question and My Answer," in R.G. Wasson, C.A.P. Ruck, and Albert Hofmann, *The Road to Eleusis: Unveiling the Secret of the Mysteries* (New York, Harcourt Brace Jovanovich, 1978) 28.

poppies,[26] but she punished Erysichthon severely for having dared to cut down her holy trees.[27]

To recapitulate, then, the list of the living beings that went by the name "wolf" among the German peasantry of the last century, according to Mannhardt, looks like this:

1. the wolf
2. the mole cricket
3. the black weevil
4. the larva of the corn-moth, or cornworm
5. the hamster
6. the cockchafer or May bug and its larva
7. ergot of cultivated grains and burls on trees

All of these, as well as the wind, are represented in the domain of Apollo's epithets and cult. The correspondences are not one to one, inasmuch as one of these beings may be represented in more than one of his epithets, or, contrariwise, more than one of them represented in only one of his distinctive titles, nor could exact correspondences have been expected in terrains so different as Greece and Germany.

As for the epithets of Apollo, or of any god, for that matter, in a polytheistic system, it is only right to make clear, at the outset, that they are not the residue of once independent gods of limited functions ("Sondergötter"), as was once believed by such great scholars as Hermann Usener and Walter F. Otto. Instead, they identify the god's activity as extending in certain directions, and covering certain areas, or "contexts," without necessarily specifying the mode of that activity. Each one of them carries with it a great many connotations, as do animal names used in everyday language, as Leach has shown.[28] Together they form a structure that defines and specifies the nature of the divine being they modify. We have seen the wolf in the epithet Lykeios; it remains for us to discover the wider context of his name in the deity bearing that epithet.

We meet up with the mole-cricket, with its double nature, in two places in Apollo's domain. As a cricket, on the one hand, it may correspond to Apollo's epithet Parnopios, found at Athens, and denoting a sort of locust found among the grain. A bronze statue of Apollo Parnopios by Pheidias stood across from the Parthenon on the Acropolis.[29] The story Pausanias tells to account for this epithet relates how Apollo once freed Athens of a plague of locusts when they were ravaging the land.[30] We have a report of a Locust Apollo, among the Aiolic Greeks, who had a month named Pornopiōn after him.[31] On coins of Metapontum in Magna Graecia Apollo Parnopios appears holding an ear of grain, and in Seleukeia in Kilikia, prayers were offered to

---

[26] For documentation of these symbols see K. Kerényi and C.G. Jung, *Essays on a Science of Mythology: The Myth of the Divine child and the Mysteries of Eleusis* (New York 1949, etc., translated from the German of 1941) 130-144.

[27] Call. *Hymn* 6.

[28] Edmund Leach, "Anthropological Aspects of Language: Animal Categories and Verbal Abuse," in Eric H. Lenneberg (ed.), *New Directions in the Study of Language* (Cambridge, Mass., M.I.T 1964) 23-64.

[29] Paus. 1.24.8.

[30] *Ibid.*

[31] Strabo 13.64 (613). He explains that the Boiotians, who are Aeolic Greeks in his view, called locusts (πάρνοπες) πόρνοπες. Among the Oitaians of Magnesia, he tells us in the passage immediately preceding this one, there was a cult of Hēraklēs Kornopiōn, the Locust Herakles, who was also said to have rescued the land from a plague of locusts.

Apollo Sarpedonios to send birds to destroy the locusts.[32]

The cricket is close enough to the locust to fill its niche in folklore in a different ecological setting. Another insect, closely related to the locust and also found among the grain, is the praying mantis, nor should we ignore the fact that Apollo, as the god of Delphi and of prophecy, was the mantis *par excellence* in ancient Greece. Prophecy is thus part of the wider context of the wolf-name, for one thing, inasmuch as the mantic prophet acts through the influence of wind or 'spirit' on him. Since the insect named *mantis* is also a harvest insect with connections to the wind it would seem to present another parallel to the German wolf-list.

The locust seems to be the only insect connected with the grain represented among Apollo's epithets in Greece. Hence, taken as a generic name for the insects found in the wheat or the barley (or the rye), it must also make do for three more wolf-creatures reported by Mannhardt from his questionnaire: the cockchafer, the black weevil, and the larva of the corn moth. It is quite understandable that the Greeks should lack such names; for Greece has never been a corn bowl, the amount of grain grown having always been very small, and in fact insufficient for the growing population of late Fifth Century Athens, so that the Athenians were forced to look to Sicily, and later to Egypt, to the Crimea and to Southern Russia, to fill their cereal needs.

The mole, on the other hand, seems to have a substantial connection to Apollo, and the mole's connection to the hamster, in the context of ancient Greek and Indo-European thought, at least, seems close. The mole's relation to fields of grain derives from his burrowing underground through them. In ancient Greek thought the mole belonged to Apollo's son Asklepios, as has been conclusively shown.[33] The relation of a god to his divine son is often one of sharing and clarifying attributes. Asklepios' name seems to be derived from that of the mole σκάλοψ, or from some other animal similarly named, and his relation with the mole is made certain by the fact that his great temple at Epidauros was built in the shape of a molehill. Asklepios and the mole are both patrons of healing, and of confraternities of young warriors with wind connections. If we can recognize the mole in the mole cricket, we can discern a strong connection between Apollo and the Germanic "Wolf" here.

Furthermore, from Greek sources alone Goossens[34] has shown a relation between the mole and the wolf. It is this: he notes that the common ancient Greek name for the mole, σκάλοψ, is related to the Greek words for the owl, ἀσκάλαφος, the spotted lizard, ἀσκάλαβος or ἀσκαλαβώτης, and the woodcock ἀσκαλώπας, as well as, apparently, to the Hebrew word for the bat, עֲטַלֵּף. All these in turn, are related to a verb reported in Hesychius: σκαλπάζειν, glossed ῥεμβώδως βαδίζειν, that is, "to walk in a zigzagging, staggering manner," (like the related German *sich schleppen*, although Modern Greek σκαλπάζω means "to gallop"). He compares the Indian god Rudra Vaṅku, *R. V.* 1.114, Rudra "the staggerer," and Apollo Loxias, "Apollo who proceeds athwart," one of the epithets applied to the oracular Apollo of Delphi. It derives from the word λοξόν, "athwart," or "at a zigzag," and is glossed λοξαβάτης, a word whose meaning is the same as that of σκαλπάζων. Goossens suggests that the

---

[32] Zosimos 1.57.

[33] H. Grégoire and R. Goossens, *Asklépios, Apollon Smintheus, et Rudra, Études sur le dieu à la taupe et le dieu au rat dans la Grèce et dans l'Inde* (Koninklijke Belgische Akademie. Klasse der Letteren en de Morele en Staatkundige Wetenschappen. Verhandeling tweede reeks, Boek XLV, Brussel 1949).

[34] In his *Esquisse d'une étude comparative*, in *op. cit.* (previous note) 134-142.

wolf too can be called *loxias*, because of his loping walk, and, writing of the animals who form the entourage of Apollo and Asklepios: the snake, the wolf, the dog, the rat, the swan, the dolphin, etc., he maintains that their grouping is not accidental, and characterizes them as a complex whose key is probably the belief in "animal medicine."

One of the animals whose names resemble that of the mole in Greek, the lizard, under another name, reappears in an Apolline, oracular context, similar to that of the epithet Loxias, in the story of Galeos, or Galeotes,[35] and of the family of the Galeotai.[36] These names refer to the lizard, and to a family of seers found mostly in Sicily. Two Hyperboreans, Galeotes and Telmissos, were told by the oracle of Zeus at Dodona to go one toward the rising sun, and the other toward the sunset, and to construct an altar, each of them, at the place an eagle would steal his sacrificial meat; Galeotes went to Sicily and Telmissos to Karia. The Hyperboreans provide a connection with Apollo here, as does the fact that an inscription[37] shows the small town of Telmissos in Karia had a famous oracle of Apollo. Furthermore, in the Germanic linguistic area too the lizard as a prophetic animal is encountered; for an Old German name for the lizard was Hagedisse, "witch."[38]

The hamster corresponds to Apollo's famous epithet Smintheus. Apollo Smintheus is the great god of Chryse and Killa and Tenedos (all places in and around the Troad) to whom the priest Kalchas prays in the first lines of the *Iliad* (1.39) for his help in averting the plague. Hence, like Asklepios, Apollo Smintheus is a god of healing, and according to the Greek apophthegm a bearer of plague as well, since ὁ τρώσας ἰάσεται, "he who has wounded shall heal." In consonance with this saying is the story that a priest of Apollo named Krinis at Chryse in Mysia angered the god by reason of his impiety, whereupon Apollo sent mice to destroy his plants; later, in answer to the priest's entreaties, Apollo came with his bow and shot the mice, and Krinis founded a temple to Apollo Smintheus.[39] Indeeed, the word σμίνθα, σμίνθος, explained with the Greek μῦς,[40] "mouse," is a Kretan word,[41] current of old in the Cypriot dialect of Greek, where it denoted the domestic mouse,[42] and also in the Troad, where the god was at home,[43] as well as in other Aiolic-speaking areas. The report that it is Kretan may derive from the story that the people of the Troad had originally come from Krete, a story told of many peoples all over the Greek-speaking area.

Apollo Smintheus was the god of Chryse in the Troad, and Hesychius[44] contends that the god bore the epithet Lykaios there as well. A possible support for this contention comes from Philostratos[45] who says Palamedes understood from the fact that wolves came down from Mt. Ida in the ninth year of the siege of Troy that Apollo was giving a sign that a plague was in the offing. Both these sources are suspect, but

---

[35] Steph. Byz. s .v. Γαλεώτης.

[36] Aelian *V. H.* 12.46, and elsewhere.

[37] Ditt. *Syll.* III3 1044.

[38] L. Hopf, *Thierorakel und Orakelthiere in alter und neuer Zeit* (Stuttgart 1888), 181.

[39] Σ *Il.* 1.39, in the name of Polemon.

[40] Hes. *s.v.*

[41] Σ Lyc.; Serv.

[42] Hes. *s.v.*

[43] Indeed Servius recognizes this fact when he says it is also Phrygian.

[44] *S. v.* Smintheus.

[45] *Heroicus* 10.4 p. 710f. Cf. also Tzetzes *ad Hesiodi Theogonian* 326ff. in Gaisford *P. G. Min.* v. 2.

may show some verisimilitude, if mouse and wolf were associated in later antiquity.[46] Strabo describes the temple of Smintheus at Chryse in his day.

The cult of Apollo Smintheus existed on the islands off the coast of the Troad, as well. Archaeological evidence from Arisba and Methymna on Lesbos shows it on that island, and Strabo[47] tells of temples of the god on Tenedos, as well as at Larissa in the Troad, south of Alexandreia Troas on the coast over against Tenedos, where there are hot springs, and at Parion in the part of Mysia called Pariane. The coins of Antigoneia-Alexandreia of the Roman period showed Apollo treading on a mousehole.[48] He seems to have been worshipped farther afield, on three other Aegean islands (besides Tenedos) at least: Nisyros (where a calendar month was called Sminthios), Keos (where there were temples of Apollo Smintheios at Koresos and at Poiessa), and Rhodes.

The earliest extant reference to this god may be of the fourteenth century B.C.E. from the island of Lesbos, if he is to be identified with the pre-Greek god of Lesbos (Lazpash) to whom the Hittite king Murshilish was referred, when he was ill, in order to restore his health, as G.P. Carratelli[49] maintained on the basis of Smintheus' role as a god of healing in the *Iliad*. If Apollo Smintheus is that ancient god of Lazpash, he would be a pre-Greek god later identified with Apollo, as G.L. Huxley[50] held, and the etymology of his name given by Goossens[51] from the same root that appears in the Hebrew שממית, *semamith*,[52] would gain verisimilitude. To Goossens' way of thinking, names from the same root given to the mouse and to the lizard, recall the alternation of an owl-name with the name of the mole-god, in the case of Asklepios, as well as the epithet Loxias, as we have seen.

The mouse appeared on coins of Tenedos along with the likeness of a reaper's basket, just as it appeared on the coins of Metapontum along with an ear of grain,[53] confirming the animal's association with the harvest. Concerning Rhodes, a holiday called Sminthia was celebrated there in memory of a time mice attacked the vines there and were destroyed by Apollo and Dionysos, who shared the epithet Sminthios on the island.[54] The same epithet is found in numerous places in Italy too: there was an Etruscan *nomen gentile* "sminthe," and another "sminthinal," and a Mars Sminthius is known from a mirror found in Volsinii.

According to Aelian[55] Apollo Smintheus guarded the grain from the inroads of the mice after sacrifice was made to him at the behest of the Delphic oracle, consulted during a plague of mice. Thus the primary connection of the cult of Apollo Smintheus is with the harvest, although it is also connected with three other wolf-themes we have already encountered: prophecy; the phenomenon of the sinkhole; and *Canis Lupus*, in

---

[46] D.J.N. Lee *op. cit.* (Chap. 1 p. 18 n. 89 *supra*) compares the Greek word λυκάβας "year," to the Old Irish *luch*, gen sing. *lochad*, "mouse," and concludes that the word, which can mean literally "the wolf's going," refers to a New Moon Feast in the spring, and that Apollo Lykeios is another Mouse Apollo. If he is right the approximation of Lykeios and Smintheus will have found even more corroboration.

[47] Strabo 13.605.

[48] *PWRE* 2 col. 102.

[49] *Jahrbuch für Kleinasiatische Forschung* (Heidelberg 1951) 159-163.

[50] *Achaeans and Hittites* (Belfast 1960) 13.

[51] *Op. cit.* nn. 32 and 33 *supra*.

[52] Proverbs 30.28, "a sort of lizard," probably a gecko, from the context.

[53] Pollux 9.84.

[54] Apollonios *Lex. Hom.* 143.

[55] *V. H.* 12.5.

whose ambience the mouse appears in one ancient monument, at least. We shall treat these themes in order.

According to the inhabitants of Alexandreia in the Troad the Sibyl Herophile, of the oracle of Marpessos, was a priestess of Apollo Smintheus.[56] There was a monument to her in the grove of the god. At Methymna on the island of Lesbos, moreover, there was found an inscription mentioning a προφητὴς τοῦ σμίνθεως Ἀπόλλωνος, showing that there was an oracle of the mouse-god there as well. In fact Aelian[57] calls the mouse "the most prophetical animal," μαντικώτατον. If the mouse epiphany (of Apollo) is closely related to the mole of Asklepios, as Grégoire and Goossens have demonstrated,[58] yet another trait connects them here; for the dream oracle of Asklepios at Epidauros was the most famous of his sanctuaries in Hellas.

Furthermore, a famous oracle, that of Marpessos was located at a place on the river Aïdoneus (named for the god of the dead, Hades) where it falls into a sinkhole, and rises again once before it is swallowed up entirely.[59] Here we discover another association of the sinkhole: it was conceived of as an entrance to the underworld; hence the river bears the name of the god of the dead. There are two facets to this connection: one is the fact that the sinkhole is associated with death and the dead, since it is an entry-way beneath the surface of the land, and the other, the fact that the destination of the water (which we have seen personified as the bull) is revealed as the kingdom of Hades, or, what amounts to the same thing, the point of origin of the wolf who is personified as the wind, namely, the netherworld. In Chap. 3 *infra.* we shall see that a common ancient belief held that winds issued from subterranean vents.

We have encountered the motif of prophecy among the animals in Apollo's entourage in the figures of the locust, or the mantis, of the lizard (*galeōtēs*), and of the mouse, and we may recall here too that, according to Suidas, at Eleusis, the cult site of the goddesses of the grain, the Apollo celebrated at the festival of the first-fruits, the Thargelia, mentioned above, was Apollo Pythios, the oracular god of Delphi, and that Apollo Karneios, the god of the Dorian Karneia in Sparta and elsewhere, is associated with the grape-harvest and with prophecy. Nor should the occurrence of prophecy in an agricultural context associated with the mouse cause us any surprise. The need for foresight in assessing the harvest was one of the chief motives for divination and prophecy in antiquity, as is shown by the story told by Hieronymos of Rhodes of the philosopher Thales of Miletos,[60] who, wishing to demonstrate how easily wealth can be acquired, showed great sagacity in predicting the olive harvest, cornered the market by renting all the oil-presses, and won himself great wealth and fame.

Another facet of prophecy is possession by a spirit from outside, and such a spirit is in itself often conceived of as a breath or a wind, comparable to the moisture-bearing wind that matures the grain and the vines. This is perhaps another source of the association between the harvest and prophecy which we can document from Athens and from Sparta.

The mouse and the wolf appear together on a Bologna kylix where the Athenian

---

[56] J.G. Frazer, *Pausanias's Description of Greece, Translation and Commentary* (London, Macmillan 1898) Vol. 5.289 reports that twelve miles south of this Alexandreia a temple of Apollo Smintheus was discovered in 1853 by Captain Scott, and excavated in 1866 by Mr. W. Pullan for the Dilettanti Society.

[57] *Ibid.* 1.11.

[58] *Op. cit.* n 32 *supra.*

[59] Paus. 10.12.5.

[60] Diogenes Laertius 1.26.

king Kodros is shown going off to war holding a shield on which a mouse is depicted sitting upright on his haunches on the back of a wolf who is pawing the ground. No satisfactory explanation of this portrayal has ever been suggested. Nevertheless, it must represent the ferocity of the wolf, along with his terrestrial sovereignty, associated with the mouse's prophetic and apotropaic functions. Another place the wolf-name and the mouse are found associated is at Mt. Myēnon (Mouse-mountain) near the River Lykormas (Wolf-landing) in Aitolia.[61]

Strabo[62] relates that the poet Kallinos told the following story of the founding of the sanctuary of Apollo Smintheus at Sminthe in the Troad: An oracle instructed the Teukrians from Krete to settle where they would find themselves the object of an attack of γηγενεῖς, or "the earth-born," an appellation whose usual meaning is "giants." When they were in the Troad their leather shield straps were gnawed through one night, whereupon they settled Troy and founded the cult of Apollo Smintheus. The same story is found in Σ Lyk. 1303, where mice are specifically named as being the γηγενεῖς, and as the etiology for the founding of the temple of Apollo Smintheus at Hamaxitos near Alexandreia, a town mentioned by Strabo as well in this connection, in Aelian V. H. 12.5. The Hamaxitos temple, where tame mice were kept under the altar,[63] appears also on coins and in inscriptions.[64] Another version of the story recorded by Polemon[65] tells that mice gnawed through the bowstrings of the enemies of the Trojans, and so the people of Troy and its environs revered mice, whom they called *sminthoi*, and founded the cult of Apollo Smintheus.

Thus the mouse is related to the harvest of the grain, and to prophecy, and furthermore is a symbol of plague and of healing.[66] We have noted the association, or confusion, of Smintheus and Lykeios in two ancient sources.[67] If the confusion in evidence here between Apollo Lykeios and the famous Smintheus of the opening lines of the *Iliad* is ancient, there may have been a living tradition of Lykeios' connection to sickness and healing that may relate to the cult at Chryse and to the shield of Kodros.

Moreover, along with the mouse's connection to plague and healing, its status as a γηγενής, "an earthborn creature," too connects it with the wolf-name; for the wolf (Canis Lupus) builds its den in subterranean pits often dug out at the root of a large tree, and hence also has earthborn status as a γηγενής. Moreover, with its mythical prowess in setting the strength of the enemy at nought, the mouse is at home in the confraternityof young warriors who bear the name of the wolf so often (cf. the Mysings, and previous chapter). Coins show the cult statue of Apollo Smintheus, carrying bow and arrows, which are also symbols of the plague and connected with this god in *Il.* 1.

Farther afield in the Indo-European linguistic area the mouse and rat have specific connections with the storm and with lightning. The evidence is presented by Grohmann,[68] mostly from India. Goossens[69] admits this evidence, but shows that

[61] Ps.-Plutarch *de fluv. et mont. nominibus* 8.

[62] Strabo 13. (604).

[63] Apollon. *Lex. Hom. s. v.* Hamaxitos.

[64] Menander Rhetor *peri Sminthiakōn* Walz 9.319, 9.304; Ammianus Marcellinus 22.8; cf. also Paus. 9.12.3.

[65] In Clem. Al. 34 P.

[66] Cf. I Samuel 6.4ff.

[67] V. nn. 44 and 45 *supra*.

[68] *Op. cit.* cap. I *supra*, n. 98.

[69] *Op. cit.* (n. 33 *supra*) 164.

many other animals are also associated with the storm and with lightning. Mannhardt's results also connect a number of other animals with the same natural phenomena. Goossens believes, however, that the specific connection of Apollo (and Asklepios) to the rat is due not to its connection with the storm, but with epidemic disease. While we recognize the importance of Apollo's role as patron of medical arts, we need not join Goossens in animadverting upon the wind and storm hypothesis.

If there is any god in Greece who is connected with fungus growth on grain it is Apollo. In Rhodes, where we have seen he was worshipped as Smintheus, he is called Erysibios or Erythibios, from the Greek word for cereal rust, which like "rust," from the root of the English "red," is ἐρυσίβη or ἐρυθίβη, from the root of Gr. ἐρυθρός, "red." He shares this epithet with Demeter Erysibie in Lydia.[70] Another variant of the same epithet is Erethymios, and Apollo, the great god of the Lykians, was worshipped under that epithet in Lykia,[71] and also at Argos and on Cyprus.[72]

Robigus was the corresponding epithet of Apollo at Rome, named after *robigo*, the rust on grain. Apollo Robigus' festival, celebrated there in April, was called the Robigalia. It was famous for the sacrifice of dogs. This sacrifice, however, is associated with the wider context of the wolf-name at a reserve, for it is a reflex of the same sort of sacrifice performed at the rising of Sirius, the dog-star, at the start of the "dog-days" of September, a sacrifice offered in the context of confraternities of young men. The Robigalia marked the setting of the star.[73]

An attempt has been made to identify ἐρυσίβη, "rust," with ergot, the fungus that is found bearing the name "Wolf" in the Germanic linguistic area. C.A.P. Ruck has written that "a parasitic fungoid growth, ergot, the sclerotium of Claviceps purpurea or 'rust,' [is] named ἐρυσίβη in Greek by the metaphor of reddening corruption."[74] This identification derives from the drug experience of the author, who is sure that the drug experience was produced in the initiates into the Greater (Eleusinian) Mysteries at Athens, but, no doubt, the unexpressed reasoning behind it is that divine epithets in Greece ought not to refer to phenomena like the rust on grain, that have no utilitarian value to humankind.[75] Had there been ergot of cultivated grains in Greece, we would no doubt have encountered an epithet of Apollo referring to it, but the epithet

---

[70] *Etymologicum Gudianum s. v.*

[71] Hesychius *s. v.*

[72] Ptolem. Heph. 7.

[73] Cf. the article Sirius in *PWRE* IIIA4 col. 337ff.

[74] R.G. Wasson, C.A.P. Ruck, and Albert Hofmann, *TheRoad to Eleusis: Unveiling the Secret of the Mysteries* (New York, Harcourt Brace Jovanovich, 1978) 115.

[75] A number of objections may be raised to this hypothesis, as expressed by C.A.P. Ruck. `Rust' is certainly not ergot, and his hypothesis ignores the rust fungus and the Roman parallel, and can hardly be serious without a consideration of these things. Next, in the drier parts of the Mediterranean climatic area ergot (Claviceps purpurea) appears on wheat and barley only in exceptionally wet years. Another variety of ergot does indeed seem to occur even in drier years in Greece on certain grassy fodder plants, like darnel (Lolium temulentum), and water couch (Paspalum distichum, on which Claviceps paspali grows), which Hofmann and Ruck contend "grows all around the Mediterranean," but here again we may confront their contention with their own implied contention that divine epithets in Greece refer only to products or processes that have some utilitarian value to humankind, unless, of course, as Wasson, Ruck, and Hofmann contend, these ergots were used for producing hallucinations. (Σφάκελός too may be a term for ergot, inasmuch as it means both "gangrene" and "convulsions," as well as some plant matter, a concatenation of meaning that occurs only in the case of ergot in nature.) Again the color of the grain of ergot in these plants is purplish-brown-black, and the "metaphor of reddening corruption" is a poor excuse for an explanation if rust is ignored.

Erysibios certain refers to rust. The most that can be said is that it might refer in addition to certain kinds of non-cereal ergot.

There is therefore a striking degree of correspondence between Apollo's epithets and the range of meanings of the German "Wolf" as reported by Mannhardt. What, then, is the range of meaning covered by the German word? Mannhardt's work is limited to the wolf and the dog, whose names are used in his material to refer to the wind. In fact, the role of wind-animal in his researches was more often taken by the sow, the cow, the goat, and the rooster than by these predators; only the further connotations of the names "Wolf" and "Hund" were much more interesting and productive. His researches led him to believe that all these animals were "spirits of the grain," a concept in need of clarification.[76] Mannhardt insists on the primacy of the wind in the picture of this wolf or dog, and on his alternately beneficent and maleficent nature.

Even more compelling evidence for the identification of the wolf and the wind than that adduced by Mannhardt from the Northern European sphere comes from ancient Italy. Here we find two divinities whose cult and name evince an identification of the wolf with the wind in this area too. They are Faunus and Soranus; the former is associated with the story of Romulus and Remus and the she-wolf, according to Ennius and Fabius Pictor, whereas the latter may be named after the shrew, a mouse-like insectivore (Lat. *sorex*).[77]

The Lupercalia on the 15 of February was the festival of Faunus, it is generally agreed[78]; but the dedication of his temple was celebrated two days earlier, on the 13 of February, and that day, Faunus' festival,[79] was known as the one upon which the wind Favonius, the fructifying west (really northwest) wind begins to blow.[80] In fact in Byzantion the same month was called Lykeios[81] no doubt for the same reason as at Epidauros Limera[82] and at Lamia in Thessaly,[83] as well. Hence we see that a god who

---

[76] Lutz Mackensen, "Tierdämonen? Kommetaphern," *MitteldeutscheBlätter für Volkskunde* 8 (1933) 109-121, is undoubtedly correct in insisting that it is a mistake to view these animals as "spirits of the grain." They are rather "metaphors" for natural as well as social phenomena. J.M. Frazer based his well-known study, *The Golden Bough,* on Mannhardt's theory of "spirits of the grain," and Eitrim in his article "Tierdämonen" *PWRE Suppl.* 6a (1936) cols. 862ff. has pinpointed the ancient evidence for them. Mackensen dismisses Mannhardt's insistence that his research has "archaeological" value, and claims animal metaphors of the sort we are discussing here never implied belief and were always fundamentally "pedagogical." His is a reductionist position; for surely linguistic metaphors of the sort Mannhardt collected are ancient, and if they appear in children's games in the nineteenth century were certainly part of adult culture in earlier times. (Cf. Philippe Ariès, *Centuries of Childhood* [New York 1962] esp. Part 1 Chap. 2, "A Modest Contribution to the History of Games," p.62ff.)

[77] *V.* n. 95 *infra.*

[78] The sole source for the connection is Ovid *Fasti* 2.267f.: Tertia post Idus nudos aurora Lupercos/ aspicit et Fauni sacra bicornis eunt. K. Kerényi, "Wolf und Ziege im Lupercalienfeste," *Niobe: Neue Studien über antike Religion und Humanität* (Zürich 1949) 139-147, maintains, no doubt correctly, from this passage, that Faunus is not a wolf, but a goat. Impressively enough the name of the wolf-confraternity that worshipped Soranus (v. infra) was Hirpi Sorani, and the Latin reflex of the Sabine *hirpus*, "wolf," is *hircus*, "goat," so that the wider context of the goat-name may include the wolf-name.

[79] Livy 33.42.10 and 34.53.3.

[80] Varro *RR* 1.28f., Cic. *Verr.* II 5.27, Pliny *N.H.* 2.122; 18.337, Hor. *Carm.* 1.4.1.

[81] Cf. Bischoff, Lykeios 2) *PWRE* 13 [1927] col. 2270.

[82] *IG* 5[1].932.

[83] *IG* 9[2]75.18 etc.

was associated with the founder of Rome, Romulus and his twin brother Remus, who were exposed as children and suckled by a she- wolf and whose festival was called Lupercalia, which clearly contains the root *lup-*, which means "wolf" in Latin,[84] is attached to the wind not only in his name as it appears (Faunus:Favonius) but in the date of his festival. The cult of Faunus contains one more element to which we must return: the 17 February was the Quirinalia, a holiday in which the wolf was also honored, inasmuch as it celebrated the god Quirinus (identified with Mars, or his son Romulus, according to the later interpretations) and involved the story of the exposure of Romulus and Remus in an ark on waters of a flood, and their rescue and nurture by a she-wolf named Lupa[85] or else Luperca.[86] Thus the theme of wind—and of flood—is identified with the wolf in this three-day period, apparently.

The divine name Faunus provides another key to this identification. According to W.F. Otto[87] and to A.A. von Blumenthal[88] his name comes from the Indo-European root *dau-, "to strangle," from which a whole series of wolf-names in the Indo-European linguistic area is derived, and is identified with the wind.[89] The wolf-names include the name of the Illyrian Dauni in Italy, that of the Dacians,[90] and of the Anglo-Saxon group called the Deanas,[91] as well as the Lydian royal name Kandaules "the dog-strangler."[92] Von Blumenthal tried to show on etymological grounds, and from other data, including the connection of the god with the Lupercalia, that the Italian Faunus was fundamentally a wolf-god. He also associated the deified fructifying west wind, or zephyr (Greek ζέφυρος from ζόφος, "the dark mist") with Faunus-Favonius, and so, by way of etymology, at least, with the same mist that is identified with the wolf in the Germanic area according to Mannhardt. Favonius is the father of the crops; his son is called Carpus (Gr. καρπός, "fruit") in Ovid *Fasti* 5.197.8. The identification of Faunus and Favonius is ancient.[93]

---

[84] For the substitution of *kp* leading to *pp* (*p*) for I.-E. *qu-* cf. the wolf-name of the Paeonian king who joined the Thrakians and Illyrians in 356 B.C.E. against Philip II of Macedon. His name has three forms, appearing as Lykkeios, Lykpeios, and Lyppeios. Cf. W. Borgeaud *Les illyriens en Grèce et en Italie: Étude linguistique et mythologique* (Geneva 1943) 27. The Latin reflex of I.-E. *ᵘlqᵘos should be *luvus, whereas the form *lupus*,"wolf," is a borrowing from the Sabine according to A. Momigliano, *Terzo Contributo*, "An Interim Report on the Origins of Rome" (Roma 1966) 553 who refers to M.G. Bruno, "I Sabini e la loro lingua," *Rend. Ist. Lombardo* 95 (1961) 501-541; 96 (1962) 413-442, 565- 640, and to G. Bottiglioni, *Studi Etruschi* 17 (1943) 315-326. It may also show Illyrian influence.

[85] Lact. *Inst.* 1.20.2.

[86] Arnobius 4.3, quoting Varro. According to Plut. *Romulus* 4, *quaest. Rom.* 21, *fort. Rom.* 8, Ovid *Fasti* 3.37, Serv. *ad Aen.* 1.273, and Ps.-Aur. Vict. *Origo* 20.4, the woodpecker as well as the wolf nurtured the twins. However in Plut.*quaest. Rom. ibid.* Nigidius relates that wolves and woodpeckers are always found together. For the symbiotic relationship between wolves and crows v. Cap. 4 *infra*.

[87] S.v. PWRE 6 (1909) cols. 2054ff.

[88] *Hesychstudien: Untersuchungen zur Vorgeschichte der griechischen Sprache nebst lexikographischen Beiträgen* (Stuttgart 1930) 38. Cf. also W. Borgeaud, *op. cit.* n. 83 *supra*, on this entire con ?..x, including Kandaules "l'étrangleur de chien," 115-117.

[89] W.F. Otto *ibid.* col. 2057.

[90] Cf. Eliade, *op. cit.* n. 91 Chap.1 *supra*..

[91] H. Krahe, *Indogermanische Sprachwissenschaft* 1 (Sammlung Göschen Bde. 59 & 64).

[92] Hipponax fr. 4 D.

[93] Serv. *ad Georg.* 1.10. Controversy still rages over the etymology of these names, the connection between them, and the nature of the god Faunus. Perhaps the context in which we have seen the god and his festival exist can contribute towards a decision in the issue. G.

As for the god Soranus, identified with Apollo, his holy place on Mt. Soracte, north of Rome, was revealed by wolves, according to Serv. *ad Aen.* 11.785. It was a cave emitting an exhalation, viz. a wind so noxious that it killed the bystanders, although Pliny[94] maintains it killed not humans but only birds. The priests of this god were the *hirpi Sorani*, a fraternity called after the wolf (*hirpus* in Sabine), who W. Warde-Fowler,[95] for whom the worship of Soranus is a cult of the sun (*sic!*), claimed performed a rain or wind making rite. Even if he is mistaken, the connection of the wolves and the "wolf"-priesthood with the gas escaping in a gust from the mountain (for the exhalations ceased only when the people obeyed the oracle and accepted the wolf's life-style, thus founding the *hirpi Sorani*) is enough to show that wind and wolf are conjoined here.[96]

A similar association is found in the territory of the Sabine nation of the Hirpini (named for the wolf) who lived around Lake Ampsanctus between Aeclanum and Compsa (today, le Mufite between Rocca San Felice and Villamagna). This is a sulphurous body of water, and Dea Mephitis was worshipped there in a cave from which asphyxiating vapors issued.[97] According to Vergil[98] a passageway connected this place with the underworld.

From the comparative evidence, then, it is clear that Apollo's epithets Parnopios, Smintheus, and Erysibios, as well as Erethymios, and his connections to his son Asklepios and the functions of the mantis, are all part of the same complex of ideas that attaches to his epithet Lykeios, and to the name of the wolf. One of the essential features of this complex is the connection the wolf has with agricultural life. We have seen that the wind Favonius brings the grain to ripening in the early spring. The

---

Wissowa, *Religion und Kultus der Römer* (Müllers Handbuch der klassischen Altertumswissenschaft 1885) denied any relation between Faunus and Favonius apart from the shared etymology of their names, and K. Latte, *Römische Religionsgeschichte* (München 1960) 148, rejected von Blumenthal's strictures on deriving Faunus from the root *fav-* (A.W. von Blumenthal *loc. cit.*),and returns to the etymology from that root. Earlier F. Altheim, *Römische Religionsgeschichte* (tr. H. Mattingly, *History of Roman Religion* [London 1938]) II p. 71ff., had argued, with Otto, that Faunus was a wolf-god with wind connections.

[94] *N.H.* 2.93.

[95] *Roman Festivals of the Period of the Republic* (London 1899) 84.

[96] Another possible connection of Soranus with the wolf would be in the etymology of his name, if indeed it derives from the Latin (Sabine) word *sorex*, "the shrew," in Later Latin "mouse," as Altheim, *op. cit.* (note 68 *supra*) holds. In later antiquity Soranus was identified with Apollo (Verg. *Aen.* 11.785, Servius *ad loc.*, and *CIL* 11.7485), and his name derived from *sorex*, so that he became an Italian form of Apollo Smintheus (cf. Wissowa, *RML* I 2,2693f.) K. Latte, *Römische Religionsgeschichte* (München 1960) 148, accepts the etymology proposed by P. Cortsen, "Die Gottheit Súri," *Glotta* 18 (1930) 183, from the Etruscan Súri, a god of death. The cult is explained by Latte as relating to an Etruscan wolf-daemon that emerges from the deep to act as a psychopomp. The word *hirpus*, "wolf," is Sabine, according to Festus *exc.* 106 M. 228 L., and since the name Soranus, with the adjectival ending (a regular variant, acc. to Altheim ibid.), occurs in Sabine as well as Etruscan territory, there is no conclusive evidence that he belonged to one culture rather than another. In fact, the Etr. Súri may have been borrowed from the Sabine, in which case once again, in an Indo-European context (*v. infra*), a mouse-god would be a god of death. This is the more likely because Súri is only one of a number of Etruscan gods of death. All the male gods of Olympus too, with the possible exception of Poseidon and Hephaistos, may be construed in some sense as gods of death, but in no case would that construction suffice to determine their nature.

[97] Pliny *N.H.* 2.208.

[98] *Aen.* 7.563.

names Faunus and especially Favonius, along with the Germanic evidence from the fields of grain, point to a specific wind, and not to wind in general, as the referent of the wolf-name. In the Hellenic world the wind that is primarily the wolf-wind will be the Zephyr, the West Wind that brings the rains that finish the growth of the grain, the most beneficial of all winds.

That winds among the Greeks were prayed to and propitiated like any other gods is clear from *Il.* 23.193ff. where Achilleus prays to Boreas, the North Wind, and Zephyros, the West Wind, to light the fire of Patroklos' funeral pyre. Pausanias 2.12.1 relates that in Titanē there were four sacrificial pits for the four cardinal winds. Moreover specific winds received sacrifice. For example, Xen. *Anab.* 4.5.3f. tells how the trekking Greek mercenaries made sacrifice to the North Wind in order to persuade it to stop blowing violently in their faces.[99] At Athens, where the story of Boreas and Oreithyia was related, frequent appeals were made to Boreas the god of the north wind, especially at the time of the Persian invasions.

Nevertheless, despite the primary reference of the wolf-name in the sphere of wind to the Zephyr, the wind-dimension of the larger context of the wolf-name is not limited to the west or the northwest wind; we shall see in the next chapter that it is widely applied to winds that issue from apertures in the earth. In that case it will characterize all winds, or else those winds that are perceived as beneficial, like the wind that brings the grain to ripening that would seem to be especially associated with the wolf-complex in Rome and in the North European area.

Apollo too, as we saw at the start of this chapter, has prominent connections with the fruits of the earth. We have seen that on one of his chief festivals at Athens, the Thargelia, "Festival of First Fruits," Apollo played a prominent role in regard to Demeter, who personifies the grain. In addition, Apollo bore a number of epithets relating to his role as a god of agriculture: e.g., Aristaios (of which more *infra*), Sitalkas ("of grain's glory") at Delphi,[100] Eriphyllos ("of abundant foliage"), and Phytalmios ("of plantings"). Further, Hesychius reports that he was worshipped as Pasparios (from πασπάλη, "fine flour") in Pergamos and on the island of Paros,[101] and Plutarch[102] tells us the oracular Pythios (generally understood as "the slayer of Python") was worshipped in Eretria and Magnes as the giver of fruits, or rather of wheat.

The wolf-name has its own connection with the grain, or more precisely, with Demeter and Kore, the Eleusinian goddesses. The Attic family of the Lykomidai, which claimed descent from Lykos (Wolf) the son of Pandion, one of the earliest kings of Athens, were in charge of a chapel,[103] whose cult was connected with the Eleusinian goddesses. This cult may have been a sort of privately celebrated ritual of first-fruits (θαργήλια).[104]

---

[99] Cf. further examples in Chap 6 p. 106ff. *infra*.

[100] Paus. 10.15.2.

[101] Cf. ἡ Πασπαρειτῶν πλατεῖα, "The square of the people of Pasparē," on an inscription of Pergamos, *Ath. Mitt.* 27 (1902) p. 101f. nr. 102; and also H. Usener, "Pasparios," *RhM* 40 (1894) 461-471. The modern scientific name of water couch (*v. supra*) Paspalum distichum is a Modern Latin formation from πασπάλη and has nothing to do with Apollo's epithet Pasparios. This fodder grass, on which an ergot with especially hallucinatory properties grows, needs wetlands on which to grow, and accordingly is extremely rare in Greece, and on the Aegean islands.

[102] *Pyth. Or.* 16.

[103] Κλισίον, Paus. 4.1.7.

[104] The sources that speak of this cult are Paus. 1.22.7, 4.1.5ff., 9.27.2, 30, Hesychius *s. v.*,

With the introduction into our investigation of the material collected by Mannhardt and of the Italian evidence, the picture of the animal we are tracking has changed: the "wolf" can no longer be simply Canis lupus. It now appears that he shares the beneficent/maleficent nature of Apollo, and he has led us right back to the *Iliad*'s "toxic" Apollo, with the epithet Smintheus, who shoots his arrows and causes plague and disease. Archery and plague form one of the four characteristic activities of Apollo listed by Plato *Kratylos* 405a3, namely, toxic, "archery and toxicity," iatric, "medicine," mantic, "oracular utterance, revealing the future, and all that is hidden," and music, "music, and all the purview of the Muses." We have had occasion to speak of all them in the context of the wolf-name, with the single exception of music: Apollo Smintheus has appeared as the healer of plague, one of the patrons of iatric, like Apollo Akesios "the Healer," Apollo Nousolytēs "the Banisher of Disease," and Apollo Iatros, "the Physician." We have also seen him connected to oracular utterance, mantic, the third of the four characteristic activities of Apollo listed by Plato. The wind which emerges from the sinkhole or *katabothron* was surely thought of at one time as identical to the breath of man; for Eliade has written:[105] "The body....built up in the course of time by the Haṭha yogins, tantrists and alchemists corresponded in some measure to the body of a "man-god"—a concept that, we know, has a long history both Aryan and pre-Aryan... The point of departure for all these formulas was of course the transformation of the human body into a microcosmos, an archaic theory and practice, examples of which have been found almost all over the world.... The 'breaths'...were identified with the cosmic winds (*Atharva Veda* 11.4.15) and with the cardinal points (*Chāndogya Upaniṣad* 3.13.1-5)."

Breath in turn may have been identified with the spirit of prophecy, as it is in the Hebrew word רוח. In the same context, an ancient Greek story, quite unsubstantiated, tells that the word of the god Apollo entered the mind of the Pythia at Delphi from a chasm in the earth whose vapors (or wind) she inhaled before she uttered her oracles. This story can not serve as primary evidence for a wind-role for Apollo Pythios, the oracular Apollo. We have not encountered the last characteristic activity of Apollo according to Plato, music, unless it is to be thought of as a sort of mantic, dependent as it is, in poetry and in the wind-instruments, upon the breath of man.

It follows, then, that the wider context of the wolf-name must have been attached to Apollo in antiquity, because he is associated with so many phenomena identified with the wolf-name beyond the derivation of his epithet Lykeios from Gr. *lykos*, "wolf," Canis Lupus. Still, as we have seen in the last chapter, his association with the animal is clear. Before we take another look at Pausanias' version of the foundation legend of the famous temple of Apollo Lykeios at Argos in which the wolf figures, let us recall the fact that a statue of a wolf was set up at the altar in front of the great temple of Apollo at Delphi, one of the two greatest sanctuaries he had in Greece, the other being Delos, and moreover, that one version of his birth story told that his mother Leto was in wolf's form when she bore him.[106] The same story, as we have seen already, is found in Aelian[107] who tells us that Apollo takes especial joy in the wolf because he was born to Leto when she was in the form of a she-wolf.[108]

Plut. *Themist.* 1, and *CIG* 386 Boeckh.

[105] *Yoga, Immortality and Freedom* (Bollingen Series LVI 1969[2]) 235.

[106] This is related by Ar. *H. A.* 580a16ff.

[107] *N. A.* 10.26.

[108] The full measure of Apollo's connection with the wolf is given *s.v.* Apollo in Roscher's *Lexikon*.

Pausanias' description of the temple of Apollo Lykeios at Argos (2.19.3) gives what must have been the current foundation myth. We have quoted it in the previous chapter in part, in regard to Danaos' appearance as the stranger and his association to the wolf on that account. In fact, this story is very different from the one told by Servius (Servius-Danielis *ad Aen.* 4.377), in his catalogue of the reasons for Apollo's wolf epithet, concerning a drought and Danaos' daughter Amymōnē's discovery of a water source, told in the previous chapter. There we found Danaos in the role of a benefactor of the country in its hour of need, whereas in the story told by Pausanias he is a rival contender for the throne of Argos.

Danaos, Pausanias tells us, claimed the kingdom by right of his descent from Io. The king of the land, Gelanor the son of Sthenelas, opposed him, and the case was put before the assembly of the Argive people for judgment. When the people voted on the contentions of the opposing claimants the votes were tied, and so they put the final decision off to the next day. At daybreak a herd of cattle grazing near the walls of the town was set upon by a wolf who first attacked and overcame the bull who led the herd. When the assembly met it decided that this was an omen. Since Danaos, the stranger, was like the wolf who came from afar, while Gelanor, the leader of the city, resembled the bull, they awarded the kingdom to Danaos, and he in turn dedicated a temple to the wolf-god, Apollo.

This tale bears all the marks of being an ecphrasis of the sculpture described by Pausanias in the sequel. There he tells that there was a pedestal in front of the temple decorated with sculptures in relief. These were supposed to have been dedicated by Danaos himself, and they showed a wolf and a bull fighting, with a girl, thought to be Artemis, throwing a rock at the ox. In fact the artistic portrayal of a predator, a wolf or panther or tiger, attacking a ruminant is quite common in the archaic period. Perhaps we can elucidate its meaning to some degree with the conclusion to be drawn from the story in Servius-Danielis, namely that the ruminant represents ever-flowing water, while the wolf stands for wind. That the wolf is not always the winner in his encounter with the bull is shown by a famous denarius minted by C. Papius Mutilus, the Samnite leader in the Social Wars against Rome in the early first cent. B.C., which showed a bull goring a wolf.[109] Here the bull was to stand for Italy and the wolf Rome.

The way Pausanias tells the story of the foundation of the temple at Argos offers an explanation for the raising of the edifice but begs the question of the origin of Apollo's wolf-title. It is not claimed here that Apollo was the stranger, but that Danaos, who had come out victorious in the struggle for the throne because of the omen of the wolf's success, chose Apollo as the god to whom he dedicated a temple because Apollo was the wolf-god. The case is otherwise with the story told by Servius, where the wolf and the bull are each connected directly with a natural phenomenon.

Of more interest is the description of the holy precinct of the temple at Argos, given by Pausanias, a description we may embellish with various other ancient texts. It contained the throne of Danaos, evidently some very ancient chair, and a statue of a figure called Biton carrying a bull on his shoulders, like the Moschophoros. Next to Biton, there burned an undying fire, said to have been lit by Phorōneus. As related in the previous chapter, a *bothros*, or artificial pit, was dug in front of the temple at Argos, according to Pausanias here and to Plut. *Pyrrhus* 32.

Now Phorōneus, as Akusilaos, the historian of the Argolid related, was the first

---

[109] G.F. Hill, *Historical Roman Coins* (London 1909) 85.

human being,[110] and the author of the ancient epic poem *Phorōnis*. Clement of Alexandria[111] dates the flood of Ógygos in his time, and says that he was later than Inachos. Io, the Argive heroine and ancestress of Danaos, was called Phorōnis, or "daughter of Phorōneus," although most versions of her story make her the daughter of Inachos, the river-god, who, according to Akusilaos,[112] was also the father of Phorōneus. Phorōneus was the father of Niobē, as well, who plays so important a role in the story of Apollo, and the brother of Argos Panoptēs. He was the inventor of fire, bringer of culture, and originator of law in the state.

What concerns us here particularly is the fact that in the holy precinct of the Wolfish Apollo at Argos there was an undying fire from the earth, called after Phorōneus, who is connected with the flood, and an artificial pit. All these things are connected with the underground, which may be identified with the island of Aiolia, the domain in the Western Ocean under Aiolos' rule from which the winds issue, according to *Od.* 10.1-27f. The West, the realm of death and the setting sun, is conceptually equivalent to the pit or *bothros* where the Thrakians located the home of the winds whence they blew on the face of the earth.[113] As mentioned in the last chapter, the wolf too, *Canis lupus*, with whom Apollo Lykeios is connected, makes its den underground by preference.

Our next task is to show from ancient Greek sources that Apollo the wolf-god was a weather deity, with especial connections to the wind and the rain. Mannhardt thought this facet of the "Kornwolf" or "Roggenwolf" complex primary. It is true that agriculture is dependent on the weather, and that Apollo's agricultural connections imply a connection with the wind. Nevertheless we have seen no direct connection between Apollo and the wind at this stage of our inquiry. Thus we must demonstrate that Apollo did appear as a weather-god in ancient texts and cult, and that the wolf-name was connected with the wind and the weather in many ways in antiquity.

Ancient Greek sources demonstrate this facet of Apollo's functions. Apollo's agricultural epithets we have investigated imply an indirect connection with the wind, but Apollo does also appear directly as a weather-god in ancient texts and cult. One of Apollo's festivals at Athens was the Munychia, in the spring, one month before the Thargelia. The Munychia, named after the horse, was connected with the weather. It marked the start of the shipping season, when ships began to venture into the deep once again after the tempests of winter had subsided. Officially it was the anniversary of Thēseus' departure for Krete, when he sailed off with Minos and the other Athenian young people who were to feed the Minotaur. That journey formed a sacred cycle re-enacted each year in the Athenian calendar.

Apollo also appears as a weather-deity in Herodotos' well-known account of Kroisos on the pyre.[114] As the king of Lydia saw the flames rising about him he prayed to Apollo, and the deity sent a rain-cloud and a downpour to extinguish the flames and deliver him from death. Again we find Apollo in a similar role in Pausanias' historicizing account of the origin of the Athenian festival Pyanepsia, celebrated in October-November, quoted by Eustathius *ad Il.* 23 (p. 1283.6). At

---

[110] *FGrH* 2b23ff.= Clem. Alex. 1.21, 102.5 p.66.5 Stäh. and Eus. *P. E.* 10.12.

[111] *Ibid.*

[112] Quoted in Synkellos 119.14.

[113] Dionysophanes in Σ Ap. Rhod. 1.826.

[114] Her.1.87.1, and cf. also Bacchylides 3.29, and 55, where it is Zeus, the more familiar weather-deity, who brings the rain-cloud.

Thebes, moreover, Apollo had the epithet Chalazios, "pertaining to the hail,"[115] and so, most probably, a cult and sanctuary in that character. The god in Greece most specifically attached to the rain and other weather-phenomena is Zeus; in all the cases quoted it would be reasonable to expect that Zeus, of whom Theokritos writes ἄλλοκα μὲν Ζεὺς πέλει αἴθριος, ἄλλοκα δ' ὕει "at one time Zeus has a fair face, and another time it rains," particularly should appear, as he does indeed in Bakchylides 3.55. However, Aeschylos makes it clear that Apollo is Zeus' eldest son, and Apollo is Zeus' surrogate in many situations.[116] Even Apollo's most distinctive accomplishment, slaying the dragon, is a feat he shares with his father Zeus.[117] So it is not surprising to discover that Zeus' most characteristic domain, that of the sky and the weather, is attached to Apollo as well.

The same relationship that holds between Zeus and Apollo exists also between Apollo and his sons, especially those of them whose names appear also as epithets of Apollo. We have seen how one of the prime areas belonging to Apollo, that of healing, iatric, is pre-empted by his son Asklepios, par excellence. Another son of Apollo is Aristaios, best known, perhaps, from Vergil as the originator of the art of bee-keeping.[118] Aristaios is the god of the Etesian winds, those cooling winds that blow out of the Black Sea into the Aegean and the Mediterranean and mitigate the heat of summer. They allowed the Greeks to sail to Egypt in the sailing season, as Herodotos emphasizes in Book II of his *Histories*. He also gives a date when the possibility of exploiting them for the voyage across the Mediterranean was discovered. On the island of Keos there was a ceremony, reminiscent of the rain-making ceremony on Mt. Lykaion in Arkadia (*v.* Cap. 6 *infra*), in honor of Aristaios. We shall have occasion to examine Aristaios further in Cap. 4 *infra*.

Other wind-gods, too, are associated with Apollo in a number of connections. We are told that Boreas (the North Wind) was instrumental in bringing Leto to Delos, where she gave birth to Apollo. When Hera made the lands on which the sun shined swear to refuse to let Leto to give birth, Zeus told Boreas to bring her to Poseidon, who conducted her to Delos.[119] Boreas, too, is associated with Apollo in a number of connections. According to Sophokles, Boreas' home, to which he carried off the nymph Oreithyia, is "over the sea, at the ends of the earth and the wellsprings of Night, where the heavens open up and the ancient garden of Phoibos (Apollo) is located."[120] This is only one of many places where ancient sources locate the home of Boreas, and the source of "Phoibos' ancient garden" is no doubt the well-documented association of Apollo with the Hyperboreans, whose name meant to the Greeks "those who dwell beyond the North Wind." Apollo's home among this people was placed in the far north, and described as an earthly paradise, and indeed Servius tells us that the North Wind blows from the Hyperboreans.[121] Zētēs and Kalais, too, the winged sons of Boreas, are said to be Hyperboreans.[122]

The Hyperborean maidens Upis, Loxō, and Hekaergē, the two last of whom bear characteristically Apollonian names, were daughters of Boreas, according to

---

[115] Proclus in Photius 231.21.
[116] *Ch.* 244-263, and 269f.
[117] Joseph Fontenrose, *Python, A Study of Delphic etc.* (California 1959) chaps. 4 and 5, 70-93.
[118] *Georgics* 1.14ff
[119] Hyginus *Fab.* 147.
[120] *Frg. inc.* 870N^2, from Strabo 7.295.
[121] *Ad Aen.* 10.350 and 12.366.
[122] Σ Ap. Rhod. 1.211.

Kallimachos[123]; and the three nine foot-tall giants, children of Chionē ("Snow Maiden") and Boreas, and their descendants, were the priests of Apollo and kings among the Hyperboreans, according to Hekataios of Abdera.[124]

Fontenrose seems to have been convinced that Apollo was a weather god; he wrote of a presumed Hittite forerunner of Apollo, "he may very well have been the weather god in some localities, and it may have been this local variant that moved westward into Greece."[125] Now, in addition, we think we have shown that Apollo's epithet Lykeios connects him directly to the wind and the weather. Indeed, the wolf-name itself is attached to the wind in certain Greek texts which were quoted by Mannhardt in *Roggenwolf und Roggenhund*. We are told that the appearance of the wolf or its howl is a sign that a storm is approaching.[126] Ps.-Theophrastos tells us "the howling of a wolf portends a storm within three days. When a wolf passes through the fields, or during a storm, it means a storm at once." Aratos says essentially the same thing in verse: that a lone wolf howling, or else entering a ploughed field, in search of shelter, is a harbinger of a storm within three days. Only the *Geoponica*, which repeats the same omen, omits the mention of three days. A corollary to the wolf-name for the wind is the description of clouds which the wind, as bringer of storms, drives onward, like fleece or sheep, notoriously wolves' prey, as they are in these passages, as well as in Aristophanes *Nub.* 343.

If we look back now at the wider context of the wolf-name in Greece, we see that it appears side by side with three other motifs, apart from its application to the fertilizing wind which brings up the grain. These are:

1. A chasm or cave out of which some gas, or else some hot or fiery material, issues.

2. The occurrence of a flood (or, alternatively, as we shall see, of an ark adrift on the waters).

3. Human sacrifice.

The next three chapters deal with these motifs in this order, with the single exception that between the first two, dealing with the occurrence of the wolf-element in place-names and with the fish or dolphin motif in the context of the wolf-name, respectively, we shall have occasion to examine some names of heroes from the root *lyk-*, "wolf," and their stories, and thereby to augment the material for the discussion of the last two. As we continue our investigation we shall find more evidence for the wolf-name being applied to the wind or wind-like beings, but in addition we shall find that new themes, most especially those of prophecy and of wolf warrior bands, have arisen in the course of our investigation.

---

[123] *Hymn. Del.* 291ff.

[124] Diod. 2.47.7; Aelian *de nat. an.* 11.1.

[125] *Python* 406.

[126] Ps.-Theophrastos *de signis et temporibus* 46; Aratos *Ph.* 1124-1128; *Geoponica* 1.3.

CHAPTER III
THE WOLF-NAME IN TOPONYMY

In various places in the last chapters we have seen subterranean phenomena connected with the wolf in Greece: The wolf of Servius led us to the dry sinkhole, with wind issuing from it. We have also discovered that the precinct of the temple of Apollo Lykeios at Argos contained the undying fire of Phorōneus, and that he in turn has connections with the original flood, at Argos termed the flood of Ógygos. An undying fire in the ground comes *ipso facto* out of a chasm or cave; for gas, or else some hot or fiery material, does not issue out of solid earth. The flood, too, is universally thought of as a subterranean, as well as a celestial, phenomenon, because rising flood waters are thought of as causing it, in addition to torrential rains. The site of the flood story on Mt. Parnassos is adjacent to the oracular sanctuary at whose the entrance the wolf's statue stood in the area of Delphi too, and there the Pythia was said to have inhaled gases from a cleft in the ground. Moreover, Fontenrose has traced the features shared by Lykaon, the Arkadian wolf-hero, and other heroes of flood-stories, like Philemon, of the story of Baukis and Philemon, and others.[1] Mannhardt found that the wolf-name was used for fire as well as wind, etc., in the Scandinavian sources. In our investigation of the occurrences in the Greek area of the wolf-name in connection with caves and winds, or gases, issuing from beneath the ground, we shall ascertain that in certain cases these winds, or gases may be inflammable, and that the wolf-name is applied indifferently to such a spot, whether or not the gas-jet from the earth has been kindled by lightning. Hence in certain cases the term "wolf" expresses the meaning "fire," as well as "wind."

Virtually every place in Greece and Asia Minor whose name is derived from the wolf-name is connected in one of three ways with the wind: Either

(1) a nearby locality is named for the wind (Zephyrion, Anemosa, Anemoreia), on the face of it showing the area to have been windy, or

(2) the locality itself contains a cave, chasm, or sinkhole out of which there issues a gust of wind, or

(3) it is in an area connected with flood stories linked in turn with stories of exposed children suckled by a wolf that contains a place where some flammable underground gases escape through a fissure in a continuous gust of wind.

Numbers (2) and (3) identify our wolf wind with the underworld, and furnish another link between the underworld wolf (cf. Acca Larentia) and the fructifying wind.

In general, wolf-names are extremely common elements in toponymy, all over the world. Some of them may indeed be connected with the lairs of actual wolves, and each should be judged on its own merits. Nevertheless in cases like that of the river Lippe in Germany, whose name is derived from the Illyrian *Lupia, as is that of the Italian city Lecce in Apulia,[2] they represent some derived signification of the wolf-name such as we find in Greece and its area.

In our survey of localities named for the wolf we shall discover examples of all these categories. To begin with, in what can hardly be a simple coincidence, a place

---

[1] Joseph Fontenrose, *Philemon, Lot, and Lycaon* (U. of Calif., Berkeley, 1945). In this work evidence is gathered for the connection of the wolf-name with the mist and wind, and the wolf-god's relation to flood-stories in Greece and Anatolia is discussed.

[2] W. Borgeaud, "Les Anthestéries, Delphes, et le Déluge," *Mus. Helv.* 4 (1947) 213 and 215, as well as already in his *Les Illyriens en Grèce et en Italie* (Geneva 1943) 15.

named for the wolf (i. e. containing the root *lyk-*, in the Greek-speaking area) lies in relative proximity to another named for the wind at three or four separate and distinct points in the Ancient Greek world:

(1) On the plateau of Mt. Parnassos in Phōkis there lies the site of ancient Lykōreia. Some miles to the east is the town of Anemoreia, the modern Arachova, whose name shows the same formation with the root *anem-* substituted for *lyk-*.

(2) In the upper valley of the Helisson in Arkadia, near the town of Mainalos, there existed in antiquity the towns of Lykaia and of Anemosa.[3] Between them were located Mainalos and perhaps Dipaia,[4] but nevertheless the location of a wind toponym in the vicinity of a site named for the wolf is a striking parallel to the situation in Phokis in (1).

(3) The land of Kilikia Tracheia is not only adjacent to Lykaonia, but historically, as when they both formed part of the kingdom of Kappadokia after the war of Aristonikos in the second century B.C.E., the two have been a single unit, while the rest of Kilikia was subject to another ruler. Kilikia Tracheia is where Cape Anemurion (modern Anamur) and the town of the same name are located. The town of Zephyrion was not far away to the east on the coast near Tarsos.

(4) The town of Lyktos (Lyttos) in Krete had as its port the town of Chersonasos, located near Cape Zephyrion, named for the zephyr, according to Ptol. *Geogr* 3.15.14.

The first of these areas, the heights of Mt. Parnassos, is the locale of the most famous of all Greek flood stories, that of Deukalion and Pyrrha. Here, not far from Anemoreia, are both Lykōreia (both names possibly from ὄρος, "mountain") and Lykosura, "Wolf's-tail"(?), both named after the wolf. Fontenrose[5] asks, regarding this area and others to which a flood story is attached, why the wolf-name is connected with the flood. His answer is that the name derives from the presence of mists, clouds, and thunderstorms. The wind, however, which we have seen connected with the wolf, brings the clouds, rain, and thunderstorms, and the top of Parnassos is extremely windy. I have it in a reliable personal communication from Prof. Julia W. Loomis that the wind howls like a wild thing around the semicircle of peaks that comprise Mt. Parnassos. This in itself is enough to account for the names Lykōreia and Anemoreia, perhaps, and a similar wind-tunnel in the valley of the Helisson in Arkadia may have been the reason localities called Anemosa and Lykaia are found there; for Pausanias[6] tells of a sanctuary of Boreas, the North Wind outside the gate of Megalopolis on the road to Mainalos along the river Helisson, and again of a place called Lykoa with a sanctuary of Artemis Lykoatis, in the same area. Nevertheless, in our survey of place names connected with heroes' names and ethnic appellations from the root *lyk-* and from other roots which signify the wolf of the other two categories, where a gust of wind issues out of a cave, chasm, or sinkhole, or some flammable underground gases escape through a fissure, we shall find other cases where such names occur in areas that are sites of a flood story, like the summit of Parnassos. Flood stories seem often to be connected to places where there are ground-fires and frequent volcanic activity.

In all the areas Fontenrose discusses[7] the wolf-name recurs; in Lykaonia, in Lykōreia on Mt. Parnassos in Phōkis above Delphi, and in Arkadia at Trapezus,

---

[3] Paus. 8.30.1.

[4] Ernst Curtius, *Peloponnesos* (Gotha 1852) I p. 314.

[5] *Op. cit.* (n. 1 *supra*) 101.

[6] 8.36.6f.

[7] *Ibid.* (n. 1 *supra*), and for Lykoreia *v.* his *op. cit.* (Chap. 2 n.117 *supra*) p.415ff.

beneath the mountain Lykaion, on its northeastern flank. Pausanias[8] describes the situation at Bathos near Trapezus: "As you go down again from Trapezus to the Alpheios there is a place called Bathos on the left, not far from the river. Here every other year Mysteries of the Great Goddesses are performed. There is a spring here called Olympias, which is dry every other year, and near the spring fire issues from the ground." According to Curtius[9] this Bathos is the deep gorge between the modern Kyparissia and Mavria. Modern observations have confirmed Pausanias' report of ground-fires and Curtius[10] derives the modern place-name Bromosella in the area from the same phenomenon. The ground-fire of Bathos is reminiscent of that of the Chimaira near Olympos in Lykia, which we will have occasion to consider below. Pausanias goes on to describe the cult at Bathos where sacrifice was made to the Astrapai (Lightning-flashes), Brontai (Thunderclaps), and Thyellai (Stormwinds).

He also tells that the Arkadians claimed that this, rather than the famous Phlegraean (Burning) Fields in Pallene in Thrake, was the site of the primeval battle of the gods and the giants. In the region of the modern Paleokastro, too, the ancient Lykosura, south of Mt. Lykaion, there are reports of places where misty or windy exhalations issue from fissures in the ground, and there may be fires there as well, resulting from the ignition of escaping ground gases by lightning.[11] Arkadia, where many places bearing the wolf-name are located, was once called Lykaonia according to Dionysius of Halikarnassos.[12] It is true that at the localities Lykaia or Lykoa in Mainalos and Lykuria in Pheneos in Arkadia no chasms emitting gas or mist are attested, but, as we have noted, there were ground-fires at Bathos near Trapezus. The presence of wolf-names in Arkadia points to their antiquity among the Greek tribes; for the Arkadians were among the earliest Greek immigrants into Hellas, and their eponymous ancestor Arkas was the son of Lykaon. From the case of Bathos we see that a ground-fire can be connected with the wind, as we have already said, no doubt because when such a fire is extinguished the natural gas it feeds on issues from the ground in a rush of wind. This is the most likely explanation of the appearance of names from the *lyk-* root in such localities.

Moreover, any place a rush of wind issued from the ground excited reverence, and so could invite the foundation of a cult. Arkadia is full of sinkholes, and of a sinkhole an early twentieth century Greek peasant of Anatolia explained, "It leads to the World Below" (πάει στὸν κάτω κόσμο),[13] no doubt giving utterance to a common sentiment. In this context we may recall that the chasm through which Herakles drew up the dog Kerberos from Hades was in Mariandynē in Bithynia, whose king was named Lykos.[14] The name Lykos, "Wolf," seems to be especially suited to a sinkhole; for Pliny tells of a river Lycus in Asia that sinks into the ground and bursts forth again.[15] Again, according to Curtius,[16] "most ...(of the sinkholes of the Peloponnesos) are dry in the summer, so that the large cavities serve as stalls for the

---

[8] 8 .29.1
[9] *Ibid.* (n. 4 *supra*) 1.304
[10] *bid.*
[11] Cf. Paus. 8.29.1.; Pliny *N. H.* 2.106 and 110.237; Aristotle *De Mir. Auscultationibus* 127, p. 842B.
[12] *Ant. Rom.* 2.12.
[13] W.R. Halliday, *Greek Divination* (London 1913) 119.
[14] According to Ap. Rhod. 2.139ff.
[15] *N. H.* 2.106, and cf. also Ovid *Met.* 15.273-274.
[16] *Op. cit.* (n. 4 *supra*) 1.36.

herds of cattle or as dens of foxes and jackals." When wolves were common in Greece they may have served for dens of wolves as well; or else foxes and jackals may even have been grouped together with wolves under the generic name *lykos*. This may be another link between the animal name and the wider context of the wolf-name.

Apollo is associated with a chasm in the curious story of the origin of the cult of Apollo Gypaieus at Ephesos in Asia Minor,[17] where the wolf-name is attached to a mountain at whose foot there exists a chasm. "Two shepherds who herded their flocks at the foot of Mt. Lysson in the environs of Ephesos espied a swarm of bees in a deep cavern, difficult of entry. One of them determined to go down in a basket, while the other let him down upon a line. The one who descended into the chasm found honey and a great deal of gold, and loaded the basket three times and sent it up. When there was no more gold he called out that he would come up next, but as soon as he had said the word a suspicion entered his mind, and he put a rock into the basket in his place and gave the signal for it to be hauled up. When the basket was near the edge the hoister dropped it down into the chasm, in order to do away with the other, and buried the gold in the ground. He concocted a convincing story concerning his friend's disappearance, when asked about it. When the shepherd in the chasm saw he had no way of escape, Apollo appeared to him a dream and told him to take a sharp stone and cut his mouth with it in several places, and then to lie still. When he had done so, vultures descended on him, thinking him dead, and one of them took hold of him by the hair with its talons while the other lifted him with its talons by his clothes, and they bore him up to the ravine above. He walked to the city hall and told the whole story. The Ephesians found the swindler guilty, and dug up the gold, whose location he told them of against his will. Half of the gold they gave to the wronged party, and the other half they consecrated to Apollo and Artemis. The shepherd, saved from death and honored with the gold, became one of the richest men, and on the summit of the mountain he built a temple to Apollo which he called the temple of Apollo Gypaieus ('Lord of the Vultures') in memory of his experience."

Mt. Lysson, like Lyktos in Krete (*v. infra*) is named for the wolf. A number of other geographical wolf-names seem to be associated with a similar natural configuration, namely with a sinkhole, Greek κατάβοθρα or ζέρεθρον, which would become a vent for subterranean wind in the dry season. Siderides, in his article on such sinkholes in Greece,[18] describes the violent gusts of wind which issue from the galleries of the sinkhole of Palaiomylos ("Old Mill") in Lake Kopais in Boiotia (many of the sinkholes were used to power mills) when dry; and he writes of a similar current of air at the sinkhole at Verzova in the plain of Tegea-Mantinea in Arkadia.[19] That is enough in itself to explain the wolf-name, if we are justified in deducing from the sinkhole at Argos that Apollo Lykeios or some other patron of the "wolf" held the patronage over all of them. Siderides treats of the story of Lykaon and the flood in the plain of Megalopolis[20] and explains, relying on Philippson,[21] that this plain was once a lake some 10 to 20 km across, before the river Alpheos dug the deep, picturesque canyon of Skorta at Karytaina. It may be that even earlier there was a sinkhole in the plain, which, stopped up, created the lake, and that the names Lykaon and Lykaion

---

[17] Konon 35, *FGrH* 1.202.

[18] N.A. Siderides, "Les Katavothres de Grèce," *Spelunca, Bulletin et mémoires de la société de spéléologie* 8 (nr. 63/64, 1911) 6.

[19] *Ibid.* 31.

[20] *Ibid.* 16.

[21] A. Philippson, *Der Peloponnes* III 1.

derive from that feature of the geography. According to Apollodorus,[22] and Nonnos,[23] who follow a tradition that locates the great flood of Deukalion in the plain of Thessaly, the floodwaters subsided and the waters filling that plain were released and land revealed once more when Poseidon struck the rocks apart at Tempē and allowed an outlet for the river Peneios. This myth parallels the accepted geological explanation for the topography of Thessaly, and most likely was the result of scientific speculation on natural philosophy in antiquity. Relying on M. Martel, *Abîmes*, Siderides writes of temporary lakes at the sites of sinkholes in the Mantinea-Tegea basin: Milyas or Mantinike, northwest of Mantinea, Argon-pedion, Verzova (Sarantapotamos) or Garatis, and Taka.

This last, Siderides tells us, was totally dry in September 1891, having begun to empty out at the end of July. The Verzova sometimes used to form a lake which overflowed into the course of Ophis and sent its waters from Tegea to Mantinea, but Siderides built a dam to hold them in. Dionysius of Halikarnassos follows a report according to which a great flood covered all the valleys of Arkadia and turned them into a great lake when Dardanos and his sons Idaios and Deimos ruled that land.[24] The lake in the plain of Megalopolis might thus have been a lake formed at a sinkhole, as well.

The sinkholes of Arkadia are located in twelve or so so-called kettle-basins, of which seven are contiguous. Hence virtually all the rivers and lakes of Arkadia are in basins drained by sinkholes. Lykuria and Lykorrheuma very likely have their names from them. Strabo remarks that the water in the vicinity of Asea in Arkadia is driven underground and gives rise to both the Alpheios in Elis and the Eurotas in Lakonia.[25] Bury de St. Vincent thought the reference here was to the sinkhole called Taka,[26] which we have already noticed as the site of a temporary lake in the Mantinea-Tegea basin, but we have seen that the Taka sinkhole was totally dry in September 1891, and so could not possibly have been the source of these two streams, as Martel already surmised. At Lykuria there were no ground-fires; however Lykuria is located on the the plateau of Pheneos in northwestern Arkadia. From Konon[27] we learn of an entrance to the underworld in the territory of Pheneos. The people of Pheneos had revealed to Demeter that a sinkhole in Kyllene was the gate of Hades into which Pluto had made off with her daughter Kore, and she requited their good offices with her benefits and never allowed more than one hundred of the citizens to fall in any war. And indeed there is more than one sinkhole in the territory of Pheneos. Lykuria is located on Pheneos' eastern boundary, where it borders Kleitor.[28]

Pausanias[29] tells us that the plateau of Pheneos "lies below the plateau of Karyai, and once the waters rose on it and flooded the ancient sity of Pheneos, so that in our times there are signs left on the mountains of the high-water mark. Five stadia distant from Karyai is the so-called Oryxis (Excavation) and another mountain Skiathis; beneath each mountain there is a sinkhole into which the water from the plateau flows.

---

[22] 1.7.2.

[23] *Dionysiaca* 6.366ff.

[24] *Hist. Rom.* 1.61.

[25] 6.2.9.

[26] *Relation du voyage de la commission scientifique de Morée en 1829* (Paris, Strasbourg, 2 vols. in 8 & Atlas, 1837-1838).

[27] *Narr.* 15.

[28] Paus. 8.19.4.

[29] 8.14.1ff.

These sinkholes are artificial, according to the people of Pheneos, and were made by Herakles. Herakles dug through the middle of the plateau of Pheneos to make a channel for the river Olbios, which some of the people of Arkadia called Aroanios..."[30] He goes on to say[31] that this river had left the bed dug for it by Herakles, but the road to Kleitor ran along the channel dug by Herakles on its way to Lykuria. According to Frazer[32] the lake of Pheneos is drained away at intervals into the River Ladon, leaving a rich, swampy tract.

The sinkholes in the plateau of Pheneos are associated with Poseidon rather than with the wolf-name, which we have associated with Apollo. Pausanias,[33] in the sequel about the town of Pheneos some fifty stades away from the sinkholes, tells of the sanctuary of Artemis Heurippos ("horse-finder") and the statue of Poseidon Hippios ("the horse Poseidon"), allegedly erected there by Odysseus, who had lost his mares and found them in Pheneos. Curtius surmises that "the runaway mares are a figurative expression for the waters that disappear into the katabothra without a trace and then suddenly reappear."[34] If we are to follow the indications, the cult of Poseidon Hippios at Pheneos will point to sinkholes perennially full of water. In fact Strabo goes on to quote Eratosthenes, in the same passage, as having written that "near Pheneos, the river called Anias," the river formed where the Olbios and the Aroanios flow together,[35] "forms a lake at the door of the city, and flows into certain sinkholes, which they call *zerethra*. However, when these are stopped up, as sometimes happens, the water overflows into the plain and flows into the Ladon and the Alpheios, so that once even the area around the temple at Olympia was flooded." Thus usually the sinkholes drained a lake, and were perennially full of water. A confrontation between Apollo and Poseidon, like that we know from the story of Amymōnē in Servius-Danielis, would appear natural here; we do not possess any such story, although a parallel may exist in the confrontation between the two divinities in the myth of the Aloadai, from Thessaly, specifically the area of Tempē, an area whose connection with Poseidon we have noted: Otos and Ephialtes, the famed Aloadai, the sons of Poseidon,[36] who wanted to pile Mt. Ossa on Mt. Pelion and reach higher than Olympus, were slain by Apollo.[37] According to Ps.-Apollodorus their sin was the plan to turn dry land into sea and sea into dry land[38]; their grave and that of their mother Iphimedeia were shown in a precinct of Dionysos, in Anthedon in Boiotia, on the shores of the Gulf of Euboia, west of Chalkis.[39] In this story Poseidon's progeny promote a rupture of the normal face of the land, with its corollary of improper drainage, whereas Apollo stands for the undisturbed, normal course of events in which surplus waters are carried off, and lands drained.

Despite all this, the wolf-name does recur in the plateau of Pheneos, in the place-name Lykuria. In an earthquake region, where changes in the configuration of the land are not uncommon, at one time or another one or more of the sinkholes here may have

---

[30] Cf. also Catullus 65.109.

[31] 8.19.

[32] On Paus.(Cap. 2 *supra* n. 37) *ad loc.* and cf. also *J. H. S.* 22.228-240.

[33] 8.16.4.

[34] *Ibid.* (n. 4 *supra*) 1.191.

[35] According to Frazer (Cap. 2 *supra* n. 55) on Paus. 8.14.3.

[36] *Od.* 11.305ff.; Hesiod fr. 19 (MW).

[37] *Od.* 11.318.

[38] 1.7.4.3.

[39] Paus. 9.22.6.

been dry. If Herakles' presence here may be connected with keeping the sinkholes in working order, a work he was renowned for at Lake Kopais in Boiotia, there is also a tradition in Pheneos of a confrontation between Herakles and Apollo. Herakles is said to have stolen the tripod from Delphi and brought it to Pheneos. Apollo was angry with Herakles over the theft; a thousand years later he flooded Pheneos as punishment for its part in the affair.[40] Indeed fifteen stades north of Pheneos there was a temple of Apollo Pythios,[41] the Apollo of the oracle at Delphi , whose cult-epithet is discussed below. It is worth remarking here that the other example of a flood in which Apollo had a part, that which afflicted Troy in punishment for the Trojans' breaking their word to pay for the building of their walls, was caused by Apollo in conjunction with Poseidon, who had served King Laomedon in fortifying the city as well.[42]

Another feature of the landscape of Pheneos is the river Styx, which falls from a height directly into a sinkhole. In antiquity there was a low wall of unmortared stones at Nonakris built around this sinkhole,[43] in connection with which we encounter the wolf-name in the plateau of Pheneos for the second time. The ancient town Nonakris was named after Lykaon's wife, and Ovid tells us that Pallas, Styx's husband, was a son of Lykaon.[44] This agrees with Dionysius of Halikarnassos,[45] according to whom Pallas the son of Lykaon was the father of Nikē (Victory), whereas Hesiod,[46] telling much the same story, omits the name of Pallas's father and adds three more children of Styx, daughter of Ocean, and Pallas: Zēlos (Competition), Kratos (Strength), and Bia (Force).

Curtius compares Stymphalia to Pheneos and says that it repeats the same features on a smaller scale.[47] At Stymphalia, however, we do not find the wolf-name. The sinkhole here is at the foot of the cliffs of Apelauros, and the water entering it was, and still is, supposed to feed the river Erasinos in Argos; it appears as a perennial stream that falls into the lake in winter and directly into the sinkhole in summer, as Pausanias expressly states.[48] Hence we need not expect to find the wolf-name here. Strabo[49] relates that in his time Stymphalos was fifty (-five?) stades from the Stymphalian Lake, although it had been on its shores in earlier times, when the flow of water into the the underground outlet of the lake, leading to the Erasinos River in Argos, had been stopped in the wake of an earthquake that caused the sinkhole to fall in.[50] The wolf-name does recur in the mountains of Apelauros; for the valley called Lykorrheuma, where there may have been a sinkhole that was dry in the summer, is located there.[51]

There was yet another place named Lykaia in Arkadia, in Kynuria.[52] Its location is unknown, and so it is impossible to tell what, if any, source of wind there might have been in its vicinity.

---

[40] Plut. *de sero numinis vindicta* 557C and 560.
[41] Paus. 8.15.5.
[42] *Il.* 7.452; Ovid *Met.* 11.206-207.
[43] Paus. 8.18.4ff.; Herod. 6.74.
[44] *Fasti* 5.97.
[45] 1.33.
[46] *Theog.* 383f.
[47] *Ibid.* (n. 4 *supra*) 1.200.
[48] 8.22.3, and he calls the sinkhole τὸ βάραθρον.
[49] 8.8.4.
[50] *Ibid.* (n. 4 *supra*) 1.207.
[51] *Ibid.*
[52] Paus. 8.27.4.

To return to the subject of ground fires, the land of Lykaonia in Anatolia, the area around modern Konya, is known for its salt flats, and for volcanic activity. Also in Anatolia, in the land named Lykia, separated from Lykaonia by the wild land of Pisidia, are found the mountains named in antiquity the Mountains of Hephaistos, that is, of fire,[53] where there was an emission of gas which could be set afire with a torch.

This was no doubt a reference to the ground-fire, known since the fourth century B.C.E. as the Chimaira[54] and today called Yanar Taš, the 'Burning Rock,' about 800 or 900 feet up in the hills to the west of the site of the ancient city Olympos in eastern Lykia. According to Bean, who visited the site twice, the "fire has been burning since classical antiquity at least.... As a whole the hillside is thickly wooded, but at one point is an open space almost bare of vegetation, some fifty yards wide and long, strewn with white and grey stones. Towards the bottom of this the fire is burning in a deep hole two or three feet in width; at night it is visible from far out to sea, but by day it is much less spectacular. The flame hardly rises above the mouth of the hole; its volume is about that of a small bonfire... This is very much the same that Beaufort saw in 1811, but other reports vary considerably. Spratt in 1842 says that in addition to the large flame there were smaller jets issuing from crevices in the sides of a crater-like cavity five or six feet deep.[55] Von Luschan in 1882 also saw a main vent and numerous small ones, and Hogarth in 1904 found almost invisible flames rising from a dozen vents."[56]

Bean goes on to relate[57] that "the main flame will succumb to a glass of water, though it reignites itself in ten or fifteen seconds.... Hogarth was told by his guide that fire would break out wherever water was poured, and on making the test found it to be so. Neither in 1952 nor in 1967 was the present writer able to confirm this." Ktesias of Knidos,[58] however, in the fourth century, stated that water feeds this fire, rather than extinguishing it, but that it can be put out with earth.

It is remarkable that in later antiquity this natural phenomenon was given the name of the Chimaira, a monstrous fire-breathing animal,[59] that fell prey to the hero Bellerophontes; for the application of the name of an animal, albeit mythological, to a ground-fire supports our identification of the wolf-name with similar ground surface phenomena. In fact the Chimaira of Homer and the mythological tradition about it was supposed to have come from Lykia,[60] or from Karia,[61] but Strabo does not locate it in this part of the country at all, but in the region of the steep mountains named Kragos and Antikragos west of the Xanthos valley, "in whose vicinity the myths tell the story of the Chimaira took place; and not far away is the Chimaira, a ravine extending up from the shore." Hence the identification of Yanar Taš with the

---

[53] See M. Delcourt, *Hephaestus* (Paris 1957) 175. She quotes Pliny *N. H.* 2.106 to the effect that the gas emitted there could be set afire with a torch, and Maximus of Tyre 8.8 ("Mount Olympos in Lykia belches forth fire, not like that of Aetna, but tranquil and compact; this fire constitutes a temple and a portent for them.") Cf. also Picard in Daremberg-Saglio *Dictionnaire des Antiquités etc.* 1919) *s. v.* Vulcanus, and L. Malten, *Jahrbuch des deutschen Archäologischen Instituts* (1912) 232 and 328, who would like to imagine gas vents near Kragos.

[54] Ruge in *PWRE* (Stuttgart 1899) 3 col. 2281.

[55] T.A.B. Spratt, *Travels and Researches in Crete* (London 1865) 95-96.

[56] George E. Bean, *Turkey's Southern Shore* (Praeger, London, N.Y.1968) 167.

[57] *Ibid.*

[58] *FGrH* 688F45e.

[59] According to Homer, *Il.* 6.179f., "a lion in front, a snake in back, and a goat in the middle."

[60] Strabo 14.3.5, and Eustathius *ad Il.* 6.179f.

[61] *Il.* 16.328.

Chimaira is not original and may go no farther back than Ktesias. Accordingly, we must admit that the original appellation of the Burning Rock is hidden from us in the mists of prehistory; it may, however, be associated somehow with the name Lykia for the whole country.

Today it is generally accepted that the names Lykia and Lykaonia signify "land of the wolf." Thus, Cornelius, writing of the incursions of the Manda-Warriors, the earliest Indo-European invaders of Anatolia, tells unequivocally how "other groups of adventurers who called themselves 'Luquoi,' 'Wolf-people,' penetrated into the land since named from them 'Lugga-udne,' i.e. 'Lugga-land,' or 'Lykaonia,' in the Hellenic period,"[62] and explains[63] that "despite the hypothetical nature of the connection, the noun Luggaudne and the adjective 'luwili' [from which 'Luwikia,' 'Lykia,' is derived] together, like those of the Italian tribes of the Piceni and the Vitali, to whom names corresponding to animal-names were given, seem to point to a form with a labiovelar *luqu-, corresponding to Lat. lupus and Gr. λύκος." Years earlier the derivation of the name Lykia from an earlier *Luwikia had been taken to mean "of Luwian descent." [64]

The controversy on this score has been long and vehement. In 1955 Guthrie wrote, in accord with the view of Wilamowitz and of Nilsson,[65] that no one at that time believed that Lykia has its name from the wolf. These authors were of the view that Apollo's epithets Lykeios and Lykios were geographical, like Artemis' epithet Leukophryene, and, signifying "the Lykian," had nothing at all to do with the wolf. In fact in antiquity the epithet Lykios, in contradistinction to Lykeios, was understood to refer to Apollo as "the Lykian god," and seems not to have been identified with the wolf- name until the Roman period,[66] although it certainly must have recalled, as far back as we can trace it, the Lykian cult of Leto near Xanthos and the Lykian version of Apollo's birth-story, noted above, according to which Leto bore him when she was in the shape of a she-wolf.

Recent discoveries such as those presented by Laroche,[67] tend to confirm the hypothesis put forward by Kretschmer,[68] that the Greeks rediscovered their own god Apollon Lykios in the principal god of that people; although according to Laroche Apollo and Artemis were purely Greek gods introduced into the divine precinct (the Letōon) of the great Lykian mother-goddess Eñi ("Mother"), identified with Leto, and the principal god of the Lykians was Trqqñt:Tarkunt, a storm-god, identified with Zeus in Lykia, whose name leads us to Kilikia and to Etruria (with Tarchon and Tarquinia, etc.).

A posteriori Apollo's epithet Lykios might refer to the wolf, in view of the analogy of other such alternations in animal names in o-stems, e. g. hippios, which

---

[62] Friedrich Cornelius, Geschichte der Hethiter (Darmstadt 1979) 23 and 45.

[63] Ibid., n. to p. 23.

[64] Gregory Nagy puts it thus in "Greek-like Elements in Linear A," GRBS 4 (1963) 209. Cf. also L.R. Palmer, "Luvian and Linear A," Transactions of the Philolological Society (1958) 75-100, and Enc. Brit. (14th ed.) s. v. 'Anatolian Languages.'

[65] J.F. Guthrie, The Greeks and their Gods (Boston 1955); U. v. Wilamowitz-Moellendorff in Hermes ; M. Nilsson, Geschichte der griechischen Religion (Munich 1941) and Minoan-Mycenean Religion 443 n. 1.

[66] Cf. R.P. Eckels, Greek Wolf-Lore [Philadelphia 1937] 64f.

[67] Emmanuel Laroche, "Les Dieux de la Lycie Classique d'après les textes Lyciens," Actes du Colloque sur la Lycie antique: Bibliothèque de l'Institut Français d'Études Anatoliennes à Istanbul (Paris 1980) 1-6.

[68] P. Kretschmer, Einleitung in die Geschichte der griechischen Sprache (Göttingen 1896) 370f.

occurs in composition in Homer, but alone first in Pindar, and *hippeios*, the regular Homeric adjective from ἵππος, "horse," *kaprios* and *kapreios*.[69] If such is the case then the existence of the fiery Yanar Taš, the Burning Rock, or Chimaira, a truly remarkable phenomenon, may have something to do with the toponym Lykia. Moreover, and most important, we are led to assume that a tribe or nation bearing a specific animal or theophoric name often tended, at a remote period, to fix its habitation in a spot to which the general context of its animal or theophoric name applied, or alternately to take its name from the geologic features of the land in which it dwelled. That would be the case here as well as in the Arkadian or Lykaonian landscape; and the case of the Dacians and their land Dacia would constitute another example.

Mircea Eliade[70] associates the name of the Dacians of old with the ancient Indo-European root *daw- meaning "to strangle," and applied like the German "würgen," from which the word 'warg,' a Germanic synonym for 'wolf,' is derived, to the wolf. Eliade does not, however, associate the location of the Daci with their name, but rather explains its application to that people from the warrior confraternity named after the rapacious carnivore that formed its nucleus and traces the survival of these conceptions. We are in a position, now, to understand that the settlement of the ancient Daci in modern Romania, the land of the once productive oilfields of Ploeşti, as well as others, must not have been fortuitous, just as the other Indo-European groups named for the same animal settled in similar areas: the Anglo-Saxon group which called itself the Deanas, "Wolves," from the same root, have left their name in the form Dean (or -dean) all across Southern England where today there are productive oilfields (not to speak of dean-holes), the Lugga of Anatolia settled in Luggaudne, the area of the ground-fires of Lykia or Lykaonia, and the Hyrcanians of ancient Iran, settled in Vehrkana (Hyrcania) named for the wolf, dwelt near the volcanic range in which the great peak of Demavend is located.

At Lykoreia on Mt. Parnassos, whose proximity to Anemoreia we have already noted, an ancient hypothesis which could explain the wolf-name posited a wind which issued from the Korykian Cave there. Nowadays, however this hypothesis is not accepted. Fontenrose writes[71] that "if in allusion to an oracular chasm we see memories of the Corycian cave, then everything is accounted for except the toxic vapors; and they seem to be no more than late fantasies, due perhaps to an old tradition that the harmless vapors or cold currents of air which were seen or felt as the issued from the cave, perhaps on a chill morning, had the power to inspire men with prophecy," but he concludes that "we have no real evidence for chasms and exhalations..."[72] Perhaps, however, one piece of real evidence does exist; for there is a sinkhole here which may provide an explanation for the persistent ancient tradition of a wind issuing from the earth in the region of Delphi. Fontenrose reports that there is "a sink (katavothra) in the southwestern corner of the Arachovite meadows of the Parnassian plateau, where the waters of the winter rains collect, fairly near the Corycian Cave."[73] We hardly need search any farther for the source of the names Lykoreia and Anemoreia, nor for the origin of the "Delphic chasm"! When the sinkhole is dry, in the summer, a steady gust of wind must indeed issue from the earth

---

[69] Cf. E. Schwyzer, *Griechische Grammatik* (Munich 1939) 1.466.

[70] *Op. cit.* (Chap.1 n. 91 p. 19 *supra*) 15-31.

[71] In his discussion of the oracular chasm at Delphi in *Python* 414-415.

[72] Idem, *The Delphic Oracle* (Univ. of California 1978) 203.

[73] *Python* 547.

at Lykoreia.

In the same way, we discover a sinkhole quite near the Kretan town of Lyktos (Lyttos). We have already noted the proximity of Lyktos to Cape Zephyrion. In an inscription from Andros[74] there appear Lyttians of the seacoast (Λύττιοι οἱ πρὸς Θαλάττῃ) as well as Lyttian uplanders (τοῖς ἄνω). Stephen of Byzantium[75] says the town is named after Lyktos the son of Lykaon, but that some say its name is Lyttos because it located on a height; for they say an upland or a height is called λύττος.

Many features in this region of Eastern Krete, the land of the Eteokretans in antiquity, recall the wolf-complex we shall meet in the following chapters: nearby was the city of Milētos, named after Milētos, the son of Apollo and Akakallis, who was exposed as a child and suckled by she-wolves sent by Apollo.[76] On Krete Lyktos is the birthplace of Zeus,[77] whence he was taken to the Aigaian Cave, the cave of the she-goat, Amaltheia.[78]

Lyktos, moreover, was also known as Karnessopolis,[79] a name which conceivably might derive from Apollo's cult-epithet Karneios and the Luwian ending ass- "sanctuary." It was the home of Meriones, the henchman of King Idomeneus.[80] Clement of Alexandria informs us that Antikleides of Athens, in his Nostoi,[81] told that the people of Lyktos sacrifice humans to Zeus. Felix Jacoby, in his note on this, compares Servius who tells us that "when Idomeneus, King of the Cretans, of the stock of Deucalion, met with a storm as he was returning home after the fall of Troy he vowed to sacrifice whatever he came upon first, and it happened that his son ran to him first of all. When he sacrificed him, as some say, or wished to sacrifice him, as others maintain, a plague broke out, and, driven out, he took Cape Sallentinum in Calabria and founded a town nearby, so that 'Idomeneus of Lyctus surrounded the Sallentine fields with an army' (Aen. 3.400)."[82] Jacoby also quotes the report that the Kuretes of old on Krete used to sacrifice children to Kronos[83] in the same context. We may remark in this connection that Idomeneus was the son of Deukalion, the hero of the best-known Greek flood-story.

Ancient Lupiae corresponds to the modern Lecce. Lupiae was a city of the Salentians, said to have been founded by a certain king of the Messapians (Dauni) named Malennius son of Dasummius,[84] and once thought to have been located near the small beach at San Cataldo, 7.5 m east of the modern Lecce, where in 1928 there were found Cyclopean walls,[85] but it has been demonstrated that Lecce itself is ancient Lupiae; for ancient Calabrian cities had two parts, one inland, and one a harbor on the

---

[74] IG 12.5.723.

[75] S. v. Lyktos.

[76] Nikander in Antoninus Liberalis 30, Herodoros of Herakleia FGrH 31F45.

[77] Hes. Theog. 477ff.

[78] This is most likely the cave of Ida, according to the foremost expert on the caves of Krete, P. Faure, Fonctions des Cavernes Crétoises [Paris 1964] 95, although it is not near Lyktos.

[79] S. v. in Hesychius.

[80] Il. 2.646 and 19.611.

[81] Clem. Al. Protr. 3.42.5, FGrH 140F7.

[82] Servius ad Aen. 3.121. Sallentini is another name for the Dauni, as are Messapii and Iapyges, according to F. Altheim ARW 219, 32, cited in W. Borgeaud op. cit. (Chap. 2 n. 83 p. 36 supra) 101, so that we are dealing here again with a people whose name is derived from the wolf.

[83] Istros, the slave of Kallimachos, FGrH 334F48.

[84] Hist. Aug. M. Antonin. 1.

[85] Baedeker's Southern Italy and Sicily, 17th Rev. Ed. 1930.

coast.[86] Surprisingly the modern name does not derive from the Latin form Lupiae, or from the Messapian (Salentine) form Luppa, but from an alternate Illyrian form *Lukpa or *Lukka[87] corresponding to, and no doubt influenced by, some Greek form like Lyktos. This area of Italy is associated with the name of the hero Diomedes, whose connection with human sacrifice in a wolf-context is discussed in Chap. 6 *infra*, as is his connection with the Dauni, who are the same as the Salentians. Much of Apulia and ancient Calabria (Messapia, Ἰapygia) has clear wolf-connections. Pliny tells of a wondrous lake in the land of the Salentini, near Manduria, whose waters are never diminished by what is taken out of it, nor increased by what is added.[88] This may be the lake of Anduria near Casalnuovo, and it may hide a sinkhole.

Spratt, after following Strabo in locating Lykastos near Lyktos in Krete, describes the location of Lyktos:[89] it is "upon the summit of a narrow but tortuous ridge overlooking the plain [Pediada] upon its eastern margin." He goes on to relate that the city was situated at the point where numerous narrow ridges branch off from the main ridge, and that the ravines below contain most of the remains of the ancient town and continues: "Immediately under the summit, and due east of Lyttus, is another very large mountain basin also called Lasethe [like the Lasithi mountains which rise to the southeast of Lyktos, the third in height in Krete, reaching almost 7000 feet in height], which is at an elevation of 3000 feet above the sea.... This remarkable basin has no outlet, being perfectly enclosed by mountains.... Its rivers and torrents, consequently, have no visible connexion with the lower coast streams, but, after uniting in one torrent bed, the waters fall into a large cavern at the west extreme of the plain, and thus escape to the sea through the bowels of the mountains by what the Greeks call a katavothron, but to reappear, according to the native opinion, as the Aposoleme River, to the northwest, some seven or eight miles distant."

Hence Lyttos too, whose name must originally have been *lykjos, "Wolfish," like λύσσα, "rabies," or "raging madness," from *lykja, "the wolf's disease," lies close to a spectacular sinkhole, whence its name may derive; for the same name, in the form Lysson, appears as the name of a mountain containing a chasm in the foundation story of the cult of Apollo Gypaieus at Ephesus quoted *supra*.

According to Faure[90] there are a number of sinkholes in Krete, aside from the high plateau of Lasithi. One is ἡ τρύπα τοῦ ξεροκάμπου (i tripa tu xerokampu), two km north of Hagios Nikolaos on the Gulf of Mirabello, another τὸ βουλιασμένο ἀλώνι (to vuliasmeno aloni) on the north side of Mt. Stroumboulas, and yet another Omalos (ὁμαλός), like Lasithi a high limestone plateau. The first of these is certainly dry in summer, located as it is, like Lasithi, on the east side of Krete, and bearing the name of "the dry field." Yet it has no locality bearing the name of the wolf nearby. The ancient name of Hagios Nikolaos was Kamara, and it actually was the port of Latos, named after the mother of Apollo and Artemis. Omalos in the White Mountains on the western portion of the island is probably never dry, nor is τὸ βουλιασμενο ἀλώνι (to Vouliasmeno aloni) near the center of the island; their case will be the same as the sinkholes in Arkadia named for Poseidon.

In Athens there is another place named after the wolf where there seems to have been a sinkhole, parallel to Lyttos and to the Arkadian sites we have looked at

---

[86] M. Mayer, *Philologus* (1906) 514, 517.
[87] V. n. 83 *supra* and esp. W. Borgeaud *op. cit.* (Chap. 2 n. 83 p. 36 *supra*) 120.
[88] N. H. 2.106.
[89] T.A.B. Spratt, *ibid.*
[90] *Op. cit.* (n. 73 *supra*) 27 n. 7.

cursorily. That is the Lykeion (Lyceum), the precinct supposed to be named after the hero Lykos son of Pandion,[91] located near the sanctuary of Herakles at Kynosarges ("White Dog" or "Swift Dog") and not far from Alopekai ("Vixens"), so that Jane Harrison thinks of the wolf as part of "a very nest of totemistic remembrance."[92] We may disregard the totemistic hypothesis,[93] and hazard a guess that the location of a wolf-precinct here is rather connected with the precinct of Gaia Olympia within the precinct of Olympian Zeus, and with the grave of Deukalion shown in the same hallowed area.[94] According to the *Marmor Parium* [95] heavy rains during the reign of King Kranaos had forced Deukalion to flee Lykōreia on Mt. Parnassos and take refuge at Athens, where he was known as the builder of the temple of Olympian Zeus. In the precinct of Gaia within the temple precinct people pointed to a hole in the ground a cubit wide, a long dry sinkhole identified as the hole into which the waters of Deukalion's flood had drained away. This story was of paramount importance in connection with the Athenian festival of the Hydrophoria,[96] a festival of Dionysos celebrated every spring in commemoration of the victims of the flood. Moreover, once every year on a certain day honey-cakes were cast into this sinkhole;[97] Plutarch[98] remarks that the festival of the Anthesteria commemorated the victims of the flood, on the day of the Chytroi, as Theopompos tells us,[99] and it is not unlikely that all these celebrations were one and the same.[100] Hence the sinkhole here, like the one into which the Styx falls, and others elsewhere, was of considerable cultic and mythic significance.

The location of the Lykeion close to the sanctuary built by Deukalion of Lykoreia who had come from the general area of Delphi does not appear to be accidental, in light of the evidence we have presented. In fact, the explanation of topographical names containing the root *lyk-* in terms of features of the natural landscape can be paralleled in the case of a few other place-names, like Olympos, perhaps, or mountain names from the roots *tur* or *taur*, and possibly also in the case of Henri Grégoire's tentative suggestion concerning the origin of the place-names resembling Gortyn-Kroton from an ancient word for "a height."[101] The meaning of similar place-names like Kastabos of Lykia, and Kastabale in Kappadokia and Kilikia, is lost today, as are those of many other such families of place-names. The towns and regions whose name contains the root *sid-*, Sidon, Isinda, Side, Sinda, Sindita, Sindaga, Sind, and Hindustan, if they all belong together and are named after the pomegranate, as Pestalozza[102] would have it, do not seem to have got their names because of any shared feature connected with their location. We are in a rare case, then, being able to establish such a connection.

We have noted another sinkhole associated with Apollo Smintheus in antiquity,

---

[91] Paus. 1.19.3.

[92] Jane E. Harrison, *Mythology and the Monuments of Ancient Athens* (London 1890) 120.

[93] Cf. Chap. 1 n. 92, *supra*.

[94] Paus. 1.18.7-8, and cf. also Strabo 9.4.2.

[95] Ep. 2-4.

[96] Photius *Lex. s. v.*, quoting Apollonios.

[97] Paus. 1.18.7.

[98] *Sulla* 14.

[99] *FGrH* 115F347.

[100] L. Deubner, *Attische Feste* (Berlin 1932) 113.

[101] H. Grégoire, *op. cit.* (Chap. 2 n. 32 *supra*) 29.

[102] U. Pestalozza, 'Iside e la melagrana,' *La Religione mediterranea.Vecchi e nuovi studi ordinati a cura di Mario Untersteiner e Momolina Marconi* (Milan 1952).

and he is a deity we have found to be closely connected with Apollo Lykeios. This was at the oracle of Marpessos of whose famous Sibyl, called Herophile, a name given to the Erythraean Sibyl as well, the inhabitants of Alexandreia in the Troad (where the Sibyl Herophile of Marpessos was also said to have resided) told that she was a priestess of Apollo Smintheus.[103]   Only Pausanias, here, and Tibullus[104] give the name with a "p"; elsewhere we find Marmyssos, Marmissos, Marmessus, and Mermessos.

The oracle was situated at the spot on the river Aïdoneus, which bears the fuller or expanded form of the name of the god of the dead, Hades, where it falls into a sinkhole, and rises again once before it is swallowed up entirely. The oracle has been located northeast of Ilion, west of the river Kalabaki, but the river Aïdōneus and its sinkhole have not been found.[105]

We may go on to examine the roots of two other Apolline epithets which often accompany his wolf-name in cultic and geographic contexts and are clearly related to it: Pythios and Delphinios, the roots that appear in Apollo's sanctuary at Delphi, where his oracle bore the name Pytho.

The root *delph-* of the Greek word for dolphin often appears in conjunction with the root *lyk-* in cultic and geographical contexts in Greece, and a third root often is joined to these two, namely the root *pyth-*, which combines three areas of meaning in Greek: 1) 'the snake or dragon that Apollo slew at Delphi,' and hence, in the plural, 'ventriloquists,' Gr. πύθων (python), Iranian *Pathana*, the name of a mythological monster, Hebr. פתן, 'viper'; 2) 'to rot, make or become putrid,' Gr. πύθω, πύθομαι; 3) 'to learn, inquire,' Gr. πυνθάνομαι, πεύθομαι, Skt. *budh-*. i.e. *bodhati*, 'to wake, be awake, observe, learn, understand, be aware,' Rus. будить, пробуждать, 'to awaken.' The names built up from these roots have various relations: One may be part of an area's toponymy and the other of its cultic conformation or mythical history, or both may belong to one or the other of these realms. Their frequent conjunction in well-known localities warrants further investigation.

We have seen the second root, *lyk-*, occurring frequently in connection with the wind, aside from its primary employment in the name of the wolf. Traditions of winds blowing out of caverns or of gases escaping from underground attach to places named after the wolf. Alternatively, near a place named for the wolf we have found a town named for the wind; that collocation presumably denotes a wind tunnel, or some other especially windy district.

Why do names derived from the root *delph-* occur so frequently in the same complex?   The most common use of the root in Greek is in the word δελφίς, "a dolphin," (if we disregard those uses derived from the cult-site Delphi). We may perceive a more general meaning for its occurrences in words of widely different signification: δέλφαξ (and perhaps δέλφος as well) means "a full-grown pig,"[106] or perhaps "a sow," according to Athenaeus,[107] who connects the word, correctly, with a word δελφύς, "the womb": κυρίως δ' αἱ θήλειαι οὕτως λεχθεῖεν ἂν αἱ δελφύας ἔχουσαι, "The word properly signifies the female of the species who possesses a womb." The reason he gives is absurd; for it is for another reason and not because sows possess a womb that they are called δέλφακες.

---

[103] Paus. 10.12.5.
[104] Tibullus 2.5.67 (Quidquid Amaltheia, quidquid Marpesia dixit).
[105] R. Kiepert, "Gergis und Marpessos in der Troas," *Klio* 9 (1909) 10ff.
[106] Hdt., etc.
[107] 9.374D.

The Greek root *delph-* derives from an I.-E. **gwolbh-*; the basic meaning of both seems to be "fetus."[108] By metonymy the pregnant womb, or simply the belly, is signified by these roots, as in Sanskrit: *garbhas*. Thus the Greek ἀδελφός, "brother," derived by Aristotle[109] from α (="together") and δελφύς, i.e. "together in the womb," has the alternate, primary, meaning, to judge by its use, of "twin," like the parallel ἀγάστωρ, that is to say, "together as fetuses." Other Indo-European languages are even clearer on this point: English "calf,"with its double meaning of "cow's young" and "the swollen part of the leg," points to these two significations. The word originally meant a fetus of any kind. The word "mooncalf" demonstrates that meaning; originally it meant "an abortive shapeless fleshy mass in the womb," a misbegotten monstrous birth; later it came to mean a false conception regarded as produced by the influence of the moon (*OED*). The calf of the leg, on the other hand, is so called because it represents a swelling of the body very like a pregnant belly. The Gaulish word *galba*, "a fat man" attests to the same complex of meanings.

The semantic connection of the pregnant womb and the fetus with with the pig and the dolphin is as follows: We may assume the pig's name to be prior to the dolphin's in Greek. The Greeks are generally considered to have been a continental, inland people before they reached Greece, and, besides, land animals are more familiar than marine. The dolphin was likely named δελφίς from the pig (unless the name came directly from the newborn child, or the fetus). Both the dolphin and the pig are portly animals with smooth skins (specifically the domesticated pig) and an affinity for wetness. Also both species have small eyes, and the beaked dolphin's snout may rather remotely have recalled that of the pig. Support for this derivation comes from the name of the porpoise, a cetacean very similar to the dolphin, which is the Old French porc-peis, "pig-fish."

The pig, δέλφαξ, on the other hand, shares its name in Greek with the fetus, or the newborn child. Both tend to be wrinkled and grayish-pink, but most strikingly, newborns tend to have flattened noses and tiny eyes, like pigs. "Piggies" can substitute for babies in fairy tales. Furthermore, the flesh of man masqueraded as the flesh of pig in the terminology of those American cannibals who invited the early European adventurers who stepped on their shores to feast with them on "long pig." These are some of the factors that explain the semantic connection between Gr. δέλφαξ, "pig," and Indo-European *gwolbh-, "fetus." The Greek word is the name of the pig, not, as Athenaeus would have it, because the sow has a womb, but because of a superficial, striking resemblance. In the same way, due to a superficial resemblance, the delphinium plant is called after the dolphin.

At the outset of our investigation we noted that the pig-name was given to the wind, according to Mannhardt's researches, just as was the wolf-name. Perhaps the dolphin which can function as a harbinger of wind and tempest, as we shall see, does so as a reflex of a larger category that includes the sow (Ger. Sau) in the Indo-European linguistic area.

The name of the dolphin is not rare in Greek toponymy. Delphi and Delphinion are two of the better known cases. They seem to be connected with Apollo's cult title Delphinios. On the face of it that title recalls the dolphin; and indeed the *Homeric Hymn to Apollo* would have both the place-name Delphi and the cult epithet

---

[108] For the semantic sphere of *gwolbh- see Otto von Sadovszky, "The Reconstruction of I.E. *pisko- and the Extension of its Semantic Sphere," *The Journal of Indo-European Studies* 1(1973) 81-100. The following discussion is indebted to that paper.
[109] *Historia Animalium* 510b13.

Delphinios recall the dolphins who led the Kretan sailors to the bay of Krisa and the site of Delphi. We find Apollo bearing the title Delphinios in Krete, Thera, Chios, Aegina, Sparta (in the form Delphidios), Krisa, Chalkis, Delphinion, Athens, Miletus, Olbia and Massilia (Marseille).[110] All of these, except Athens and Sparta, are coastal areas, and in Krete there are two attestations of seaports. Apollo Delphinios, moreover, is recognized as a god of seafarers.

Nevertheless, the origin of the epithet and its appropriateness to Apollo are in dispute among scholars.[111] The argument has centered about the city where the cult can be considered to have been "at home." Some have thought that place was Delphi, while others have opted for Krete or Chalkis, or elsewhere. Another question in dispute is whether it applies to Apollo in his role as god of colonization, inasmuch as the dolphin is a marine animal and the colonies were founded by people who reached them in ships, or in his role as dragon-slayer, being connected first and foremost with the cult-site Delphi, or whatever. It seems simplest to keep the dolphin of the Homeric *h. Ap.* in the foreground, and see the god as the patron of sailors and seafarers, but in fact the root *delph-*, as we have seen, can not be explained so easily, with its wide semantic field. Perhaps the complex of names it appears in may serve to illuminate its meaning to the Greeks of the Dark Ages of Greece and earlier.

Perhaps Greece's most celebrated shrine was that of Apollo at Delphi. It was right near Lykōreia, as we have seen, a site that preceded it as the Oracle of Apollo, according to certain sources. Furthermore, a wolf's statue stood before the great temple of Apollo at Delphi itself. Three elements come together here: the wolf, the *lyk*-name, and *delph*- name. A number of tales attempt to explain the name Lykōreia. According to a late false etymology[112] it derives from λύκων ὡρυγαί, "the howling of wolves," and was named by refugees from Delphi who were led to its high ground providentially by the howling of wolves during the flood. After the waters subsided Delphi was resettled from it.

The last feature of the story, that Lykōreia was the mother-city of Delphi, is repeated in more common, and apparently more ancient, because more naive, traditions. These too relate the town to the flood, in different ways. We learn that Deukalion was king there when the flood began,[113] and that it was at Lykōreia that Deukalion landed his ark.[114] We learn that the inhabitants of Delphi had earlier resided at Lykōreia, and once were called Lykōreis.[115] The Korykian Cave, probably the earliest sanctuary in the area of Delphi, was in the territory of Lykōreia. Menander Rhetor is referring to Lykōreia when he states that Delphi was founded right after the flood. All this has led J. Fontenrose to conclude that the original seat of the Delphians, and the original seat of the Delphians, and the original oracle of Apollo, was at Lykōreia, "the wolf-town," founded by Deukalion[116]

That is not all there is to the story. Fontenrose has found reason to identify Deukalion with Lykos or Lykōros, the original hero of Delphi. Relying on the verbal correspondence between the ruddy man, Pyrrhos (another name of Neoptolemos,

---

[110] A full list of these attestations can be found in *PWRE* 4.2513- 2514 in Jessen's article "Delphinios."

[111] *Ibid.* 2515.

[112] Brought by Paus. 10.6.2.

[113] Marmor Parium 4-7.

[114] Lucian *Timon* 3.

[115] *V. Schol. Vet. in Ap. Rhod.* 2.711 and 4.1490; also Strabo 9.3.3.

[116] Fontenrose, *op. cit.* (Chap. 2 n.117*supra*) 419ff.

Achilles' son, who was torn to pieces at Delphi), and Pyrrha, Deukalion's wife in the myth, he equates Deukalion with Pyrrhos. Pyrrhos, or Pyrres, whose shrine Fontenrose himself excavated at Delphi, was a predecessor of Apollo at that shrine.[117] He was said to have been buried beneath the floor of the great temple of Apollo at Delphi, before receiving a sanctuary of his own in a special precinct. Now the flood of Deukalion was commemorated each year at a Delphian festival called Aiglē, celebrated most likely two or three days before the full moon of January or February, at the same time as the Athenian Anthesteria festival, the last day of which was devoted to commemorating the victims of the great Flood; this was the same time of year when Apollo was believed at Delphi to return from his sojourn among the Hyperboreans. Moreover, Dionysos is said to have perished and returned to life in the Flood.[118] Deukalion, otherwise called Pyrrhos, in Fontenrose's interpretation, also returned alive from the flood waters; hence, in view of their spring resurrection, Dionysos, Deukalion, and Lykos-Pyrrhos may all be the same figure, appearing under different names because of minor variations in the tales told of them, and Apollo may be associated with them as well. Lykos or Lykōreus, the eponymous hero of Lykōreia, was the grandfather of the hero Delphos, through his daughter Kelaino. Since the genealogical tables also name Deukalion as grandfather of Delphos through his daughter Melaina-Melanthō (whose name, like Kelainō means "black one"), the two may again be identified. Hence we need not be surprised to discover the wolf, or a wolf-personage, paired with Deukalion. At Athens too, as we have seen, we find a collocation of the three names.

In short the name Delphi has two connotations. If in the Homeric *h. Ap.* it is associated with the dolphin, it is no less associated there with the power of prophecy and the site of the oracle of Apollo. Now, we have discussed, on p. 55 *supra*, one of the puzzles concerning the site of Delphi, namely the persistent ancient report that the Pythia, the priestess of Apollo there, gained her prophetic powers from a gas which issued from a chasm or cleft in the ground. The story has been dismissed as a fabrication, but we have suggested that it took its origin from the sinkhole at Lykōreia nearby. From the appearance there of the root *lyk-*, which denotes, *inter alia*, a wind tunnel in the earth, we may imagine that the wind, or spirit, that issued from the marked site was associated with mantic powers, and when the sinkhole, which gave the *lyk-* name its original signification, was forgotten, the story of a chasm was invented to convey the same meaning. In the next chapter we shall discuss the dolphin's association with the power of prophecy.

Just as there was a myth that told of wolves leading men to a favorable site for settlement in Lykōreia, as we have seen, so the raven or crow has the same function, in connection with Apollo, in at least one well-known Greek context: he flew before the men of Thēra who settled Kyrene guided in their ship by the god Apollo in the form of a Mediterranean seal.[119] Moreover the same bird , crowed in Apollo's ear the sad news that his beloved Korōnis (also named for the crow), the mother of Asklepios, had betrayed him with a Haemonian boy, Ischys, and caused him grief,[120] just as it grieved Athena by revealing that two of the daughters of Kekrops had opened the basket that contained Erichthonios, so that when she heard the news she dropped the mountain she had brought from Pellene to be a bulwark for the Akropolis and it became Mt.

---

[117] J.E. Fontenrose, *The Cult and Myth of Pyrros at Delphi* (Berkeley 1960).
[118] Diodorus 3.62.10.
[119] Hdt. For more on this subject see Chap. 4 section 1 *infra, s.v.* Oiolykos.
[120] Ovid *Met.* 2.531ff.

Lykabettos.[121] This is the context in which the raven is famed for being a bird of prophecy: Aristotle[122] tells us its crowing presages rain and wind (*sic!*), and Plutarch[123] calls expertise in understanding the language of crows and jays a sort of mantic power.[124]

In Indo-Iranian folklore there is another curious link between the raven and the wolf. We have noted that B.A. Rybakov[125] compares the flying dogs of the Tripolye neolithic culture to the Sassanian Sēnmurw, a great bird with a canine face that causes seeds of all plants to fall to earth from the world tree when she lands on her great nest in that tree (on which *v.* chapter 7 *infra*). The Sassanian Sēnmurw, called *Si-murg* in Pahlavi and *paskuj*, or something similar, in the languages of the Caucasus and others[126] appears as a "female raven" in the Jewish hermeneutical tradition on the *pushkanza* פושקנצא.[127] In the same way the picture of this bird with a canine face sitting in a tree at the end of a Spanish manuscript of the fifteenth century is labelled *corvus*. Now it seems the same bird is called a wolf, i.e. necessarily a flying wolf; for we hear of "the grey-blue wolf, whom they call *pashgunj*."[128] The Sēnmurw, who can be identified with the Indian Garuḍa or (Pali) Garuḷa, the steed of Vishnu, is most generally recognized as the manifestation of the *xvarena* (Mod. Pers. *farn*), the paramount symbol of warlike valor in Iran, but she is also a nurturing mother, as well as the one who causes all seeds to sprout, in her function as wind-wolf, despite her frightening, demonic nature. Hence she combines virtually all the ideological functions of the wolf in the Indo-European linguistic area.

It remains for us to introduce the symbiotic relation that exists between ravens and wolves in the wild, for which we may quote the words of one who has followed wolves in their natural habitat, on Isle Royale in Lake Superior:

> One of the few birds that regularly maintain a close relationship with the wolf is the raven. This large black member of the crow family occurs throughout most of the wolf's present range and is primarily a scavenger.....flocks of ravens routinely follow wolf-packs from kill to kill and live on the leavings of the packs. When following wolves ravens fly ahead of them, land in trees, await the passing of the wolves, and repeat the process. When the wolves attack prey, the birds sometimes swirl about them excitedly. Once I saw a raven sitting in a tree cawing as wolves harassed a wounded moose. Sometimes the scavengers even join wolves in eating the bloody snow around such a moose. Besides following wolves directly, ravens often track them....They are often rewarded by the discovery of fresh wolf-droppings, which they pick apart and feast upon before continuing on. Another aspect of wolf-raven relations can be seen in the "playful behavior" indulged in by both animals..... Lois Crisler (*Arctic Wild* [Harper, N.Y. 1958] 28) observed

---

[121] Amelesagoras fr. 1 *FGrH* IIIB330.

[122] Fr. 241.7 Rose.

[123] *Septem Sapientum Convivium* 7.152D.

[124] Cf. also Aesop no. 213 (Halm).

[125] *Op. cit.* n. 8 Chap. 2 *supra*.

[126] Hanns-Peter Schmidt, "The Sēnmurw, of Birds and Dogs and Bats," *Persica* 9 (1980) 59ff.

[127] *Tal. B.Tractate B. B.* 73a.

[128] From the Pahlavi text *Me-no-gi i Xrad* 26.49-50 quoted in Mirza Hormazdyr, "The Pahlavi Word for Monster," *Proceedings and Transactions of the All-India Oriental Conference, Sixteenth Session* (Lucknow 1951).

....activity between her free-ranging wolf-cubs and a raven and described it as follows: "He let the pups trot to within six feet of him, then rose and settled a few feet away to await them again. He played this raven tag for ten minutes at a time. If the wolves ever tired of it he sat squawking until they came over to him again.".... It appears that the wolf and the raven have reached an adjustment in their relations in such a way that each creature is rewarded in some way by the presence of the other and that each is fully aware of the other's capabilities. Both species are extremely social...[129]

Even more remarkable is the amazing performance of ravens and wolves singing together witnessed by Lawrence.[130] No doubt people have always been aware of the relationship between these two species, since myths and folktales concerning one of them so often include or are told of the other. In Greece too the story that Apollo cursed the raven that brought him the sad news of Korōnis' infidelity and changed his color from white to black seems to set the bird firmly in the context of the wolf-name we have been trying to elucidate.[131] The Greek story that the raven was once white[132] may reflect an ancient belief that because he flies through the hole in the firmament through which men glimpse the fire beyond, namely the sun, he has turned black, being covered with soot like a chimney-sweep. Thus he appears to be the counterpart of the wolf at Delphi who represents the mantic power at the oracle, because he is able to pass beyond the bounds of the seen into the realm of the unseen.

The theme of the wolf and the raven is much better attested from Germanic mythology and from the myths and social organization of the Indians of the Northwest Coast of North America. We shall have occasion to return to these themes, but for now let us note that the Teutonic god Oðinn kept two wolves at his side who accompanied him into battle along with his two ravens Huginn and Muginn, and tore the bodies of the fallen. The Germanic name Wolfram, moreover, derives from *wulf-hraban*, "wolf-raven."

Another bird that, like the raven, has mantic powers is the dove. At the famous oracle of Zeus at Dōdōna Peleiades, or Doves, had a special place. The oracle at Dōdōna was founded at the behest of a dove who showed the ancient inhabitants of the place a holy oak.[133] According to Herodotos and those who follow him the mantic priestesses of Dōdōna were called after the dove as well: Peleiades.

Doves are also associated with the raven more simply; the two birds have a similar gait when walking, and again, the dove and the raven are the messengers sent out by Noah in the Biblical flood story (Gen. 8.7-12). Moreover, it seems that the dove and the wolf are somehow associated as well; for a plant named for the dove in Greek is also called after the wolf: the plant named peristerion, after the dove, Gr. περιστερά, and described by Dioscorides,[134] has been identified with Lycopus exaltatus, the tall wolfsfoot. Hence the dove, too, seems to have a place in the wider context of the wolf-name.

In the fifth chapter of this book we shall investigate the dolphin as another

---

[129] L. David Mech, *The Wolf* (New York, Natural History Press, 1970) 287.

[130] R.D. Lawrence, *In Praise of Wolves* (Totem Books, Toronto, 1987) 194-195.

[131] Cf. G. L. Huxley "White Ravens," *GRBS* 8 (1967) 199-202, who also cites Ovid *Met.* 2.535-541, Call. *Hec.* fr. 260 56ff. (Pfeiffer), Hyginus *Fab.* 202, and Apollod. 3.10.3.

[132] *Ibid.*

[133] Hdt. 2.55.

[134] 4.59.

parallel to the wolf, along with Apollo's epithet Delphinios. The comparison of wolf and dolphin will lead us through the sea-lion and the whale to the Pacific area, and specifically to the Pacific Northwest of North America, where the chief culture hero of the Tlingit and of the other peoples of the area is the Raven.[135]

The dove and the dolphin appeared together in the strange statue of Demeter Melaina that stood in a cave at Phigaleia in Arkadia described by Pausanias.[136] Here a stone statue portrayed the goddess with a horse's head, holding a dolphin in one hand and in the other a dove. There can be no doubt that the dove, the counterpart of the raven, appears here in conjunction with the dolphin to show that sky and sea both are in the hands of the fructifying earth with her cereal crops.

In the Greek tradition the raven makes a third to the wolf and the dolphin as an animal connected with Apollo's wolf epithet. Our investigation of the wider context of the wolf-name has led us to the conclusion that it is connected to the wind, and more particularly to that wind which issues from the bowels of the earth. This may be all wind, in the primitive view, for we know from general Greek tradition of the cave of the winds, as well as of a great bag of wind, provided by Aiolos, "the steward of the winds" (*Od.* 10.19ff.), which may lead to the conclusion that the wind is not something that blows free, but rather a small part of an immense surge of moving energy that is pent up somewhere out of sight, or beneath the surface of the seen, which amounts to the same thing. Now each of these three animals is connected with one of the three great divisions of the world. A tripartite division of reality of a sort appears in Poseidon's words in *Il.* 15.189-192:

> All things are divided three ways, and each (god) has his own domain: I have received the grey sea to dwell in always, since we cast lots; Hades' lot fell out in the misty dark; and Zeus received the wide sky... The earth is held in common....

To the casual observer as well all things are divided three ways: into the earth, the sea, and the sky. The dolphin or whale, of whom we shall learn more in the following chapter, regularly emerges from the surface of the sea in order to breathe and goes under again, and this activity of his must have appeared to those ignorant of its true cause as if he were relaying messages from under the sea.

Furthermore the concept of the wellsprings of the deep and the windows of heaven, familiar from the Biblical flood story,[137] was widespread. It is in the Welsh tradition, however, that we find a third hole in the "skin" of reality, as it were: here we find that there are "three wells of the ocean," one of which is identified with the "sea-flood," i. e. the ebb and flow of the tide, the second with the rain falling through the air, and the third, named Dyfrdonwy, is said to "come through the veins of mountains like the flinty feast made by the King of Kings."[138] This hole under the mountains is the one to whom the wolf belongs; and just as the animal in this case appeared as the messenger from that unseen realm beyond the surface of things, so the storm and the wind, and prophecy, and fire, and martial courage, all things we have seen bearing his name in the wider context of the wolf-name, may well seem to come from beneath the earth under the mountains, as well.[139]

---

[135] Viola E. Garfield & Linn A. Forrest, *The Wolf and the Raven* (Seattle 1948).

[136] 8.5.8.42.

[137] Gen. 8.2.

[138] *Bulletin of the Board of Celtic Studies* 5.124 and *The Myvyrian Archaiology of Wales*, 2 ed. O. Jones *et al.* (Denbigh 1870) 25, quoted in A. & B. Rees, *Celtic Heritage* (London 1961) 52.

[139] À propos, Jarich Oosten, "Theoretical Problems in the Study of Inuit Shamanism," in Mihály

In the last chapter we have seen that the idea of the macrocosm and the microcosm is exceedingly ancient. There we quoted Mircea Eliade to the effect that in India the "breaths were identified with the cosmic winds (*Atharva Veda* 11.4.15)."[140] Now we shall see that the wolf we have come to know in the macrocosm from the wider context of the wolf-name reappears in the microcosm in an ancient Roman spell against flatulence:[141]

> When you lie down in bed rub your stomach and say thrice: "The wolf went along on the road, on the path; he was eating up the solids and drinking up the liquids." This physic is quite effective for digestion in practice.[142]

The relations between the macrocosm and the microcosm are reversed here, we may notice, insofar as the relation of the hidden "outside" of the sensible world, where the cosmic wolf resides, to its more or less orderly manifest inside answers here to the relation of the wolf of the private person, i.e. his hidden, unseen, unfathomable innards where reside heartburn and gas pains, and his inscrutable, suspect heart, to the manifest, open, clear human face.

A striking corroboration of Apollo's rôle of revealer of the hidden world implicit in his links with the animals, the wider context of whose names we have been investigating, comes from the demonstration that Apollo's gesture on the Parthenon frieze, where he bares his nakedness by drawing aside his cloak, is the same as that of a number of other classical statues of the god. This baring, or revelation of the hidden, was considered perhaps the most important of his functions by the Greeks of the classical period in their portrayals of the divinity.[143]

The same concatenation of ideas, the hidden over against the manifest, is met with in the toponymy of the island of Dēlos, the most famous site of Apollo's birth, where Leto is said to have borne Apollo "on rocky Dēlos, leaning against the long ridge, the Kynthian hill."[144] The scrub-covered granite hill called Kynthos, from the Greek verb κεύθω, "to hide," is the most conspicuous feature of the island of Dēlos, whose name means "manifest." The first part of the *Homeric Hymn* deals with the appearance of Dēlos out of the waves to provide a place where Apollo might be born,

---

Hoppál and Otto von Sadovszky (edd.) *Shamanism Past and Present* Part 2 (Budapest 1989) 336, tells that in the séances of the shaman among the Inuit (the *angakkoq*) the symbolism of the breathing hole (*aglu*) that connects this world with the nether and the upper worls is found; the shaman passes from one world to another like a seal that surfaces (*nuqqaqtoq*) through the hole in the ice. We can now comprehend the importance of the duck or some other diving bird that appears as the primeval creator of the world in tales from far and wide collected by M. Eliade, *Zalmoxis, the Vanishing God* tr. W.R. Trask (Chicago 1972) Chap. 3 pp.95-106; these birds function on land, in the sea, and in the air, i. e. in the realms of wolf, raven, and dolphin, and like all of them disappear from view, for they dive below the surface of the sea. The mythological significance of Penelope's name is hereby explained, as well. Why else should her parents have named their daughter "Duck"?

[140] Cap. 2 *supra* n.104.

[141] Marcellus *de medicamentis* ed. Helmreich 20.78 in R. Heim, "Incantamenta Magica Graeca et Latina," *Fleckeisens Jahrbücher für classische Philologie Suppl.* 19 (Leipzig 1893) 487.84 (in Cap. V: *Similia similibus*).

[142] Cum te in lecto posueris, ventrem tuam perfricans dices ter: Lupus ibat per viam, per semitam, cruda vorabat, liquida bibebat. physicum hoc ad digerendum de experimento satis utile.

[143] Evelyn B. Harrison, "Apollo's Cloak," *Studies in Classical Art and Archaeology* (New York, J.T. Augustus, 1979) p. 93.

[144] *H. Ap.* 16-17.

since all the lands under the sun had been bound by an oath to Hera to deny Leto a place to lie in of Apollo. Thus Dēlos, as the place where Apollo became manifest, is itself an island that was made manifest out of the hidden undersea realm, where it existed as a reef before. Still, the hill on the island is named for the hidden realm.

The cult of Apollo Aiglētēs (also known as Apollo Asgelatas[145]) on the island of Anaphē is attributed to a similar occurrence, where the hidden manifests itself. Apollo caused the island to appear out of the waves during a storm in which Jason and his men on the Argo were caught on their return from Kolchis with Medea. "The men on the Argo prayed much and besought aid greatly, and Apollo held up an arrow above them and dissipated all their sorrows. A great light shot down from on high, and from the abyss the earth released an isle on which they anchored. They named it Anaphē ('lighting up, kindling') after the occurrence, since it had seen the sunlight for the first time, and built a temple to Apollo Aiglētēs ('Giver of Splendor')."[146]

---

[145] In the inscription of Timotheos, *CIG* 2.2477, from the island.
[146] Konon 49 *FGrH* 1.210.

CHAPTER IV
HEROES OF GREEK MYTH WHO BEAR THE WOLF-NAME
OR PARTAKE IN ITS WIDER CONTEXT

In our survey of place names containing the root *lyk-* in the last chapter we have encountered names of heroes derived from the same root. In this chapter we will treat, in the first section, some of those heroes of Greek myth who are named Lykos, and, in alphabetical order, some of those in whose name the root *lyk-* appears, then, in the second section, some of those who are said to have close connections to the cult of Apollo Lykeios, and, finally, in the third section, some of those who show features associating them with the complex of ideas we have dealt with in the previous chapters.

In the course of our investigations into these figures of mythology we shall find lines of thought leading backwards to the agricultural sphere we have delineated, and forwards into themes of outlawry and death, and of immortality in humans and other living things. Outlawry and death are associated with the wolf-figure as symbolic of initiation and of crossing borders, in general. The second of these great themes, that of immortality, is a facet of Demeter's sphere among the divine functions, no less important than her association with the grain, treated at greater length in Chap. 6 *infra*. Furthermore, a number of connections with other Greek divinities, and other mythological themes, emerge from the study of these heroes. For example, Hermes and Dionysos appear here not infrequently in their functional relationships with Apollo.

1.HEROES IN WHOSE NAME THE ROOT *LYK-* APPEARS
Lykos

We have already met one famous hero of this name, the Athenian hero, son of Pandion, the founder of the cult of Apollo Lykeios at Athens, after whom the Lyceum (the Lykeion), the school of Aristotle at Athens in later times, was named.[1] His name arose in the context of the proximity of his precinct to the that of Gaia Olympia within the precinct of Olympian Zeus, where the grave of Deukalion was shown,[2] along with the sinkhole where the waters of the flood of Deukalion disappeared, according to the Athenian tale. The Lykeion, we noted, is near the sanctuary of Herakles at Kynosarges ("White Dog" or "Swift Dog") and not far from Alopekai ("Vixens"). The connection this Lykos son of Pandion has with the flood story suffices to refute the view that the name Lykos was originally that of a Thrakian god whose worship spread over Boiotia, Attika, and part of the Peloponnesos, who was identified with Apollo.[3] Rather it would seem this Lykos, and the other twenty odd heroes of the same name, are reflexes of the wider context of Apollo's divine nature expressed in his wolf-epithet.

This Athenian Lykos is known in the sources as the ancestor of the family of the Lykomidai, a race of priests and prophets, as the founder of Lykia in Asia Minor when he was exiled from Athens, and as the restorer of the mysteries of Andania, in Messenia.

---

[1] Chap. 1 p. 3 *supra*. Paus. 1.19.3.
[2] Paus. 1.18.7-8, and cf. also Strabo 9.4.2.
[3] Sam Wide, *Skand. Arch.* 1 (1891), and *Lakon. Kulte* 12.383. Cf. also *PWRE* 13.2 col. 2398ff.

The Attic family of the Lykomidai, which claimed descent from Lykos (Wolf) the son of Pandion, were, as we have seen,[4] in charge of a chapel (κλισίον[5]) where a cult connected with the Eleusinian goddesses was celebrated.[6] Because this family was also involved with prophecy, which properly belongs to Apollo, we may perhaps assume this was a sort of privately celebrated ritual of first-fruits, like the public festival of the Thargelia at Athens in which Apollo and Demeter were associated.

Strabo[7] emphasizes the Atthidographers' agreement that Pandion, king of Athens, had four sons, Aigeus, Lykos, Pallas, and Nisos, the last of whom inherited Megara and founded Nisaia. He goes on to quote Sophokles to the same effect:[8] Aigeus, speaking, says,

> "My father set the shore aside for me and sent me there, assigning me the best part of the land, while to Lykos he will assign the garden of Euboia over on the other side, and for Nisos he has chosen the bordering land of Skeiron's shore, while to Pallas, the unyielding breeder of the earthborn, there has fallen the southerly portion of the land as his lot."

Apollodorus[9] tells much the same story, adding that Pandion, the son of Kekrops and Metiadusa, ruled in Athens after his father's demise, but was forced to go into exile in Megara by a revolt of the sons of Metion. There he married Pylia, the daughter of Pylas, and reigned over Megara. After Pylas killed his paternal uncles he handed over the sovereignty over Megara to his son-in-law, himself retiring to the land of Messenia in the Peloponnesos, where he founded Pylos. In Megara Pylia bore him his four sons, and he died there. Subsequently his sons returned to Athens, defeated the sons of Metion and divided the land up among themselves, although the supreme sovereignty fell to Aigeus.

Lykos became an exile, like his father Pandion before him, and two stories were told of his adventures. According to Pausanias[10] he was driven out of Athens by Aigeus and migrated to Arene in Messenia, where he revealed the cult of the Great Goddesses, i.e. Demeter and Kore, celebrated in later years at Athens by his progeny, the Lykomidai, to Aphareus, his wife Arene, and their children. So he restored the mysteries, originally founded by Kaukon in Andania, by revealing the rites of the goddesses to them there. Pausanias, however had already written in his guide to Messenia:[11]

> Lykos the son of Pandion, however, brought even greater honor to the Mysteries of the Great Goddesses many years after Kaukon, and the thicket where he purified the initiates is still called Lykos' wood. A poem of Rhianos of Krete tells of a wood called "Lykos' wood" in this land in the following lines: "And near rugged Elaion and above/ Lykos' wood." It is clear that this Lykos was the son of Pandion from the inscription on the statue of Methapos; for Methapos too made certain improvements in the rites of the mysteries. This Methapos was an Athenian by birth, an

---

[4] Chap. 2 p. 39*supra*.

[5] Paus. 4.1.7.

[6] The sources for this cult are Paus. 1.22.7, 4.1.5ff., 9.27.2, 30, Hesychius *s. v.*, Plut. *Themist.* 1, and *CIG* 386 Boeckh.

[7] 9.1.6.

[8] Nauck 872.

[9] Apollod. 3.15.5.

[10] 4.2.6

[11] 4.1.6-9.

aficionado of the mysteries and the inventor of all sorts of religious rites. He set up the mysteries of the Kabeiroi in Thebes, and erected a statue in the booth of the Lykomidai bearing a long inscription containing all we need to substantiate our account: "I sanctified the temple of Hermes and the paths of holy Demeter and her firstborn, Kore, where they say Messene taught by Kaukon, the seed of Phlyos' famed son, set up a contest in honor of the Great Goddesses, and I stood amazed at all the Attic rites which Lykos the son of Pandion established in wise Andania." This inscription makes it clear Kaukon, a descendant of Phlyos, came to Messene, and also proves what I have written relating to Lykos, and especially that the mysteries had existed at Andania from ancient times.

Prophecy (which we have seen may be associated with wind, when the human body is considered as a microcosm), the land of Lykia, and the founding of the cult of Apollo Lykeios connect this Lykos with the Apolline wolf-complex we have been investigating; what is new in his contribution to the wider context of the wolf-name is the theme of becoming an exile, found also in the story of his father Pandion. This is the theme that was chosen by Immerwahr[12] to represent the meaning of the wolf-complex. It is the theme found in the English expression "lone wolf," and widely encountered in the Teutonic cultural area, and elsewhere in the Indo-European area.

Most important, however, for our purposes, is the association of this Lykos with the mysteries of the Great Goddesses, with Demeter and Kore. These goddesses function chiefly in the agricultural sphere, the sphere of the growth of the grain, and their mysteries are those of the rebirth of the dead the way the seed of grain regenerates when buried in the earth. The same connection we find here holds, as we have noted above, in the festival of the first fruits at Athens, the Thargēlia, shared by Apollo and Demeter.

2. A second Lykos too we have already met in passing. He is connected with Delphi, rather than with Athens, and he appears as an attacker of the temple site, who tried, during the First Sacred War in the early sixth century, to steal the tripod of Apollo, the holy symbol of the temple and of the oracle, but was stoned to death during the attempt.[13] This role is attributed to Herakles, as well.

This Lykos (Lykōros) has been identified with Pyrrhos-Neoptolemos, the son of Achilleus, who was torn to bits by the angry crowd of Delphians when he attempted to desecrate Apollo's temple and carry off the tripod, and at a further remove, with Dionysos, the god whose σπαραγμός, "being torn to bits," was famed among the Greeks, with Delphos, the predecessor of Apollo at Delphi,[14] and with Deukalion as well.[15]

The identification of these figures is something we have found corroborated in the juxtaposition of names from the roots lyk-, delph- and deuk- in many Greek cities. Names from the root delph-, recall the dolphin, of which we shall treat infra in Chap. 6, and Deukalion recalls the flood-story, which we have encountered in the history of Lykos 1, as well. As for Pyrrhos, he is the hero whose grave was shown on the sacred precinct at Delphi; his name means "the red," and the flaming red color, associated by Fontenrose with the Biblical Adam (from Heb. אדם, "red"),[16] may recall Antisthenes

---

[12] H. Immerwahr, *Die Kulte und Mythe Arkadiens* I (1891).

[13] *Hippocratic Corpus* 9.412 (Littré)

[14] Aesch. *Eum.* 15f.

[15] Fontenrose, *op. cit.* (Chap. 2 n.117*supra*) 422 (cf. also p. 412ff.).

[16] Fontenrose, *op. cit.* (Chap. 2 n.1 *supra*).

of Rhodes the Peripatetic's anti-Roman report of the great red wolf that devoured all of the Roman general Publius on the coast of Aitolia, except for his head, which continued uttering dire prophecies concerning Rome under the influence of Phoibos Apollon Pythios, whereupon the people built a temple of Apollon Lykios (sic!).[17]

Lykos, "Wolf," and the other heroes who attacked Delphi, fell before the power of the god Apollo. Here the wolf is subordinate to Apollo, and we may surmise that the epithet Lykeios means "master of the wolf," in the first place (with all that the wolf-name implies), and not "incarnation of the wolf." The wolf's subjection to Apollo, the chief representative of the strength of the Olympian gods of the younger generation in the Greek tradition, also belongs, at a further remove, to the context of Apollo's most important feat in mythology, the slaying of the dragon. In general, dragons in mythology stand for interrupted traffic; they sit at the crossroads and prevent passage onward. What the wolf represents is precisely passage between realms, and the master of the wolf, like the slayer of the dragon, ensures that the roads are open. Dragon-slaying appears among the accomplishments of two of the most famous Apollonian "wolvish" heroes, as well, Thēseus, of whom we will treat in Chap. 5 infra, and Perseus.

3. A third Lykos is the king of Thebes, father or uncle of Megara, the wife of Herakles, whom Herakles killed upon his return from Hades, either (in his madness) along with Megara and her sons, or else because he had been oppressing them. He is to be viewed in the context of Herakles' slaying of another wolf-hero, Lykaon the son of Ares and the nymph Pyrēnē (the patroness of the Pyrenees), and also in connection with the opposition between Herakles and Apollo inherent in the famous story of the theft of the tripod from Delphi by Herakles, and in the opposition between the open sinkholes, which seem to belong to Apollo, and the clogged ones which seem to fall within Herakles' purview.[18]

4. There is another Lykos, king of Thebes, the husband of Dirkē, who so sorely persecuted Antiopē,[19] the mother of the famous twins Amphiōn and Zēthos. The intricacies of this Lykos' story have been retold, and classified, by Vian.[20] Antiopē is a key figure for an understanding of the wider context of the wolf-name, because one early version of her story makes her the daughter of a Lykurgos,[21] and other versions the wife of a Lykos[22] or of a Lykurgos,[23] whereas the vulgate makes her the victim of Lykos and Dirkē. In any case, the wolf-name is associated with the Greek term for the seal, φώκη, in this tale; for subsequently Antiopē was married to a Phokian king named Phōkos, a figure whose story we shall tell in Chap. 6 infra. He cleansed her of the stain of the cruel murder of Dirkē, and ultimately was buried next to her in Tithoreia in Phōkis.

There were many versions of the story of Antiopē. Boiotia and Sikyon were the localities where her story was located: for the earliest form of the story we have, from the Nekyia in the Odyssey,[24] makes her the daughter of Asōpos, and a river of that name is found both in Sikyon and in Boiotia. However, the form of the tale employed

---

[17] Cf. Chap. 1 p.12 supra, and nn. 53 and 54 there.
[18] Cf. Chap. 3 p. 51 supra.
[19] Paus. 9.17.3ff.
[20] Francis Vian, Les Origines de Thèbes (Paris, Klincksieck 1963) 193-201.
[21] Kypria Proklos Chrestomathia p.8 Kinkel.
[22] Hyginus fab. 7.
[23] Σ Ap. Rhod. 1.164.
[24] Od. 11.260.

by Euripides in his lost drama *Antiope*, and preserved for us by Hyginus[25] and Apollodorus,[26] has prevailed over other versions. It combines the Boiotian version where Zeus was Antiopē's lover, and that of Sikyon where her lover's name was Epōpeus, no doubt originally an epithet of Zeus, similar in meaning to πανόπτης, "he who sees all things." Hyginus[27] summarizes Euripides' play:

> Antiopa was the daughter of Nycteus, who was king in Boeotia. Jupiter, attracted by the loveliness of her beauty, made her pregnant. When her father wished to punish her for her wantonness, Antiopa escaped the danger that threatened her. She fled to Mt. Cithaeron, bore twins, and abandoned them; a herdsman brought them up, and named them Amphion and Zethus. By chance Epopeus of Sicyon had stopped at the same place she had come to, and he carried her away to his home and made her his wife. Nycteus was very upset by all of this, and when he was on his deathbed he made his brother Lycus swear not to let Antiopa get away unpunished. After he died Lycus, to whom he had left the kingdom, came to Sicyon, killed Epopeus and took Antiopa away in chains. Antiopa was handed over to Dirce, Lycus' wife, for torment, but she found an opportunity of running away and took flight. She came to her sons, but Zethus did not let her in, thinking her a runaway slave. At the same time Dirce came to that spot as a maenad of Bacchus, found Antiopa there, and led her away to be put to death. The young men, who had been told that she was their mother by the herdsman who had brought them up, set out in pursuit, and rescued her; they tied Dirce to an ox by her hair, and so put her to death. When they wished to kill Lycus, Mercury forbade it and at the same time bade Lycus cede the kingdom to Amphion.

Apollodoros[28] adds to this that Nykteus committed suicide out of despair, and Antiopē's chains fell off her miraculously, so that she was able to escape from her bondage, and also tells that Antiopē bore the twins at Eleutherai in Boiotia when she was being led back to Thebes in chains, and that Zēthos was a herdsman whereas Amphiōn was a lyre-player.

The common features of all the versions appear to be that Antiopē is the mother of twins, and in fact of a pair that since antiquity has been considered the double of the noted divine twins in Greece, the Dioskuroi,[29] and also the daughter-in-law of one of twins, and is somehow related to a figure that bears the wolf-name. Another interesting feature of her tale as told by Euripides is that Dirkē appeared in it as a maenad on the hills, so that Lykos, her husband and cohort, the enemy of Antiopē, is also an ally of Dionysos and of the maenads. Inasmuch as Lykos is, as we have seen above, a name for Dionysos, the name Lykurgos, from the Greek root *erg- "to work, wreak," can mean "the one who wreaks vengeance on the wolf," like that Lykurgos who pursued Dionysos himself with an ox-goad,[30] and Antiopē, in other versions of her story, is the daughter or wife of Lykurgos (or of Lykos, in Hyginus *fab.* 7, which is either an error or a syncopated form of Lykurgos). We have seen above that Lykos,

---

[25] *Fab.* 8.
[26] 3.5.5.
[27] *Loc. cit.*
[28] *Loc. cit.*
[29] Cf. Eur. *Her.* 29f., where Amphiōn and Zēthos are called "the two white colts," an epithet usually applied to the Dioskouroi.
[30] *Il* 6.130ff.

"Wolf," was one of the heroes who attacked Delphi and fell before the power of the god Apollo. If this is so, Antiopē and her son Amphiōn will be Apollonian figures. It remains for us to examine what the role of the twins here is.

A west Greek parallel to the twins Amphiōn and Zēthos may be furnished by the two sons of Boreas, the North Wind, Kalais and Zētēs, called twins by Ovid,[31] the famous heroes of the story of the Argonauts. According to Hesiod,[32] they called on Zeus Aineios, a god of Kephallenia, when they were being pursued by the Harpyies. This was when the latter were chasing them to the Echinades,[33] islands in the West of Greece; these islands are prominent in the story of Lykurgos and Butēs, also sons of Boreas. Zētēs appears as the husband of Aēdōn, in place of Zēthos, in one version of her story.[34]

The tale of twins associated with the wolf or the wolf-name here is parallel to the stories of Autolykos and Philammon, and of Milētos and Kydon, treated below under Milētos, and to the Roman story of Romulus and Remus, where the theme of twins is also associated with a flood.[35] If we examine the pairs of twins associated with Antiopē, we find there are four of them: (1) Lykos has a twin brother Nykteus (these are heroes of the Boiotian city Hyria), (2) Amphiōn and Zēthos are Antiopē's twin sons according to the most common form of the story, (3) in the Korinthian story,[36] where Antiopē is taken to wife by the god Hēlios, she is the mother of twins named Aiētēs and Aloios,[37] (4) in the version of her story where she is the wife of Lykurgos, she is the mother of twins named Ankaios and Epochos.

Amphiōn is clearly marked as an Apollonian figure by the music of his lyre. The Theban myth told how he and his brother Zēthos had built the walls of Thebes; how the stones brought by Zēthos were set in place in the wall by the music Amphiōn played on his lyre. He is also known as the husband of Niobē, and so the father of the children killed by Apollo and Artemis when their mother boasted that they surpassed the children of Leto in their beauty.

The tale of Antiopē, the maenad who fled to Mt. Kithairon and was there beloved of Zeus, who appeared to her in the form of a satyr, a Dionysiac figure; and was later abandoned to her cruel fate, until she was finally purified and wed by Phōkos, is reminiscent of that of Ariadnē, abandoned on Naxos by Thēseus, and saved by Dionysos.

5. Another King Lykos appears in the story of the Argonauts. On their way to Kolchis the Argo put in at the land of the Mariandynoi. There the ship sailed far up the river Acheron[38] and were received kindly by the king of the country, Lykos the son of Daskylos, the son of Tantalos. Since the seer Idmon had died at Herakleia, immediately prior to this (and Tiphys the helmsman of the Argo, as well), during the laments for Idmon, Lykos joined the Argonauts in the mourning ceremonies. This Lykos was the grandson of the river Lykos, also in the land of the Mariandynoi, through his mother Anthemoeisia. The land of Lykos and the Mariandynoi had other associations with death as well; it was known as the place where Herakles brought

---

[31] *Met.* 6.712.

[32] Σ Ap. Rhod. 2.297.

[33] Apollod. 1.9.21.

[34] Eustathios *ad Od.* 19517; Chrestomathy of Helladios (Phot. *Bibl.* p. 531 Bekker).

[35] Livy.*V.* the previous chapter for the flood.

[36] Eumelos *fr.* 2 Kinkel; Diophantus in Σ Ap. Rhod. 3.242.

[37] In this version she is the grandmother both of Medea and of the Aloadai, Otos and Ephialtes.

[38] Herodor. fr. 50, and Ap. Rhod. 2.752; the name is that of the famous river of Hades.

Kerberos up from Hades, and where the plant aconite arose from the poison dripping from the dread creature;[39] furthermore there were mountains in it named ἄκρα Ἀχερούσια, "the peaks of Acheron."[40]

5. Another Lykos was a king of Libya, the son of the god Ares, who sacrificed strangers to Ares, his father.[41] In Chap. 6, *infra*, the theme of human sacrifice will be shown to be part of the wider context of the wolf-name.

The *lyk-* element is found, in the names Autolykos, Harpalykos, Lykaon, Lykomedes, Lykoreus, Lykortas, Lykurgos, and Oiolykos, from myth and mythological history, aside from the name Lykos.

Autolykos

Among the stories told of Autolykos, he is said to have been Herakles' teacher in the art of wrestling. Since he was at home on Mt. Parnassos, the holy mountain of Apollo above Delphi, the Harpalykos who appears in Theoc. 24.111ff., must be a avatar of Autolykos. In Theokritos' poem on the youth of Herakles, this Harpalykos, identified as a son of Hermes, is said to have come from Panopeus, the modern Phanoteus near Lebadeia on Mt. Parnassos; nobody dared compete with him because of the frightful scowl he bore on his face. Theokritos names him as Herakles' teacher in the arts of the pancration and in boxing. Here we see "the very wolf" alternating with the "ravenous wolf," a fact which need not occasion us any surprise.

Harpalykos—Harpalykē

These figures of Greek myth appear together in the best-known occurrences of the names, Harpalykos being Harpalykē's father. It is noteworthy that *harpax* is the name of one of the five species of wolf listed in Ps.-Oppian *Kynegetica* 3.293-335. Thus his name would signify "the ravenous wolf" or simply "the wolf." In one of the places where Harpalykos appears alone,[42] he is identified as having been one of the sons of the Arkadian Lykaon. Although the sources for the myth are Roman, we have just noted under Autolykos the name Harpalykos which occurs in Theok. 24.111ff., as that of Herakles' teacher in the arts of the pancration and in boxing, who was a son of Hermes from Panopeus with whom no one dared compete because of the apotropaic scowl he bore on his face. Hence it is likely that the Roman story is also originally Hellenistic, and was committed to writing in the period when the Alexandrians were busy collecting various versions of Greek myths.[43]

Another Hellenistic source quotes Aristoxenos to the effect that Harpalykē died of unrequited love for a youth named Iphiklos and that maidens held a singing contest in her memory; one of the songs sung in this contest was called Harpalykē after her.[44] This version seems to come from Thessaly,[45] as may also the version of the story

---

[39] Ovid *Met.* 7.408-419, Pliny *N. H.* 27.4, *et al.*
[40] Xen. *Anab.* 6.2.1, Ap. Rhod. 2.351, Pomponius Mela 1.97.103, and Dionys. *Per.* 788.
[41] *V.* Diomedes and especially n. 103 *infra*.
[42] Apollod. 2.4.9.
[43] Cf. A.S.F. Gow, *Theocritus* II (Cambridge 1952) 433, and Roscher *Lex.* 1.2 col. 1835 *s.v.* Harpalykē.
[44] Athen. 14.619E.
[45] Cf. S. Eitrem in *PWRE* 7 col. 2403.

preserved for us by Hyginus[46] and elsewhere.[47] Here she is the daughter of Klymenos and Epikastē, and she is also associated with death. She took a gruesome form of revenge on her father Klymenos for having had incest with her, and feasted him on human flesh, either that of her brother[48] or of her son Presbon, the child of her incest with him.[49]

This version of the story is a mirror image of the story of Oidipus, and in fact legitimizes the wolf-connections of the Oidipus myth both through its material and through the name Epikastē, which is the name of Oidipus' mother, usually called Jokastē (Jocasta), in *Od.* 11.271ff. It also connects the story of Harpalykē with that of Atalanta; for according to the Boiotian-Thessalian version of her story Atalanta was the sister of Klymenos, both being the children of Schoineus, the son of Athamas, the founder and eponymous hero of the town of Schoinus where the river of the same name empties into Lake Hylike in Boiotia, or alternatively of another town of the same name in Arkadia near Methydrion in the valley of the Helisson on the road to Megalopolis. According to the Arkadian version of her story Atalanta was the daughter of Iasos, one of the sons of the Arkadian Lykurgos. Both she and Harpalykē are famous huntresses, and the latter, like the former surely belongs to the sphere of Artemis, which includes slaying small animals, as well as child-murder, a theme we shall examine in connection with Athamas.

The various versions of the story of Harpalykē are noteworthy for manifesting the connection between the wolf-name and death, which we shall examine below, as well as the connection between the wolf-name and swiftness, shown already in the name Harpalykos which may signify "snatching (or rapid) wolf," and recalls the fleetness of the wind or of the young who are as fleet as the wind. The best known version is the only other ancient source relating to the wider context of the wolf-name, besides the foundation myth of the temple of Apollo Lykeios at Argos appearing in Servius-Danielis, that contains a name similar to the name Amymōnē.

Vergil tells of the armored Thrakian maiden Harpalyce who could outrun steeds and the current of the swift river Hebrus (or, according to Ribbeck's emendation of the passage, Eurus, the east wind).[50] This Harpalyce was the daughter of Harpalycus, the king of the otherwise unknown Thrakian tribe of the Amymonii,[51] or the Amymaei,[52] The same sources go on to tell that her father fed her on the milk of cows, mares and, wild beasts, and trained her in masculine pursuits after she was orphaned of her mother. When he was murdered by his subjects in revenge for the severity with which he had ruled them she took to the forest in her grief and led the life of a hunter and a brigand, until the farmers set their nets for her, caught her like a beast of prey and put her to death. Thereupon there arose a quarrel among them over the ownership of a kid she had stolen, and much blood was spilt. In commemoration of this fight a yearly festival featuring the mimicry of a battle was celebrated at her grave. We may compare with this the reports of female werewolves and the annual battle mimicry at Tongres cited in Chap. 6 *infra.*

---

[46] Fab. 206, 239, 242, 253 and 255.

[47] It also was told by Euphorion according to Parthenios 26 (ed. Gaselee *LCL* 328, 330).

[48] Euphorion quoted in Parthenios. *V.* the previous note.

[49] Σ Ovid *Ib.* 545 and Nonnos *Dion.* 12.71-75.

[50] *Aen.* 1.316ff.

[51] Serv.-Dan. *ad Aen.* 1.316ff.

[52] Hyginus *fab.* 193. In Epeiros, in Chaonia, however, there was a tribe called the Amymnoi, according to Steph. Byz. *s. v.,* otherwise known as Aigestaioi.

Harpalyce had once rescued her father from captivity among the Getae by gathering together a fighting band and making a bold incursion among them.[53] Hyginus replaces the Getae with the Myrmidons, that is the warriors of Achilleus, in this story, and tells that Neoptolemos (Pyrrhos), the son of Achilleus, had beaten Harpalycus in battle and wounded him when he stopped in Thrace on his homeward journey from Troy.

Lykaon and Hippōtēs

According to Pausanias[54] Lykaon was the son of Pelasgos, the first inhabitant of Arkadia. (He was the father of Kallisto and grandfather of Arkas, the son of Kallisto and Zeus from whom the land of Arkadia got its name.) He founded the town of Lykosura (Wolf's-tail), on Mt. Lykaion, according to Pausanias[55] the oldest town on earth, whether on the continent or on an island, the first the sun ever beheld, from which men learned to build all the other towns that exist. He also founded the games of Zeus Lykaios and named Mt. Lykaion, which was the national sanctuary of Arkadia, and the site of some of the oldest athletic contests in Greece.

We quote: "Lykaon brought a human baby to the altar of Zeus Lykaios, sacrificed the child and poured its blood upon the altar; they say he turned into a wolf from a man at once, right after the sacrifice." Pausanias goes on to justify this story as a true divine punishment in the times before the generations turned bad, and learned to pay no heed to such chastisements. "They tell that since the time of Lykaon a man changes into a wolf at the festival of Zeus Lykaios, but the change is not for life. If in wolf-shape he refrains from human flesh, he turns from a wolf into a man again after ten years, but if he tastes human flesh he stays a wolf forever."[56]

Pliny[57] quotes the story of Lykaon from a certain Greek author named Euanthes (or Neanthes, according to Jacoby's surmise in *FGrH*), of uncertain date. According to Euanthes too Lykaon was the ancestor of the Arkadians. Lykaon's progeny were cursed with lycanthropy because he had served up one of his children to the gods upon one occasion when they had paid him a surprise visit and his larder was bare. Each year one of the family of Anthos in Arkadia, Lykaon's descendants, was chosen by lot, whereupon he would hang his clothing upon an oak tree and swim across a lake, emerging as a wolf on the other side. He would remain in wolf shape for a certain period. If he could abide by the terms of the ordeal and refrain from human flesh for the term of his transformation, he would return to the farther side of the lake at the end of the period, swim across to his clothing, and resume human form.

Another heroic figure named Lykaon is the son of Priam killed by Achilles after having been sold by him once into slavery across the sea.[58] He evinces traits we have seen associated with the wolf-name, having been shipped over the sea and returning quite beyond expectation, traits that recall the connection of the wolf with shifting frontiers, visiting from one world to another, and reappearing or remanifestation after an absence or disappearance.

The hero Hippōtēs of Dorian myth, who wanders far afield for ten years under a

---

[53] Serv.-Dan. *ibid.*
[54] Paus. 8.2.1ff.
[55] 8.38.1.
[56] The theme of lycanthropy in Greece is treated, *inter alia*, in Chap. 6 *infra*.
[57] Pliny the Elder *N.H.* 8.34 (*FGrH* 3.11 fr. 33, under Neanthes).
[58] *Il.* 21.34ff.

ban in expiation of a crime, seems closely related to the story of Lykaon, and to Apollo, as well. Hippotes was the son of Phylas and of Leipephile, the daughter of Iolaos, Herakles' twin brother's son.[59] Returning to the Peloponnesos with the family of Herakles under the leadership of the seer Karnos the Akarnanian, Hippōtēs murdered Karnos at Naupaktos, just before the crossing into the ancestral homeland. The seer's death was henceforth celebrated at the Dorian festival of the Karneia, where Apollo, as we have seen, appears as a divinity of the harvest, as he does in the Ionian Thargēlia. The immediate result of this murder was a plague which attacked the children of Herakles, and the Delphic oracle ordered Hippōtēs into exile for ten years in order to expiate his crime and so stop the plague.[60] Karnos appears as 'Απόλλωνος φάσμα, "an apparition of Apollo,"[61] and there seems to be a similarity between the story of Hippōtēs and that of Hyakinthos, just as there is between it and the story of Lykaon in the other direction. Hippōtēs is a sort of "murderer of Apollo," at second remove, and so is an eternal enemy of the god, just as the Arkadian Lykaon, who is one of the "first man" figures in Greece, is the accursed of the gods.

Lykomēdēs

The Athenian Lykomēdēs was the ancestor of the Lykomidai,[62] while Lykomēdēs king of Skyros appears in the story of Thēseus. Another Lykomēdēs, this one from the island of Samos, appears in the genealogy of the island deriving from the ancient epic poet Asios of Samos.[63] "Lykomedes is perhaps the mythical progenitor of a Samian family," writes G.L. Huxley;[64] we may add a hypothesis to the effect that the family may have had to do with Apollo, or more likely with the cult of Demeter, as in Athens.

Lykōreus

Lykōreus or Lykōros was the son of Apollo and the nymph Korykia of the Cave of Korykos ("Bag" or "Wallet") above Delphi. The town on the Korykian heights of Parnassos above Delphi was named Lykōreia after him.[65]

Lykurgos

The Thrakian king Lykurgos , the son of Dryas (from Greek δρῦς, "tree"), who pursued and laid low the nurses of Dionysos and chased Dionysos himself with an ox-goad, an act for which he was punished with blindness and dishonor by the gods, is an ancient figure who appears as early as *Il.* 6.130ff. If his name brings us into the sphere of Apollo, his deeds and his father's name connect him with Dionysos, who under the epithet Dendrites was the god of trees.. We have seen *supra* that another Lykurgos appears as the father of Antiopē.[66] Elsewhere it is the name of her husband,[67] and

---

[59] Hes. *Ehoiai* (Fr. 252, M.-W.).

[60] Apollod. 2.8.3, Paus. 3.13.3, Diod. 5.9, Konon 26.

[61] Konon 26 *FGrH* 1.210. Cf. Chap. 2 p.25 *supra.*

[62] On whom *v. supra* p. 68-69.

[63] Paus. 7.4.1

[64] *Greek Epic Poetry* (Cambridge, Mass. 1969) 91.

[65] *V.* Chap. 3 *supra*, pp. 46 and 57.

[66] *Kypria* Proklos p.8 Kinkel.

[67] Σ Ap. Rhod. 1.164.

another Lykurgos is the grandfather of Harpalykē in one version of her story. Yet another Lykurgos, with clear wind-associations, is Lykurgos, the son of Boreas, the North Wind, and step-brother of Butēs, who was the ancestor of the ancient Athenian noble clan of the Eteobutadai,[68] in an ancient Athenian version of the story of Butēs. In another version of the story he is the son of Poseidon.[69] In the Athenian version of the story Butēs plotted against his step-brother, in consequence of which he was sent into exile, along with his Thrakian accomplices, by Lykurgos. They then seized Naxos, which had been called Strongylē, set themselves up as pirates, and would kidnap women to be their wives, since there were no women upon the island. Now, they had to go far afield for this purpose; for the Kyklades had but few inhabitants, and they had been repulsed from Euboia, so that they were forced to make their way to Thessaly. There they found a party of maenads celebrating mysteries of the god Dionysos, in a place called Drios in Achaia Phthiotis. When they approached, the women ran away and cast away their sacred objects, but Korōnis[70] was caught and forced to lie with Butēs. She prayed to Dionysos to punish him, and the god made him insane so that he threw himself down a well and died.

A similar story seems to lie at the root of the version where Butēs the son of Lykurgos avenges himself on the maenads for his father's death.[71] In this version we find another Lykurgos who is the enemy of Dionysos and the maenads, and is in a Poseidonian context; for the Eteobutadai, among whom Lykurgos was a common name,[72] held the ancient priesthood of Poseidon in the Erechtheion, while their wives were the priestesses of Athena Polias.

Oiolykos

The name Oiolykos means "lone wolf." Among the Dorian colonists of the island of Thera, modern Santorini, there appears a certain Oiolykos, son of Theras ("the beast") and father of Aigeus.[73]

This story shows the wolf-figure as the head of a band of settlers who must have formed a warrior-confraternity of the well-known sort.

2.HEROES ASSOCIATED WITH THE CULT OF APOLLO LYKEIOS

Perseus

In Kilikia, at Tarsos, the hero Perseus[74] was closely associated with Apollo Lykeios, and enjoyed almost divine status himself. His chief fame derives from his role as the slayer of the Gorgon Medusa, itself an Apollonian theme; his association with the wolf-epithet is enigmatical, but it may explain the appearance of Lykos, etc., as royal names; for Perseus is the prime example of kingship, and the progenitor of the

---

[68] Diod. 5.50.2, in his history of the island of Naxos.

[69] Hes. *Katalogai fr.* 223 M.-W.

[70] This is the name of the mother of Asklepios by Apollo, also from Thessaly.

[71] Σ Ovid *Ibis* 605. *V. s. v.* Aloadai in *PWRE* 1 col. 1592.

[72] Plut. *vit.* X *or.* 843e, and Paus. 1.26.5.

[73] Hdt. 4.149

[74] Another hero closely related to Perseus is Perseutes the hero whose cult was found in the city of Kurion on Cyprus (*v.* Oberhummer in *PWRE* 11.2 (1922) col 2210f. *s.v.* Kurion, and *infra*).

most illustrious royal lineage, in Greece.[75]   Among the children of Perseus and Andromeda we find not only the grand-parents of Herakles, but Eurystheus' father, and Thēseus' maternal grand-father as well. In Chap. 5 *infra* we note that the theme of his being enclosed along with his mother in a floating chest, mistaken for a whale or a sea-monster, places him within the context of the dolphin, and of adolescent initiations, both of which have wolf-connections.   Further traits that conceivably place him within the wind-context of the wolf-name may be the powers he was granted by Athena and Hermes, and the fact that he was endowed with the power of flight through the air by virtue of magical slippers given him by the Graeae[76]; for Perseus' career is characterized by the preternatural aid proferred him by Athena and Hermes in his quest for the Gorgon Medusa.   Hermes gave him a sickle, Athena a burnished brazen shield to function as a mirror, and the Graeae, to whom these two deities directed him, winged sandals, the Cap of Hades, and a wallet (to carry the Gorgon's head in).   By virtue of this aid, he was able to slay the Gorgon Medusa, he could fly through the air, and by virtue of the Cap of Hades he was endowed with invisibility.   The κυνέη Ἀϊδος, a dog's or wolf's head, to judge by its name, makes its wearer invisible. Invisibility is the most prominent characteristic of Hades, Greek Ἀίδης, whose name, made up of the privative ά prefixed to the root *Ϝιδ-, 'to see,' means "invisible." The appearance of the Cap of Hades in the story of Perseus implies his symbolic death; for like the dead, the inhabitants of the realm of Hades, he was invisible when wearing it.

Moreover heroes like Perseus who were set afloat in a chest on the water seem to be connected with the syndrome of wolf-Apollo insofar as he is associated with the dolphin or the sea-monster.   In a remarkable parallel Thoas of Lemnos,[77] the father of Hypsipyle, is associated with Artemis, another wolf-goddess; for his daughter Hypsipyle set him afloat in a chest when the women of Lemnos put all the men of the island to death, in order to save his life, in a dramatic reversal of the normal story of this type where the father sets his daughter afloat in a chest in order to put an end to her life.[78]   This same Thoas later became the king of the Taurians who made Iphigeneia, the heroine who is known from the cult of Brauron to have been a version of Artemis, sacrifice strangers wrecked upon the coast to Artemis.   Thoas may be another Dionysos, and his story parallels that of Staphylos and Anios, brought below, as well.   Like Staphylos of Chios, the brother of Oinopion, Thoas was the son of Ariadnē and Dionysos.[79]   Moreover, his grandson Euneos, the son of Jason and Hypsipyle, supplied the Achaeans with wine during the years of the siege of Troy. He appears at Athens as the ancestor of the Euneidai, the family of the priests of Dionysos Mélpomenos, the patron of the theatre, whose sanctuary lay in the Kerameikos.[80]

---

[75] D. E. Gershenson, "The Beautiful Gorgon and Indo-European Parallels," *The Mankind Quarterly* 29 (1989) 374-388, esp. 387.

[76] Cf. the neolithic flying wolves at the beginning of Chap. 2 *supra*.

[77] *Il.* 14.230.

[78] Cf. the myth of Auge, the mother of Telephos, as well as that of Danae.

[79] Σ Ap. Rhod. 3.997, Apollod. *Epit.* 1.9, etc.

[80] Harpokration, Hesychius, and Photius, *s.v.* Euneidai.

3. HEROES WHO PARTAKE IN THE WIDER CONTEXT OF THE WOLF-NAME

Argos

Argos is best known in the Greek-speaking area as a place-name. There was a town called Argos Hippion in Apulia in Magna Graecia,[81] but the cult of Apollo Lykeios in the town of Argos in the Peloponnese was particularly celebrated. We hear of a prophetess, Gr. προφῆτις, of Apollo Lykeios at Argos,[82] so that there may have been an oracular cult there as well.

Argos is the name of a number of figures in mythology, as well as of the town in the Peloponnesos. One of them is Argos Panoptes, the sleepless watcher of Io, who is covered with eyes,[83] like the Angel of Death in Talmudic tradition.[84] Another is his great-grandfather, the eponymous hero of the town.

The earlier Argos, the son of Niobe and Zeus, according to Akusilaos, or else of Apis,[85] has the attributes of a culture-hero, too. He is said to have brought wheat from Libya to the Argolid, where he built a temple at Charadra to Demeter Libyssa.[86] Argos had been sent to Sicily and Libya to find the wild wheat that grew there, and after he brought it back to the Argive land Triptolemos ploughed and sowed it, and taught all mankind its use. Apis had gone to Egypt, and sent cattle from there to Argos, and taught Triptolemos to sow.[87] In his reign the Greeks imported grain and began to raise wheat.[88]

Argos Panoptes, set to watch Io the heifer, is associated with cattle. As the keeper of Io his genealogy is variously given:[89] son of Arestor, according to Pherekydes, son of Inachos, according to Asklepiades, and earth-born, according to Akusilaos. This Argos Panoptes was killed by Hermes, who thereby earned the epithet Argeïphontes.

Another Argos Panoptes, the son of Ekbasos, was of exceptional strength and succeeded in overcoming a monstrous bull which had been devastating Arkadia. He wore the bull's hide, and killed Satyros, who had been lording it over the Arkadians and stealing their cattle. He was also the slayer of the monstrous Echidna, daughter of Tartaros and Gē,[90] who devoured wayfarers, and avenged the death of Apis on his murderers.

The bull's hide worn by Argos the son of Arestor is described as shaggy.[91] Like the initiates in the cave of Zeus on Mt. Ida in Krete, dressed in boars' skins, and those on Mt. Pelion in Magnesia, clad in sheepskins, or the wolfskin clad figures around Mt. Lykaion in Arkadia, Argos in the bull's hide is one of the adolescent initiates into the mysteries of the adolescent confraternity whom we shall meet again *infra*. Thus Argos Panoptes is associated with death, an integral part of the wider context of the wolf-name,[92] and also appears as a culture-hero, and a monster-killer, who, moreover, is

---

[81] Cf. p. 85 and n. 107 *infra*.
[82] Plut. *Pyrrhus* 31.
[83] Aesch. *Prom.* 569, 679, etc.
[84] *T. B. Ab. Zar.* 20b.
[85] Aug. *Civ. dei* 18.6.
[86] According to Polemon fr. 12 (Müller *FHG* 3.119)
[87] Tzetzes ad Hes. *WD* 32.
[88] Aug. *ibid.* (n. 83 *supra*).
[89] Apollod. 2.1.2ff.
[90] *Ibid.*
[91] A.R. 1.324f., and cf. also Hyg. *fab.* 14.
[92] Cf. Chap. 6 *infra passim*.

found dressed in the hide of an animal.[93] He may also be a avatar of Herakles.[94] Hence, like Aristaios *infra*, he seems to belong in the (werewolf-) Männerbund setting.[95]

Aristaios

Aristaios, the son of Apollo and Kyrēnē, is the Apollo-figure with the clearest wind connections.[96] He was worshipped on the island of Keos, where he sacrificed to the dog-star and to Zeus Ikmaios on a scorching day of late summer, and was answered with wind and rain.[97] It seems it was on this island that he was known as the initiator of the Etesian winds. He was the originator of bee-keeping as well,[98] and of cattle-raising and hunting too.[99] In Arkadia, however, he was worshipped as Zeus,[100] and his name also served as a cult epithet of Apollo. In a tomb painting from Kyrene he was shown carrying a ram on his shoulders and holding a shepherd's crook in his hand, in the midst of sheep within a circle of fish.[101]

Asklēpios

Asklēpios, the son of Apollo, has been treated at length by Grégoire and Goossens,[102] and there is no need to repeat their arguments here. The upshot of their argument is that, as we have seen,[103] he is a mole-god. Thus he seems to fall into the agricultural wolf context defined by Mannhardt. Furthermore, his medical role is part of the functions of Apollo, as described by Plato in the *Cratylus*, in the same way that Herakles, the son of Zeus, took over his functions as god of oaths, in Rome, especially. In these contexts, then he functions as a sort of avatar of Apollo Lykeios.

Athamas

We shall return to Athamas in the context of ritual human sacrifice in Chap. 6 *infra*, and he has already appeared in our discussion of Atalanta under Harpalykē above. Here we shall look at the outlines of his story.

At the sanctuary of Zeus Laphystios at Halos, where there took place initiations like in the cave of Zeus on Mt. Ida in Krete, on Mt. Pelion in Magnesia, and on Mt. Lykaion in Arkadia, the eldest surviving descendant of Athamas was sacrificed on the altar in a yearly rite.[104] This sacrifice would appear to have been somehow an expiation of Athamas' foul attempt to sacrifice his son Phrixus, according to one version of the myth, as a consequence of the jealousy which arose between his second wife Nephelē, the mother of Phrixus and Hellē, and his first wife, usually identified

---

[93] Apollod. *ibid.*

[94] J. Bayet, "Hercule Funéraire," *Mélanges d'Archéologie et d'Histoire* 40 (1923) 30.

[95] Defined by Faure, *op. cit.* (Chap. 3 n. 78 *supra*) 124.

[96] Cf. Chap. 2 *supra*.

[97] Ap.Rhod. 2.516ff.

[98] Verg. *Georg.* 1.14ff.

[99] Σ Pind. *Pyth.* 9.112.

[100] Servius ad Verg. *Georg.* 1.14ff.

[101] Cf. F.G. Welcker *op. cit.* (Chap. 1 p. 21 n. 103 *supra*) 1.489.

[102] *Op. cit.* (Chap. 2 n. 33 *supra*).

[103] Chap. 2 p. 30 *supra*.

[104] Hdt. 8.197.

with Inō, the daughter of Kadmos and aunt of Dionysos. Inō, envious of Nephelē's position in Athamas' affections as his younger and preferred wife, planned to take revenge by destroying Nephelē's son, Phrixus. She taught the women of Thessaly to parch or toast the kernels of grain that were to be planted, promising them that the return would be increased manifold. Having cast the blame for the failure of the crops on Nephele and on Nephele's son Phrixus, she convinced the king to sacrifice the boy in order to restore the fertility of the soil.

A golden ram sent by Zeus appeared at the side of the altar, rescued Phrixus, and taking him and his sister Hellē on its back, flew away with them over land and sea. Hellē fell from the sky over a body of water which bears her name to this day, the Hellespont, but Phrixus reached the land of Kolchis, where the fleece of the ram was hung up as the Golden Fleece.

Athamas, taken with madness when his plan to sacrifice his son was foiled in this way, snatched up his bow and quiver and began to pursue his remaining sons, the children of Ino, at whom he was furious for having persuaded him to make the sacrifice, now rejected by the god. He is said to have killed his son Learchos this way, or else, with no connection to the sacrifice of Phrixos, when he was aiming at a stag in the forest, an act which maddened him and caused him to pursue his remaining sons, but Ino escaped with the infant Melikertes in her arms and, fleeing all the way to Athens and beyond, leapt into the sea from the Skironian rocks on the road from Athens to Megara. Athamas then found a wolf pack, according to one version of the story, and began to run with the wolves. Only later did he return to human society.

Diomēdēs

There are two or more figures of Greek mythology of this name: aside from Jason, the hero who retrieved the Golden Fleece and brought it back to Greece, whose original name was Diomēdēs, they are Diomēdēs, King of Thrake, son of Ares and Kyrene (and so half-brother of Aristaios), the owner of the man-eating mares who was fed to his horses by Herakles, and Diomēdēs of Argos, son of Tydeus, the hero of the Trojan War, perhaps best known for having wounded Aphrodite.[105] King Juba of Mauretania in his work concerning Libya told how, after the fall of Troy, this Diomēdēs was shipwrecked on the Libyan coast, where it was the practice of the king, Lykos, son of the god Ares, to sacrifice strangers to Ares, his father.[106] Diomēdēs escaped this fate through the good offices of the king's daughter, Kallirrhoe who had fallen in love with him, and untied his bonds; but he paid her no heed and sailed away, whereupon she hanged herself. Jacoby dismisses this story as a romantic invention,[107] and criticizes Gruppe[108] for labelling it "above suspicion," but in fact a similar story was told in Southern Italy where Diomēdēs was worshipped as a god, in Metapontum and Thurioi. Among the Dauni of Apulia, where Diomēdēs was said to have founded Argos Hippion, "Argos of the Horse," and other geographical features are named after him too,[109] he was said to have been killed by King Daunos.[110] We have seen that Daunos and Lykos are identical names, both meaning "wolf."

---

[105] *Il.* 5.
[106] Plut. *Parall. Graec. et Rom.* 23.
[107] *FGrH* in his commentary on 275F5.
[108] *Gr. Myth.* 1380.2.
[109] Strabo 6.3.9.
[110] Σ Lykophr. 592, [Ar.] *mirab. ausc.* 80.

Diomedes is also associated with a strange rite practiced in Salamis on Kypros, said to have originally been associated with Aglauros and Achilleus.[111] Human sacrifice was practised in a sacred precinct of Athena, Diomedes and Aglauros there. This sacrifice is also said to have been in honor of Zeus, whether correctly or incorrectly, we can not tell.[112] Our sources tell us that Salamis was called Korōnia ("Raven-town") of old, and that in the month called Aphrodision in Kypros, the people of Salamis sacrificed one of the ephebes to Agraulos, who may originally have been the same as Achilleus, and the nymph Agraulis. In the time of Diomedes, the sources continue, the rite was changed somewhat, and the sacrifice devoted to Diomedes. The man marked out for sacrifice was carried three times around the altar by the ephebes, and then struck in the stomach with a lance by the priest. Later he was cremated. Aglauros is a form of Agraulos, which is a name that derives directly from the sphere of ephebic life; for it means "bivouac," and one of the earmarks of the training of the ephebes was sleeping out in the fields.

Milētos

Milētos, the eponymous hero of the city Milētos was the child of the nymph Akakallis and Apollo,[113] and his mother exposed him in the woods, fearing that her father would discover her clandestine love. Apollo sent wolves to care for the child, and a she-wolf suckled him. He fled to Anatolia out of fear of Minos, and founded the city there that bears his name.

Apollo and Akakallis were the parents of Amphithemis and Garamas, as well as Milētos.[114] Akakallis bore Kydōn to Hermes, at the same time. Kydōn and Milētos, the twin Kretan sons of Apollo, were brought up by a bitch[115] and a she-wolf respectively. This makes the case of Akakallis parallel the birth of the twins Philammon and Autolykos ("the very wolf"), the former the son of Apollo and the latter of Hermes. The people of Elyros on Krete related that Akakallis bore the twins Phylakides and Phylandros to Apollo, and these children, like Milētos, were exposed, and tended by an animal, but by a goat, this time, a statue of which was erected in Delphi by the people of Elyros.[116]

Another account[117] makes Apollo and Areia the daughter of Minos the parents of Milētos. Areia hid the child from her husband Kleochos in a yew-tree (σμῖλαξ), but Kleochos found and raised him, and named him after the tree; for σμῖλαξ=μῖλαξ, i.e. *milax,* from which the name Milētos is derived.

Oidipus

We have already noted Oidipus' connection with the wolf-name at second remove in our discussion of Harpalykē *supra.* There we saw that in one version of her

---

[111] Porphyr. *de abst.* 2.54ff., as well as Eus. *praep. ev.* 4.16.2f.24.

[112] Lact. *inst. div.* 1.21.

[113] His story has already been mentioned in connection with Kaphauros in Chap. 1 *supra*; it is found in Antonius Liberalis 30, and in Apollod. *Bibl.* 3.5, as well as in the scholia cited in the following note.

[114] Ap. Rhod. 1.85, Σ *ad loc.,* Σ ad Theoc. 7.12, and Ant. Lib. 30.

[115] Cf. the coins of Kydonia in Krete *Cat. of the Greek coins in the Brit. Mus.* Pl. 7.4-7.

[116] Paus. 10.16.3.

[117] Σ Ap. Rhod. 1.85 (=*FGrH* 31F45).

story Harpalykē the daughter of Klymenos, took a gruesome sort of revenge on her father Klymenos for having had incest with her, and feasted him on human flesh, either that of her brother or of her son Presbon, the child of her incest with him. Epikastē is the name given to Oidipus' mother, usually called Jokastē, in *Od.* 11.271ff. and so, Oidipus emerges as a sort of half-brother of a girl named after the ravenous wolf. Here we may note two more connections this hero shares with the wider context of the wolf-name, as elucidated *supra*, the agricultural dimension of the theme of incest, on the one hand, and the form of Oidipus' death in the legend, also a form of incest in a certain sense, on the other.

The theme of autochthony, with its corollary of child rejection or child-murder, shown to be central to the Oidipus myth by Lévi-Strauss,[118] provides a link between the agricultural context of the wolf-name and the theme of human sacrifice to be examined *infra* in Chap. 6, for if human beings are authochthonous, that is, born directly from the earth, then they are the plants' kindred, and belong in an agricultural context.

Another facet of the myth of Oidipus comes to light both in the incestuous relations he has with his mother Jokastē or Epikastē, and in the manner of his death depicted by Sophocles.[119] There he is accepted wholly and bodily into the cleft of the earth in the sacred precinct of the Erinyes or Eumenides, the divinities most closely associated with motherhood, in a sort of return to the womb. Such a return is a *sine qua non* of rebirth in certain forms of initiation, e. g. in the Indian types where the womb is identified with the cow and the pot (*hiraṇyagarbha*).[120] In the following chapter we shall see that the wolf's maw may stand for the same thing.

Staphylos

The legend of Staphylos, the son of Dionysos, from the islands of the Aegean Sea parallels to some extent the Lykos-Lykeios relationship at Delphi between Apollo and Dionysos, and the two deities' alternation there in the course of each year. Staphylos' daughter Rhoiō, named for the pomegranate (ῥοιά), bore Anios, the hero of the islands, to Apollo or to Zarex the son of Karystos. Anios was the first king of Delos and first priest of Apollo there, taught prophecy by Apollo himself and given divine honors as a *daimon*. By Dorippē he was the father of Oinō, Spermō, and Elais, called the Oinotropoi, or "wine-growers," though their names denote wine, grain, and olive oil.[121] The name Anios also appears to derive from the agricultural sphere; for it seems to be from the verb ἀνύω "to bring to maturity, to speed, fulfill." Wine, grain, and oil are the three staples of the ancient mediterranean world,[122] and grain, at least, belongs to the sphere of agriculture that falls within the purview of Apollo. Wine and oil seem to be associated with Dionysos; for the olive is a tree, and Dionysos had the epithet Dendritēs, "of the trees."

Thus Oinō, Spermō, and Elais combine the spheres of Dionysos and Apollo; for their father Anios is from the sphere of Apollo, whereas Staphylos ("the cluster of grapes"), their great-grandfather, is the son of Dionysos, and his grandson the son of

---

[118] Claude Lévi-Strauss, *Structural Anthropology*, tr. C. Jacobson & B.G. Schoepf (New York: Basic Books 163-1976) Chap. 11, "The Structural Study of Myth," 206-232.

[119] Soph. *O.C.* 1544ff.

[120] M. Eliade, *Rites and Symbols of Initiation* (New York 1958) 57-58.

[121] Tzetzes ad Lyc. 580ff. et al.

[122] Cf. Deut. 11.14.

Apollo.

Anios is called a *daimon*,[123] and he may have enjoyed divine worship. Staphylos shut his daughter Rhoiō up in a chest when he found her to be pregnant, and threw her into the sea. Washed up on the shores of Delos, she gave birth to Anios.

Melanthos and Xanthos, Hippōtēs and Karnos, and Achilles and Tennes

Long ago Usener pointed out that the relationships between Melanthos and Xanthos, Hippōtēs and Karnos and Achilles and Tennes, are reflexes of one tale.[124] For him this tale was the alternation of light and darkness in nature; Vidal-Naquet has shown rather, at least for the first of these alternations that it involves the struggle between age-classes and the initiation of young warriors into the ranks of adult warriors.[125] The wind-wolf is involved in this struggle as well, because the myth that pictures Apollo, the god of the mature and reasoned warrior, subjugating and controlling the high spirits and ravenous appetites of the young, represented by Dionysos, is found also in the story of Apollon and Lykos, at Delphi, where the grave of Lykos is found in the precinct of Apollo. This may be the prototype of the alternation of the victorious warrior and his unfortunate mate, his victim, so that we may perhaps find justification for adding Apollo and Hyakinthos and Achilles and Tēlephōs to the list as well.

CONCLUSION

The heroes treated in this chapter show only a few links to the wind. On the other hand they introduce us to a realm which has been investigated quite fully by Gernet and others in the Greek cultural area, and is related to that of the Sakā Haomavargā of Iranian tradition.[126] These last form an important source; for if they were indeed werewolves, they show that the *haoma*, or some sort of drug, was involved in the frenzy of the Indo-European wolf-warrior. In Greece, despite the attempt of Wasson *et al.* to show that drugs were used there too, the situation is less clear, and the preponderance of occurrences of the wolf-name in the wind-context, in Greek myth, cult,and toponymy, would seem to indicate that the full Indo-European theme is missing here. Eleusis, the subject of Wasson's work, may or may not be pertinent here.

It is striking that we have been able to find so many figures of Greek mythology with connections to the wider context of the wolf-name, and surely there are many more. It may even be that this context is crucial to the nature of the ancient Greek hero and heroine; for it involves initiation, as we have seen, and that is the chief theme of myth.

---

[123] D. S. 5.62.1f.

[124] Hermann Usener, *Sintfluthsagen* 95.

[125] P. Vidal-Naquet, "Le chasseur noir et l'origine de l'éphébie athénienne," *REG* 80 (1967) 30-31.

[126] This name is found at the end of the uppermost row in a list of 29 countries who brought tribute, in the funeral inscription of Darius at his grave in Nakš-i-Rustam near Persepolis. *V.* Herrmann in *PWRE* 1A2 cols. 1778-1779. Geo Widengren writes the name Haomavarka, i.e. "haoma-wolves," thus identifying them with a werewolf confraternity, and he has been followed in this by Alföldi and others.

CHAPTER V
THE DOLPHIN AND THE WOLF

The dolphin, as much as the wolf, is connected with the wind or storm. That is perhaps the reason that Apollo Delphinios, rather than Poseidon, was the preferred god of seafaring men in antiquity. An ancient handbook of dream interpretations tells us: "A [dolphin] swimming in the sea appearing [in a dream] is a good sign, and the point he appears at indicates the direction the wind will blow from.... A dolphin appearing out of the water is not a good sign: it means one of your friends is going to die."[1] Here the dolphin marks the direction wind will come from; yet other ancient sources relate that squid darting out of the water or dolphins swimming toward land in a bay, or a harbor, signify the onset of a storm to pilots.[2] This is in fact accurate. All over the world dolphins and porpoises swim into bays, and squid jump out of the water, if a storm is brewing.

Further, in the story of the foundation of Delphi,[3] Apollo in dolphin form raised a strong wind astern in order to drive the Kretan seamen who founded his Delphic sanctuary to Krisa. We shall see *infra* that the dolphin, in the form of Apollo Delphinios, is connected with wind in the myth of Thēseus, and in Athenian cult as well.

The dolphin is connected with the wolf as well as with the wind or storm. In a parallel between wolf and dolphin, dolphins drive schools of fish on before them just as wolves drive flocks before them. This is the way the dolphin figures most prominently in the *Iliad*:[4] ὑπὸ δελφῖνος μεγακήτεος ἰχθυες ἄλλοι φεύγονται "pursued by the dolphin with the immense maw the other fish fill the recesses of the spacious harbor, frightened, and rightly; he devours any he catches..."; the dolphin has a voracious appetite,[5] and we hear tell of dolphins driving fish directly into fishermen's nets.[6] Furthermore the root of the Greek word for the dolphin, *delph-*, is associated with wolf-names like Lykos, as we have seen in Chap. 3 *supra*, and Vergil describes the man-eating Scylla in terms of both of these animals:[7] *delphinum caudas utero commissa luporum*, "uniting dolphins' tails to her wolves' belly." The Telchines are connected with the wolf; in addition there may be a connection between the Telchines and the dolphin, because Athenaeus quotes the author of the history of the Telchines to the effect that the dolphin, as well as the pilot-fish, is a holy fish.

An indication of the close connection of Apollo and the dolphin is the name Eikadios, "Twentieth," an epithet of Apollo, and the name of an Apolline hero. The twentieth day of each lunar month was sacred to Apollo.[8] The name recurs in an Arkadian list of kings where Eikadios and Koroneia appear as the parents of Dorieus,

---

[1] Artemidorus Daldianus *Oneirocrit.* 2.16 (133.5f. Pack).

[2] Cic. *Div.* 2.70; Pliny *N. H.* 32.15, in the name of Trebius Niger. Squid live on the high seas and are known to jump more than a foot out of the sea, like flying fishes. Epicharmos in Athen. 7.316e and 323f. calls them "flying squid," and Varr. *L. L.* 5.79 explains their Latin name *loligo* as a variant form of *volligo*, from *volare*, "to fly."

[3] *H. H.* 2.

[4] 21.22f.

[5] Oppian *Hal.* 2.551.

[6] Pliny *N.H.* 9.3.

[7] Verg. *Aen.* 3.428.

[8] *Et. M.* 298.1 *s. v.* Eikadios.

an eponymous hero of the Dorians.[9] This pair seems to represent the Arkadian reflex of the couple Apollo and Koronis, the parents of Asklepios, known from Thessaly. (Cf. the section on Asklepios in the previous chapter; here, once again, we find Apollo associated with the name of the raven.)

Eikadios, however, is also the name of a Lykian hero intimately associated with the dolphin. In Patara in Lykia, he was known as the son of Apollo and a heroine Lykia, and reputed to have been the founder of the city and of the cult of Apollo there. In fact, he was thought to be the real Apollo Delphinios who suffered shipwreck while en route from Patara to Italy, and was saved by a dolphin which brought him to the neighborhood of Mt. Parnassos, where he founded Delphi, named after the dolphin.[10]

A number of other heroes of Greek myth were dolphin-riders, among them the Lesbian hero Enalos, and Taras and Phalanthos, each of them a reputed founder of the colony of Spartan *Partheniai*, Tarentum (Taras) in Italy; these heroes' stories are rather attached to Poseidon than to Apollo, despite the fact that Apollo is the patron of newly founded colonies in general, but the story of the musician Arion transported by the dolphin, told by Herodotos, seems to lead us back into Apollo's purview again. Stories of humans saved from the sea by dolphins are authenticated, and Pliny gives a list of cases up to his time where dolphins became attached to humans and served them as marine steeds.[11]

In the mythological context the importance of these stories, and that of Eikadios, lies in the fact that the dolphin appears in them ias a nourishing animal, like the she-wolf we have encountered which suckles the sacred children, the saving mother, one of the important rôles played by the mythic figures in adolescent initiations. The other rôle the dolphin plays is that of the devouring monster (and surrogate parent) evinced in the stories of Jason and Herakles in the sea-monster's maw.

Perhaps the most striking connection of wolf and dolphin in Greek mythology is their association with Amymōnē, Danaos' daughter, whom we have learned of as the herald of the battle between the wolf and the bull that took place at Argos before Danaos founded the temple of Apollo Lykeios there. Amymōnē rode on a dolphin at the fountain of Lerna, that marsh on the east coast of the Peloponnesus that was famed for being bottomless.[12] The fountain of Lerna was Poseidon's creation,[13] and Poseidon is Amymōnē's mate in the common myth of the founding of the temple of Apollo Lykeios at Argos. The dolphin, as a marine mammal, is connected with him as well as with Apollo, and Amymōnē serves as a link between the two gods. In one passage in Ovid, at least, Neptune appears in the form of a dolphin.

In the myth of Thēseus, and hence in Athenian cult, the dolphin, in the form of Apollo Delphinios, is connected with the wind. Thēseus dedicated his suppliant's badge to Apollo at the Delphinion in Athens, before setting out for Krete.[14] That act, we may assume, included a prayer for a fair voyage with favorable winds; the dolphin-god would be able to guarantee that. The sixth day of the month Munychion was an Athenian festival when unmarried young girls came as suppliants to the Delphinion, to make sacrifice to Apollo Delphinios; for a festival of Artemis on this day commemorated Thēseus' departure for Krete. Thēseus was supposed to have left for

---

[9] Σ Eur. *Or.* 1647.
[10] Servius ad *Aen.* 3.332.
[11] *N. H.* 9.3.
[12] Lucian *Dial. marit.* 8 [6].
[13] Hyginus 2 and Eratosthenes *Katast.* 31.
[14] Plut. *Thes.* 18.

Krete then, on the day that opened the new sailing season each year.

The appearance of young girls as suppliants of Apollo Delphinios received an etiological explanation. They were supposed to be commemorating the prayer for the fourteen young Athenians taken along with Thēseus by Minōs, the King of Krete, in the period of the Kretan thalassocracy, to be fed to the Minotaur, the last such batch sent out and the only ones to escape. This supplication recalls certain aspects of ephebic practice. The confusion of boys and girls, or the transformation of one into the other, is a characteristic trait of ephebic education which we may be able to connect with the wolf. It occurs twice in the story of Thēseus, both times within the sphere of Apollo Delphinios.

The old Attic story of Thēseus' first arrival at Athens shows ephebic traits properly belonging to the warrior confraternities of the Indo-European linguistic area:[15] "He was wearing an ankle-length tunic and his hair was neatly braided. When he reached the temple of Delphinios the builders on the roof asked mockingly what a girl of marriageable age was doing wandering around by herself." Theseus did not leave any doubt, however, about which sex he really belonged to. He showed at once that he was a man, for he "did not say anything to them but...unhitched the oxen from their wagon and threw them up higher than the roof they were making for the temple."

Again, a similar thing happened when the fourteen chosen Athenian youths and maidens were to leave for Krete. There were to be seven of each, but Thēseus substituted two young boys for two of the girls. He took the two boys, kept them out of the sun to whiten their skin, and had them bathe often and use creams and bandages to improve their complexions so that they might be passed off as maidens.[16] This story was used to explain the events at the Athenian festival of Dionysos called the Oschophoria, celebrated in the month of Pyanepsion, to commemorate Thēseus' return from Krete. Pyanepsion was at the beginning of the winter (November-December) and marked the beginning of winter maneuvers for the ephebes, who constituted the standing army at Athens. When he landed at Phaleron, Athens' port at the time, Thēseus established this festival at the temple of Athena Skiras there, as a holiday of thanksgiving to Ariadne and Dionysos, who had saved him from the Labyrinth according to what appears to be the oldest version of his story. In the procession, a central part of all Athenian festivals, two boys of noble lineage, called Oschophoroi, led the line. They were dressed in the same kind of long Ionian tunic Theseus wore when he came to Athens, and may have been meant to represent the two boys passed off as girls. This may be a late (sixth century) etiology, but in any case it extends the ephebic theme of Thēseus' entry into Athens to his later adventures, and is in no way out of place among them. In the Oschophoria it was mandatory for both boys to have had both parents alive. As is well known, when Thēseus returned to Athens from Krete, he was an orphan, and hence a king, unbeknownst to himself, so that having both parents alive may imply directly that kingship, and manhood, for that matter, which do not belong to the ephebes, are both inherited states, since manhood implies ownership of property. Hence the boys in the procession at the Oschophoria must have had both their parents living.

A further narrative of Thēseus and the dolphin is found in the myth that tells how Thēseus plunged into the sea on the same voyage.[17] In Bakchylides' version of the

---

[15] Paus. 1.19.1.

[16] Plut. *Thes.* 18.23. L. Deubner, *Attische Feste* (Berlin 1932) 142 thinks this story is late, probably of the sixth century B.C.E.

[17] Bakchylides 17 tells the story, and it is mentioned by Pausanias and others. H. Jeanmaire,

story Thēseus was accompanied by dolphins as he dived to retrieve the golden ring Minos had cast into the waves. He came to the house of his father Poseidon at the bottom of the sea and was received there by Amphitritē: "The dolphins who live in the sea swiftly bore the great Thēseus to the house of his father, Lord of Horses" (97-100).

Again according to Bakchylides, Thēseus emerged out of the depths with the "wreath dark with roses." That wreath was Amphitritē's and it had been given to her by Aphroditē on the occasion of her marriage to Poseidon. It is called a golden wreath,[18] and *coronam...compluribus lucentem gemmis*, "a crown glistering with many gems."[19] No doubt it was identified with the glistering crown given Thēseus by Ariadne (who also may be equivalent to Aphrodite, it seems, if her name is to be identified with that goddess's epithet Ariagne, "very holy") to light up his way out of the labyrinth after he slew the Minotaur, according to one ancient version of that myth. According to the Greek astronomers the constellation Corona Borealis is that crown set to shine forever in the night sky.

We need not wonder at Thēseus' appearance at the bottom of the sea. That is where the "ephebic" hero in Iranian myth goes to retrieve the symbol of courage, the glistering, shining splendor there hidden, the *xvarena,* which corresponds to the Rheingold in Teutonic myth. Thēseus' leap into the sea, then, is another act that seems to recall initiation rites, inasmuch as it parallels the Iranian story of Franghrasyan (Afrasiab) leaping into Vourukaša in the Avesta in order to procure the shining *xvarena.* In any case Thēseus' dive itself recalls the natural behavior of the dolphin.[20]

The figure of the god Dionysos, who appears in two tales, at least, in the rôle of one who dives down to the bottom of the sea, and returns, is more important for our investigation, however. His is the same rôle that we have posited in Chap. 3 *supra* for the dolphin,[21] and just now seen in Thēseus. (Jason and Herakles appear in similar rôles below.) In the *Iliad*[22] Dionysos is found fleeing into the depths of the sea before the raging Lykurgos, where, in the depths, he found refuge in the lap of Thetis. The amphora into which the remains of Patroklos were placed is said to have been the gift of Dionysos to Thetis,[23] presumably for having taken him into her arms when he fled into the sea. The other tale of a similar nature told of Dionysos relates how Perseus pursued him and forced him to the bottom of the swamp of Lerna.[24] In two other ancient parallels to these stories Dionysos appears emerging out of the sea. One is a story from Methymna on the island of Lesbos telling how fishermen hauled up a face made of olive-wood out of the sea; they were told by the oracle at Delphi that this was an image of Dionysos Phallēn which they were to worship, whereupon they sent a

---

Couroi et Courètes. Essai sur l'éducation spartiate et sur les rites d'adolescence dans l'antiquité hellénique (Lille 1939) p. 323ff., and esp. p. 330f., adduces examples of ancient Greek initiatory practices from Thēseus' visit to the realms of Poseidon and Amphitrite.

[18] Paus. 1.17.3.

[19] Hegesianax *Astron.* 2.5.

[20] With this we can place Thēseus in the context of the three names, from the roots *lyk-, delph-,* and *deuk-.* We have seen in the previous chapter that his story relates him to Lykomēdēs and to Deukalion; now we find he is related to the dolphin. Furthermore, like Phorbas or Phlegyas, he was said to have once cleared the road to Delphi of highwaymen. Cf. Σ Aesch. *Eum.* 13, and Σ Aristides p. 324.20ff. Dindorf. So he is once again connected with a place named from the root *delph-.*

[21] P. 67 *supra.*

[22] *Il.* 6.135ff.

[23] *Od.* 24.74.

[24] Σ T ad *Il.* 14.319f.

bronze copy to Delphi and kept the original image for themselves.[25] The second tale, quoted from a certain Sokrates *On Sacred Objects*, which relates how the Argives used to call Bull-born Dionysos out of the water with trumpets, and throw a lamb into the deep for Pylaochos (The Gatekeeper),[26] makes clear the identification of the deep with the other world; for the epithet Gatekeeper, here apparently given to Dionysos, is usually applied to Hades, the god of the world of the dead. We made this point at the end of Chap. 3 *supra*, and here we have another place where Dionysos seems to be identified with the figure of Lykos, the wolf who passes from the outside world to the known world. In fact, in the case of the god Dionysos his epiphany is of paramount importance. It is he who comes over the sea in a bark, and in a Naxian tale sailors who accompany him turn into dolphins.[27]

In view of these things, and of *Il*. 21.22f., quoted above, we may view the dolphin as the "the wolf of the sea." Evidence of sea-monsters in antiquity, and comparative evidence.points to the same conclusion Most Greek references to the dolphin are unequivocal; they refer to the common dolphin *Delphinus delphis*, black above and white below. In Aristotle, however, we find the dolphin classed with the whale,[28] and in fact it must have been confused with various species of marine mammals. There surely once was a time when the Greeks were not familiar with these species. The ancient invaders from northerly regions far from the sea who were their ancestors (see above) must not have distinguished one large sea mammal from another. This must be the origin of the belief in strange sea-monsters like the *skolopendra* that survived throughout Greece.[29] Only later were known species "distilled," as it were, out of the general category of κῆτος, "sea-monster," "great fish," or "sea-serpent." To complete our survey of Greek beliefs about the dolphin, we need to investigate the wider context of the words κῆτος and βάλαινα, "swollen monster," "whale."

First, however, let us note, in this context, that the seal partakes of some of the dolphin's and wolf's association with weather and storms. The Greeks believed the seal to be immune to lightning, and thought its skin protects against it;[30] and people used to hang the skin of a seal on a vine in order to protect it from hail.[31] The Mediterranean seal, *stenorhynchus albiventer*, is termed φώκη, *phōkē*, in Greek.

The seal-name appears in Greek toponymy and in myth as part of the context of the wolf-name, in the name of the land Phōkis, the land in which Delphi with its sanctuary of Apollo stood, and in the name of the eponymous hero of the land, Phōkos. Nikander relates, in connection with his version of the wolf that ravaged the flocks of Pēleus, that a statue of a wolf stood on the border of Phōkis and Ozolian Lokri.[32] Psamathē ("sand-woman") is the name of the Nereid who had lain with Aiakos in the form of a seal and borne him Phōkos. She was said to have sent a monstrous wolf against the flocks of Pēleus ("man of the mud") after he and his brother Telamon, the two sons of Endēïs, murdered Phōkos, her son and their half-brother. This giant wolf was later turned to stone by Psamathē herself, upon the intercession of Thetis, the

---

[25] Paus. 10.19.3.
[26] Plut. *de Is. et Osir.* 364F.
[27] Aglaosthenes in Hyginus *poet. astr.* 2.17.
[28] Ar. *Hist. An.* 1.5, 489b2.
[29] Ar. *ibid.*, Theophr. *H.Pl.* 7.11, Hesych. *s.v.*
[30] *PWRE* 1A (1914) col. 949 Gossen.
[31] *Geoponica* 1.14 quoting Philostratos.
[32] Ant. Lib. 38.

Nereid who was married to Pēleus.[33] Another version of the story has Thetis herself turn the wolf to stone; in this version the wolf appeared to punish Pēleus for having killed Eurytion accidentally.[34] In this myth a Nereid, a nymph of the sea, who is the mother of a hero, named for the seal, appears as the mistress of the wolf whose statue was set up at the entrance to a land named after the seal.

There is another Phōkos, the son of Ornytion, son of Sisyphos, whom some called the ancestor of the people of Phōkis, instead of Phōkos, the son of Psamathē and Aiakos.[35] This Phōkos was the husband of Antiopē,[36] the mother of the famous twins Amphiōn and Zēthos, whom he had married after cleansing her of the stain of the cruel murder of Dirkē, and next to whom he was buried in Tithoreia in and Phōkis. Hence his story is associated with the wolf-name as well, in the person of Lykos, husband of Dirkē, and king of Thebes, treated in the last chapter.

The sea-serpent or great fish, κῆτος, is closely related to the snake or dragon, δρακών. Two ancient monuments illustrate the relation between the fish, the κῆτος or dolphin, and the snake. The first is a red-figured stamnos in the British Museum showing the contest between Herakles and the river-god Acheloos.[37] Here the river-god has a serpent's body and a fish tail, along with a human torso and a bull's horns. Thus the serpent and the fish are combined in a composite figure that might stand for the dolphin, or for any standard cetacean. The second monument provides even clearer evidence. A vase in the Vatican Etruscan collection shows Jason emerging from the jaws of a snake-like sea-monster, while the Golden Fleece hangs on a branch above him and Athena stands nearby.[38] Jason is not known to have been swallowed by the monster who guarded the Fleece from any literary source. A close parallel to this story in myth is Herakles' three-day sojourn in a sea-monster's maw, either in the story of the rescue of Hesione,[39] or in that of the sea-monster sent by Poseidon as a punishment for Laomedon's non-payment of the fee for the construction of the walls of Troy by him and Apollo, into whose gullet Herakles leapt in order to destroy it from inside.[40] We note the composite nature of the monster; it is a sea-serpent.

A clearer identification of dolphin and snake emerges from the Bible, as well as from other ancient Near Eastern texts. The name Leviathan, given to the Biblical sea-serpent,[41] seems to be applied to the dolphin or some similar creature in Ps. 104.26, "That is where the ships go: where that Leviathan whom thou hast made to play therein (in the sea) is"; for the only animals seen to sport near ships are porpoises and dolphins. It has been argued from the association of Leviathan and ships in this verse that "Leviathan must be something visible from the ships at sea, something that occurs to the mind when thinking of ships and sights seen at sea."[42] Etymological considerations may combine with the context here to give the meaning "dolphin" for לויתן, "Leviathan." One of the meanings of the Hebrew root lwy (לוי) is "to

---

[33] Tzetzes on Lyk. 175 and 901, and Ovid *Met.* 11.346ff.

[34] Nikander in Ant. Lib. 38 .

[35] Σ *Il.* 2.517.

[36] Paus. 9.17.3ff.

[37] *CVA British Museum* 3,III 1C Pl. 19, 1b, reproduced in Fontenrose *op. cit.* (Chap. 2 n. 116 *supra*) 233.

[38] The vase is shown in Jane E. Harrison, *Themis, A Study of the Social Origins of Greek Religion* (Cambridge 1927²) 435.

[39] Apollod. 2.5.9.10.

[40] *Il.* 20.145ff. and Σ A, B, and D, *ad loc.*

[41] Job 26.12 ;Isaiah 27.1.

[42] Meïr Weiss, *The Bible and Modern Literary Theory* (Jerusalem 1962) 58 (in Hebrew).

accompany." This is probably a folk-etymology, but in the context here it is not inappropriate. The Greek πόμπιλος, "a fish that follows ships" would be a parallel case; the verb is from the verb πέμπω, "to accompany on one's way, to send someone off, or away." That fish is today identified with the pilot-fish, a variety of stickleback that follows ships, on the basis of the identification made by the Baron Cuvier, against the ancient identification with the tuna (Pliny *N.H.* 9.20): "Tunny-fish follow vessels in full sail, visible from the poop for hours and for many miles; they are the fish called pompili." On the basis of this passage of Pliny, it has been held that Leviathan is a name for "tunfishes and dolphins,"[43] while another opinion would have the name Leviathan refer instead to the whale, because that animal accompanies its young.[44]

The Psalmist's Leviathan is not Lôtan, the mythical creature of the Ugaritic texts, though he seems to share his name. No doubt the use of the same name for the dolphin and the mythical creature of Ugarit reflects a period when few if any marine species were clearly distinguished, and the dolphin could be thought of as a sea-monster. It is not hard to imagine a time when the sea was *terra incognita* to the ancient Semites. The mythical Lôtan too, however, has a parallel in Biblical literature. In the Ugaritic Ras Shamra texts Lôtan (Leviathan) is conquered by Baal and Anat in a scene that has been thought to correspond to Leviathan falling prey to the Lord in Isaiah 27.1, Job 26.12, and Ps. 74.13-14.

Now the common dolphin belongs to the genus Delphinidae along with the grampus, the killer whale, and the pilot whale. There is, in fact, little reason to distinguish between the whale and the dolphin, and indeed Aelian explains that the whale, φάλαινα, is an animal like, or identical to the dolphin.[45] In that passage a variant reading has φώκαινα, "the seal," and indeed seals and whales are often mentioned together by the Greeks, and the poet of Ps. 104 "surely did not distinguish scientific genera, species, and families in these animals."[46]

Once the whale is brought under the same rubric as the dolphin, comparative studies give us grounds for identifying the dolphin-whale, or Leviathan, and the wolf. The common attribute of both the Leviathan and the Teutonic Fenris-wolf is their maw or gullet. Both are capable of swallowing the sun, and threaten to do so. The wolf is a voracious creature in Greek tradition, as well as in The Three Little Pigs, our wind-wolf story from the Teutonic linguistic area, and so is the whale, or great fish, in stories, from the Greek linguistic area and from elsewhere, in which he swallows a man (Jason or Herakles, or the Tlingit culture-hero Raven) and regurgitates him.

If we look a bit closer at the motif of threatening to swallow the sun, or the sun and the moon, clearly we must try to answer the question why man and a heavenly body alternate as victims of the ravening monsters. The Greek story, of Theseus and the Athenian Youths and Maidens, along with the Iranian tale of Franghrasyan in Vourukaša,[47] hold the key to this alternation. To repeat the parallel here: the hero wearing the shining, or fiery crown, be he Thēseus or Franghrasyan,[48] is like the sun, and like Āpām Napat of the Sanskrit sources; the Avestan source which gives the name *xvarena* to the shining treasure of the warrior at the bottom of the lake,

---

[43] B.D. Eerdmans, "The Hebrew Book of Psalms," *Oudtestamentische Studien* 4 (1947) 470-471.
[44] G.R. Driver, "Mythical Monsters in the Old Testament," *Studi Orientalistici in onore di G. della Vida* I (Rome 1956) 240.
[45] *N.A.* 4.5.
[46] Weiss *Op. cit* (n. 42 *supra*) p. 204.
[47] P. 88 *supra*.
[48] P. 87-88 *supra*.

identifies it as the special glory of the warrior, the possession of Khshsathra, the patron of Dumézil's second (warrior) function in Iran.

If the great fish or the wolf is going to attack one of the heavenly bodies he must traverse the air to get at least as high as the moon, and unlike the old woman in Mother Goose who went to sweep cobwebs from the sky these monsters could not have been "tossed up in a blanket"! These wolves, and the great fish Leviathan, like the Chinese dragon *lung*, must be embodiments of the spirit of the storm borne aloft, and so represent in their flight great winds. In fact we saw in Chap. 2 *supra* that flying wolves who are the storm-wind are known from German folk-sayings and a Norwegian riddle, and that the most telling example of such creatures in art is on neolithic pottery from South Russia of the second millennium B.C.E.

Leviathan the "fleeing serpent" of Job 26.12[49] darkens the sky and so threatens the heavenly luminaries. Verse 13 is part of a litany of praise for the Lord's great deeds: "By His wind the heavens are serene; his hand pierced the fleeing serpent." In Job 3.8 "those who curse the day" are "those who are skilled to rouse up Leviathan." Again Leviathan seems to threaten the day, or the sun; for Job, here is asking skilled men to curse the night he was born, and "if the men who curse the day are to curse the night Job was born, they should by rights stir Leviathan up to darken the stars."[50] The monster can extinguish any vestige of light in the sky, it seems.

Even stronger support for this picture of Leviathan comes from parallels in other Near Eastern texts. The Egyptian story of the battle between the serpent Apophis (or Apep) and the young sun-god Horus-Behedti is surely such a parallel. This snake is referred to as "the enemy" who "lies with his arms in chains, his whirlwind severed by the sword"[51]; he is darkness incarnate. Moreover the wind is one of his essential attributes, according to the same passage, and his dwelling place is both the eastern and the western parts of heaven. From his station he refuses to allow day to come forth and bring light either to the living or to the dead. Apophis' desire is to restore the rule of primeval darkness. It is clear then that, like Leviathan, he constitutes a peril to sun and moon, in fact, to all light-sources.

At Edfu Apophis is depicted in the shape of hippopotami and crocodiles in the Nile, animals which Horus-Behedti lances and kills.[52] There are many pictures of Horus killing Setech in the form of a hippopotamus with his lance. Hence, Leviathan is paralleled by the hippopotamus at Edfu,[53] and Leviathan and Apophis are parallel figures. We have so few and such scanty references to Lôtan from Ugarit that it is impossible to tell whether West-Semitic or Egyptian influence is to be traced there, i.e. whether he reflects Leviathan or Apophis.[54]

The two Teutonic wolves who attempt to devour the sun present another parallel to Leviathan-Lôtan. Two wolves, named Geri and Freki, belong to Oðinn.[55] Both their names mean "the greedy one." Snorri's Edda speaks of two wolves who try to

---

[49] He is the same as "Leviathan the fleeing serpent, Leviathan the twisting serpent" of Isaiah 27.1.

[50] Otto Kaiser, *Die Mythische Bedeutung des Meeres in Aegypten, Ugarit und Israel* (Berlin, Toepelmann, 1959) 145.

[51] Chapter 66 of *The Book of the Dead* .

[52] Günther Roeder, *Volksglaube im Pharaonenreich* (W. Spemann Verlag, Stuttgart, 1952) 214.

[53] We may note that the hippopotamus is a non-ruminant artiodactyl related to the pig, and if it does indeed play a dolphin-like role in Egyptian mythology, we may have discovered another link, however tenuous, between the dolphin, Gr. δελφίς, and the pig, Gr. δέλφαξ.

[54] Günther Roeder, *op.cit* (n. 52) 181.

[55] E.O.G. Turville-Petre, *Myth and Religion of the North* (New York 1964) 54 and 60.

swallow the sun,[56] Skøll and Hati, of whom one threatens to devour the sun and the other the moon. The wolf succeeds in devouring the sun, the father of the world and gives birth to a daughter before being killed by Viðarr.[57] The wolf Fenrir, son of Loki, is chained by the Ases and bites off the hand that Tyr, as a token of good faith had put into his mouth. It is Fenrir's release from his chains that bind him to the "western gate," the gate of the sunset, that will mean the coming of the *Ragnarøk* or *Götterdämmerung*, the end of the world and the death of all things. Moreover Fenrir will swallow the sun and devour Oðinn himself in the *Ragnarøk* at the end of days.[58] It is not far-fetched to identify the two wolves of Oðinn, the greedy ones, with the two wolves of *Vafthrúðnismál;* in Greece too the two primeval snakes of Delphi, with their "dolphin" names, Delphyne and her male partner, Delphynos, parallel the single primeval snake Python, and also a single mythological figure Lykos,[59] so that once again snake-cetacean figures are counterparts of the wolf.

Our identification of Fenrir with Leviathan is not new. The ninth or tenth century tall monolithic cross of Norse provenance in the churchyard of Gosforth in Cumberland, England, does the same. The sandstone monument seems to be susceptible of a pagan as well as a Christian interpretation.[60] On the south side of the cross Fenrir, in the form of a wolf-headed monster, is shown gagged by Thor's sword, in a portrayal that parallels Leviathan tamed on the north side. In any case, these two are the monstrous opponents of the Ases and of the Lord respectively.

Another facet of Fenrir that connects him with the dolphin-complex is worth mentioning here. That is his name, which, according to the most plausible etymology, derives from Old-Icelandic (and English) *fen*, "swamp."[61] The Norse Fenris wolf may not really be a swamp or water demon,[62] but the connection of the wolf with water here corresponds exactly to the wolf's control over the life-giving passageways of the universal body, a connection that recurs in folklore. Accordingly, the Fenris-wolf is the guardian of the entry to the land of the dead in old Norse mythology, along with the wolf Garmr, who seems identical with him.[63] The same rôle is played in India by the two vicious four-eyed dogs of Yama, the Sārameyās, named Śyāma and Śabala,[64] and in Greece by the dog Kerberos, the "hound of Hell," who recalls the snake, and is also identical to our sea-serpent or dolphin; for Kerberos appeared to the Greeks as a serpent-like animal. Hekataios of Miletos, at the beginning of the fifth century, wrote that the "hound of Hades," that lived at Tainaron, was a horrible snake. Even before his time Kerberos had been shown on vases with snakes' attributes. The three-headed dog is shown once with two dog's heads and one snake's head; on a number of archaic Attic vases he has two dog's heads and a snake's head for a tail; and at other times

---

[56] *Edda Snorra Sturlusonar* (ed. Finnur Jónsson 1931) *Gylfaginning* 6.

[57] *Vafthrúðnismál* 45-47.

[58] *Gylfaginning* 38 and *Vafthrúðnismál* 53. Cf. A. Olrik, *Ragnarök* [tr. W. Ranisch] (1922) 36ff.

[59] Fontenrose, *op. cit.* (Chap. 2 n. 117 *supra*) 421ff.

[60] A.B. Cook, *Zeus: A Study in Ancient Religion* II (Cambridge 1919) 305.

[61] That of Finnur Jónsson and S.N. Hagen brought *s. v.* Fenrir in Jan de Vries *Altnordisches etymologisches Wörterbuch* (Leiden 1977²) 117. The same derivation had been suggested earlier by Siegfried Gutenbrunner.

[62] F.R. Schröder, "Sinfjötli," *Hommages à Georges Dumézil (Collection Latomus* 45) (Brussels 1960) p.199 and note 4.

[63] E.O.G. Turville-Petre, *op. cit.* (n. 55 *supra*) 281.

[64] A.A. MacDonell, *Vedic Mythology* (Strassburg 1899=*Grundriss der indo-arischen Philologie* 3.1. Hft. A, 1899) 404.

snakes emerge from his back, his neck, or his stomach.[65] Plato attests to Kerberos as a "compound monster," incorporating snake elements in addition to its hound's nature,[66] and its affinity to the snake-dragon Hydra is attested both by their common parents, Typhon and Echidna,[67] and by the fact that they each have a number of heads.

The phrase "You have viewed the Three-headed one," refers to Kerberos, the three-headed dog, and the fear he inspires that strikes men dumb. The same effect is attributed to viewing a wolf; for a Greek proverbial saying λύκον εἶδες "you have seen a wolf," means "you have been struck dumb,"[68] and of the wolf the poet remarks, "had I not seen him before he saw me, I imagine I would have been struck dumb."[69] In the folklore of many peoples a wolf's gaze strikes men dumb, unless the wolf is seen first. It appears that the wolf whose gaze deprives people of the power of speech is identical to the dog of the underworld, and they may be two forms of the same creature. In ancient Italy the wolf was a symbol of the underworld, and appears on funerary monuments, and we may recall that the Norse wolves Fenrir and Garmr parallel the Indian Sārameyās. In many folktales the wolf and dog are enemies or friends and are clearly distinguished,[70] but their functions overlap here, as they do at other points as well. No doubt Apollo's wolf-titles have a chthonic basis; the dog appears in contexts that include the wolf, the serpent, the marine monster, or the giant.

In another context too dog and wolf alternate in Greece and Rome, namely, that of the bitch (or vixen) and the she-wolf, which stand for the prostitute in each respectively. The Latin *lupa*, "she-wolf," is the regular term for a low-class prostitute[71] just as the word *lupanar* denotes a house of ill-repute. In the Greek myth of Erysichthon whose appetite was never sated, his daughter Mestra, or Mnestra, was able to change her shape at will, and would sell herself in order to feed him.[72] She is called "a shapeshifting, shiny-tailed vixen," (βασσάρα)[73] and examples of her different shapes are given as "a cow, a bitch, or a bird."[74] Perhaps in the same way that the she-wolf stands for the most animal-like of all creatures, so the girl who can turn herself into any animal is the vixen or the bitch. In Greek the dog's outstanding characteristic is its lack of shame, the quality that gave the name of the dog to the Cynic school of philosophy.[75]

Another dog in Greek mythology that may have connections with Kerberos, is Orthros, the dog Herakles overpowered. He was the guardian of the flocks of Geryon, himself a three-bodied monster. It may be, however, that the name Orthros gives him away. According to Dumézil's contested etymology,[76] it is the Greek reflex of the

---

[65] S. Eitrem *s.v.* Kerberos *PWRE* 11.1 (1921) cols. 271-284. *V.* also B. Schlerath, "Der Hund bei den Indogermanen," *Paideuma* 6 (1954) 39, and Bruce Lincoln, "The Hellhound," *JIES* 7 (1979) 273-285, who holds that the name Kerberos, like Geri, derives from the growl of the ravenous animal.

[66] Pl. *Rep.* 588. Cf. Vergil *Aen.* 6.419, Hor. *Odes* 2.13.33f. and 3.11.17f., and Tibullus 1.3.71, for similar descriptions.

[67] Hes. *Theog.* 310.

[68] Pl. *Ibid.* 336D.

[69] Theoc. 14.22.

[70] Cf. the Grimm fairy tale "Old Sultan and his Friends."

[71] Cf. Juvenal 3.66, *et alibi*.

[72] Lykophron 1393 and Σ *ad loc.*

[73] *Ibid.*

[74] Apostolios 11.21 (Leutsch-Schneidewin *CPG* II p. 520).

[75] And the Homeric epithet κυνῶπις "dog-eyed," to Helen of Troy.

[76] P. Chantraine, *Dictionnaire étymologique de la lange grecque* (Paris 1968) Vol. 3 819-820 *s.*

name that occurs in Vedic mythology as Vṛtra, who was the great snake-dragon overcome by the god Indra, in the central story of Indian myth that parallels Apollo's battle with Python. Vṛtra is the Indian counterpart of the Leviathan-Fenris figure as well; for he dries up the sky by his presence and holds back the life-giving waters. He is the son of Dānu, the goddess of the waters. If there is a pair Orthros-Vṛtra, we may see an Indian serpent figure mirroring a dog-figure in Greece, both of whom function as opponents, and ultimately victims, of god-heroes. Like Kerberos, then, Orthros may be a dog with serpent connections.

All accounts agree that Herakles brought Kerberos up from Hades. One euhemeristic version, however, takes an interesting form: "Kerberos belonged to a king of the Thesprotians named Aïdōneus. He was stolen and hidden in a dark cave. Herakles in turn stole him out of there and brought him to Eurystheus."[77] (Aïdōneus is another name for Hades.) The theme of stealing something out of a dark cave, and the theme of the dog (wolf) recall the Latvian werewolf document in Appendix B. There the returning werewolves, the "hounds of God," steal grain and bring it out into the light again with them, to ensure the success of the crops. In place of the grain there appears here Kerberos, the dog-snake, and Herakles takes the place, not surprisingly, of the werewolf brotherhood, like whom he wears a wild beast's pelt, in his case a lion's skin, with the jaws gaping around his face. Thus there may be a survival of folk custom here, and not merely euhemerism.

In the more common version Herakles was allowed to take Kerberos with him to the upper world only if he could overcome him unarmed.[78] Herakles wore only his lion's skin and body armor during his struggle with Kerberos. He strangled the dog with his bare hands, though the dog's tail inflicted a nasty bite on him. In art Herakles is often pictured leading Kerberos by a chain, and holding a club or a bow, which are probably shown in order to identify him. Herakles' weaponlessness in his adventures with Kerberos and the Nemean lion connects him with the activities of the ephebic group, and with wolf-like warrior confraternities. This too is a trait that belongs to the lore of the ancient confraternities of the Indo-European linguistic area. The ephebes at Athens were set on the borders, as a φρούριον,[79] to guard against invaders virtually unarmed; and Latvian werewolves too went out without weapons. Myth here once again agrees with actual practice, ancient and modern.

The end of this episode of the Dodecathlon is Kerberos' return to Hades. The people of Argos said he ran away at the fountain Kynadra, or "dog's watering," between Mykenai and the Argive Heraion; other versions told that Herakles returned him. The Dodecathlon of Herakles provides examples, over and over again, of victory over the powers of death. The Hydra, Geryon's herd of cattle, and the apples of the Hesperides are all episodes concerned with death and immortality, as is the aid Herakles tendered to Thēseus in the affair of Peirithoos' attempt to rape Persephone, his rescue of Alkestis, and other tales as well. Of these, only the story of Kerberos is attached to specific Hell-holes, or entrances to the underworld, in Greece and the surrounding area, where Herakles brought Kerberos up to the light of day, or returned him to the land of the shades. One of these is located at Cape Tainaron in the Peloponnesos, and another in the land of the Mariandynoi around Herakleia on the

---

v. ὄρθρος seriously doubts the name in this form, or in the form ὄρθον (Hesiod), ever had an initial Ϝ, or is at all related to ὀρθός, which was once Ϝορθός.

[77] Vatican περὶ ἀπιστῶν 5 p. 322 Westermann, p.90 Festus.

[78] Apollod. 2.5.12.8.

[79] From πρὸ ὅριον, "at the border."

Black Sea in Paphlagonia. Herakles' visit to the land of the dead, burlesqued, forms the plot of Aristophanes *Frogs*. Turned inside out, as it were, and made into his assumption into Olympus, or heaven, it comprised his apotheosis, his reconciliation with and adoption by Hera, and his marriage to Hēbē, "Eternal Youth." Heaven and Hell are both part of the "outside."

Herakles is connected with openings, or passages between the inhabited world and the outside in another way, as well. He was the patron of hot springs, and *thermai*, hot springs, were known as passages to the underworld; Persephone was supposed to have descended to Hades through the spring Kyane, for example.[80] Added evidence for hot springs as gates of Hell comes from the various versions of the story of Herakles and the cattle of Geryon. That tale was located at various spots, at each one of which there are hot springs: in Lydia, in Chaonia, near Baiae, near Padua, and at Thermopylae. Geryon's close connection with the land of the dead may be deduced from his dog Orthros and from the fact that nearby a herdsman called Menoitios tended the cattle of Hades.

Herakles has other connections with water sources. He went to fetch water during the voyage of the Argo,[81] and some say he had to fight Lepreos to get to the water.[82] This fight may be compared to Herakles' wrestling match with Death in Eur. *Alk.* in his struggle to return Alkestis to life. Hylas, too, Herakles' favorite, went to fetch water in the land of the Mariandynoi, which has a number of wolf-connections and whose king was named Lykos, during the voyage of the Argo, and was seized by water nymphs at the well, and fell to his death.[83]

In Cap. 3 *supra*, sinkholes, which also function as entrances to the underworld also appeared in the story of Herakles.[84] He is said to have cleaned and opened the sinkholes of the plain of Pheneos in Arkadia, so draining the swamp there, and he stopped up and re-opened the sinkholes of Boiotia, thus causing the formation of Lake Kopais.[85] Also the lake named after Herakles at Agyrion was his work.[86]

These traits of Herakles tie him to the wolf-dolphin complex, just as do his monster-killing exploits. Even more important for our purposes is the dolphin-whale-serpent as the swallower or devourer, the rôle we have seen in the vase painting showing Jason emerging from the jaws of a snake-like sea-monster, while the Golden Fleece hangs on a branch above him and Athena stands nearby, and from Herakles' sojourn in a sea-monster's maw.[87] This is an initiatory adventure paralleled in many folktales from all over the world. Being swallowed by a monster, specifically by a sea-monster, is part of adolescent initiations in many places.[88] In much of the material from Oceania collected by Frobenius,[89] in order to elucidate the well-known Germanic folktale of Little Red Riding Hood, whose grandmother had been devoured by the big bad wolf, the hero emerges bald from the belly of the sea monster, showing that his

---

[80] Cf. Ganschinietz, "Katabasis," *PWRE* 10.2, col. 2379 (1919), for hot springs as leading to the world below, and O. Gruppe, "Herakles," *PWRE* Suppl. III, for Herakles' connection with warm springs.

[81] Hes. *fr.* 263 MW. *et al.*

[82] Zenodotus in Athenaeus 10.2.412a, Aelian *V. H.* 1.24.

[83] Concerning the name Hylas, and Apollo's epithet Hylates *v.* Chap. 6 *infra*.

[84] Pp. 47, 50-51 *supra*.

[85] Albani Tablets *IG* XIV 1293.

[86] D. S. 4.23.3.

[87] P. 90 and nn. 38-40 *supra*.

[88] M. Eliade, *Rites and Symbols of Initiation* (New York, Harper, 1958) 35.

[89] Leo Frobenius, *Die Zeitalter des Sonnengottes* I Book 2 Chaps. 4-9 (Berlin 1904) 50-220.

status is that of a newborn.[90] We may note here, in this context, that the Finnish heroes Ilmarinen and Vänämöinen in the *Kalevala* are also swallowed by a fish or by a hag who is Mother Earth and Goddess of Death rolled into one.

In Little Red Riding Hood the grandmother is reborn from the belly of the wolf, who had, moreover, impersonated the old lady. In both these roles the wolf is a maternal figure, like in the story of Romulus and Remus. In the last chapter we have indeed seen the wolf in the role of nourishing (foster-)parent. The Thyiades in the ancient rites of Dionysos used to wander over the hills in their frenzy, and were said to have given suck to whelps, as well as to fawns.[91] (In mythological thinking the biting, whelplike infant must have a she-wolf as his mother.) Nor ought we to forget that the belly is the home of another wolf who is the wind, as well, the 'lupus' that is to go 'per semitam,' "the wolf on the path," of the Latin spell cited at the end of Chap. 3 *supra*.

In fact the wolf's or whale's maw is symbolic of death and rebirth; the content of the symbol is the maternal facet of the wolf and the dolphin (sea-monster) along with these animals' rôle as couriers between the hidden world and the realm of the visible. Most pertinent to the theme of the dolphin-whale-serpent as the swallower or devourer is the special house built in the shape of a sea-monster, Barlun, in Papua-New Guinea, for the circumcision of adolescent boys. A wooden sculpture from the same area, in the Rockefeller Collection, shows a crocodile[92] whose back is open to reveal huddled, embryo-like human creatures lined up in rows, meant to represent souls of the departed in transit to the other world.

Tlingit society of the northern coast of British Columbia and the Alaskan Panhandle is divided into two moieties, one called after the wolf and the other after the raven. One of the most important myths of this tribe tells how Raven, the chief culture hero of the tribe (and hence the most common figure on the totem poles of the Tlingit), and the patron of the moiety named after him, was swallowed by a whale, and lit a fire in the animal's belly to allow himself to escape. He emerged from the side of the dead stranded whale blackened from the smoke of the fire.[93]

Raven is a sun-figure, and his story parallels that of the white raven who turned black in the Greek story.[94] Accordingly, the whale here is the swallower of the sun, a death-figure who is symbolic of the solar eclipse, just like the Fenris-wolf of Teutonicstory, or the Leviathan figure. For our purposes one facet of the Tlingit myth is even more important. The sea-monster, Gonaqadate, is a double of the whale figure, and a patron (forefather), of the wolf-moiety as well. Here is a clear indication of the close association of the sea-monster, and the wolf, one that can serve to elucidate the story of Psamathē and the wolf, cited above, from the Greek tradition.

In conclusion we may reiterate that the way the dolphin and the seal break the surface of the waves and take in air in order to breathe allows these mammals to be identified worldwide as messengers from the other world who come through the wellsprings of ocean to communicate with our world; thus they correspond to the wolf and the raven (as generic names), on the land and in the air.

---

[90] *Ibid.* pp. 63-64.

[91] Eur. *Bacchae* 699-700.

[92] Eliade, *ibid.* (n. 86 *supra*). I have seen a similar wooden sculpture in the Ethnological Museum in Stuttgart. In many places the crocodile is just "a large fish" (cf. the Biblical Heb. word תנין. The association of dolphin and crocodile seems to be established by the fact that Skt. *śiśumāra*, "child-killer," denotes the Gangetic dolphin as well as the crocodile.

[93] Garfield,V.E. & Forrest, L.A. *op. cit.* (Chap. 3 n. 135 *supra*) 103 and for Gonaqadate 117ff.

[94] Chap. 3 n. 131 *supra*.

CHAPTER 6
THE WOLF AND DEATH

We have seen the wolf connected with death in various places in the Greek-speaking area in antiquity. We found this most strikingly in the phenomenon of the sinkhole, so often named for the wolf; for one feature of sinkholes in general is revealed in the story telling how Pluto abducted Kore-Persephone and took her to Hades through a sinkhole on Mt. Kyllene in the territory of Pheneos.[1] The sinkhole appears there as an entrance to the underworld, or rather a gate of Hades. The people of Pheneos had revealed its location to Demeter and she rewarded them by never allowing more than one hundred of them to fall in any war.

A sinkhole we have seen associated with Apollo as well as with death was at the oracle of Marpessos[2] concerning whose priestess the inhabitants of Alexandreia in the Troad, where the famous Sibyl named Herophile, a name given to the Erythraean Sibyl, as well, was said to have lived, told that she was a priestess of Apollo Smintheus (who we have seen is associated with Apollo Lykeios). The oracle was situated where the river Aïdoneus, which bears the fuller or expanded form of Hades' name, falls into a sinkhole, and rises once again before it is swallowed up entirely. From these cases we were able to understand that sinkholes, wherever found, may be considered entrances to the land of the dead, and so in fact our subject has come up passim in Chap. 3 *supra.*

We have encountered another case in which the wolf-name is associated with death in the story of Lykos king of the Mariandynoi: he participated in the funeral services for Idmon the seer of the Argonauts, and in his land Herakles brought Kerberos up from Hades whereupon the plant aconite arose from the poison dripping from the dread creature, part of the tale of the voyage of the Argonauts told *supra.*[3]

Another story in which the wolf-name is associated with death is that of Euenos, the son of Ares and Demonike[4] and father of Marpessa by Alkippe. Marpessa was the wife of Idas[5] stolen from him by Apollo. Idas ventured to oppose Apollo with his bow and arrows. Earlier Marpessa had been stolen from her father Euenos by Idas, and Euenos, when he failed to regain his daughter, had killed his horses and thrown himself into the river Lykormas, thenceforth named Euenos after him.[6] This story is connected to Apollo in his mantic aspect as well, as to his connection with the wolf whose "anchorage," ὁρμή, Lykormas is, because the name Marpessa (or Marpessos) is connected with Gergis and with the Oracle of the Sibyl in the Troad, which belonged to Apollo Smintheus, as we have seen. Just as Aïdoneus is the name of the river on which the oracle of Marpessos is located in the Troad, and signifies death, so the wolf-river here is the site of the suicide of Euenos, the father of Marpessa in an Apollonian context.

Furthermore, farther afield, in Italy, we find the same association of the wolf and death in the territory of the Sabine nation of the Hirpini, named for the wolf, "hirpus," in the Samnite language, around Lake Ampsanctus between Aeclanum and Compsa, a

---

[1] Konon *narr.* 15.
[2] Paus. 10.12.5.
[3] Chap.4 *supra.*
[4] Apollod. 1.7.7.2.
[5] *Il.* 9.557ff.
[6] Apollod. 1.8.

sulfurous body of water where in antiquity Dea Mephitis was worshipped in a cave which gave off asphyxiating vapors[7] and was said to be connected with the underworld by a passageway,[8] and in the story of the modern Greek peasant of Anatolia who said of one of the sinkholes of Arkadia, "It leads to the World Below" πάει στὸν κάτω κόσμο.[9]

In ancient Greece, the most striking example of the connection of the wolf-figure and death in a wolf-epithet attached to a god is in the cult of Zeus rather than of Apollo. The myths and cult material connected with Zeus Lykaios point to his connection with the wolf, with weather, i.e. bringing the wind and the rain, and with death. Nevertheless the connection of the name Lykaios with the wolf has been disputed, as was the case with Apollo's cult-name Lykeios as well.[10] If we examine the material concerning Zeus Lykaios and his cult in the wider context of the archaic significance of the wolf-name, which we have been investigating, it soon becomes apparent that there is little room to doubt the connection of the name Lykaios with the wolf we know; and his chief associations are with death.

Apropos, we may remark that the wind (weather) is associated with death especially in the conception of a werewolf army of the dead, or of the Wild Hunt, as it is called in Germany. We shall have occasion to refer to this phenomenon further. Perhaps inasmuch as the soul is conceived of as a breath of wind when it leaves the body in death, a storm-wind came to be viewed as a whole company of dead souls passing through the air.[11]

Zeus is indisputably a wolf-god; he bore the epithet Lykeios[12] and the epithet Lykōreus as well, at the Korykian cave on Mt. Parnassos.[13] As for Lykaios, Zeus was given this epithet in his worship at Tegea,[14] as well as on Mt. Lykaion;[15] both localities are in Arkadia, and Tegea is not far from the mountain, so that we may rest assured that the connection of Zeus Lykaios with the mountain is primary. The mountain in turn is connected with the wolf and with werewolves over and over again in the literature. Hence the name Lykaios must be derived from λύκος, "wolf."[16]

Anyone who tasted human innards along with the rest of the sacrificial meat at the holy precinct of Zeus Lykaios on Mt. Lykaion in Arkadia would be turned into a

---

[7] Pliny N.H. 2.208.

[8] Verg. Aen. 7.563.

[9] W.R. Halliday, *Greek Divination* (London 1913) 119.

[10] Cf. Appendix A.

[11] L. Weniger, "Feralis Exercitus," *Archiv für Religionswissenschaft* 9 (1906) 216.

[12] Paus. 8.36.

[13] Steph. Byz. 279 Holst.

[14] Paus. 8.53.11.

[15] Paus. 8.36.6.

[16] Not infrequently forms in -αιος derive from second declension nouns. M. Nilsson, *Geschichte der griechischen Religion* 372ff. claims the epithet Lykaios is local, deriving from the mountain called Λύκαιον ὄρος in Arkadia (cf. Pind. *Fr.* 100, Theoc. 1.123, Paus. 8.41.3). This view makes the epithet of no importance for understanding the nature of Zeus Lykaios; for such cult-epithets as Artemis Leukophryene, or Lykoatis, or Poseidon Souniou, all of which are local names, are of no use in interpreting their divine nature. On the other hand the epithet Lykaios may be identical to Lykeios, since it has been shown that the adjectival ending -αιος is applied to second declension nouns outside Attica. Cf. Appendix A n. 12 *infra*. Furthermore, our interpretation of the name Lykaios agrees with the nature of Zeus Lykaios as Nilsson understood it. The name of a locality with which a god is connected is usually related to the deity's attributes if its name is identical to, or derived from, a cult title. Moreover, as we have seen in Chap. 2, there was an Apollo Lykaios at Chryse in Mysia, according to Hesychius.

werewolf.[17] A certain boxer, Damarchos of Parrhasia in Arkadia, who had won a first prize at the Olympic games, was said to have tasted human meat at a sacrifice on the mountain, become a werewolf, and resumed human shape nine years later,[18] and a similar story was told of another pugilist named Demainetos, who took up boxing after he had had lived in wolf's shape for nine years, and also won first prize in the Olympic games.[19] Theophrastus[20] considered the rite of besprinkling the altar of Zeus Lykaios on the mountain with human blood, still being performed in his day, in the third century B.C.E., to be the remnant of an ancient rite of human sacrifice.

Other ancient writers tell us a sentence of death hung over anyone who dared to enter the sacred precinct on Mt. Lykaion. One explanation of this was that whoever went into the *abaton*, that part of the holy precinct that might not be trodden upon by human feet, would die or be killed.[21] In the course of Pausanias' account, in the part of his guide-book devoted to the Lykaian Mountain in Arkadia, he gives two versions of the fate that awaited anyone who transgressed the sacred boundary.[22] First, he tells us that such a person will die within a year, and then he tells us he loses his shadow, explaining that a person who was shortly to die was apprised of the fact by the loss of his shadow.

Hyginus writes concerning the constellation of Boötes, or the Guardian of the Bear (Arktophylax), "He is called Guardian of the Bear from the story that he once was Arcas, the son of Callisto and Jupiter, whom Lycaon butchered and served up along with other pieces of meat when Jupiter came to visit, in order to ascertain whether or not the one seeking his hospitality was really divine. He suffered no less a punishment in his person; for Jupiter at once overturned the table, turned his house to ashes with his thunderbolt, and turned him into a wolf."[23]

The boxers Damarchos and Demainetos mentioned above are not the only boxers of Olympic fame to have had to overcome wolf-shape. The story of Euthymos of Lokroi Epizephyrioi[24] is the most famous example of this association. Euthymos fought with and overcame a demon, or ghost, called Heros, at a place called Temesa in Magna Graecia, where there was an annual rite of expiation in honor of Heros. The demon had been a sailor of Odysseus who had raped a girl at that place, when Odysseus put in there with his ships, and had been stoned for it. The man's ghost killed young and old, men and women alike, until the people of the place decided to sail away. They were dissuaded from this plan by the Delphic oracle who ordered them to build a sanctuary to Heros, and each year, in a ceremony of sacrifice, to marry the most beautiful young girl in Temesa to him. Euthymos saw the girl, fell in love with her, and decided to save her life. He waited for the demon in his temple fully armed, and drove him into the depths of the sea. The oracle then told the Lokrians to sacrifice to Euthymos in his lifetime.[25] A picture Pausanias saw of the confrontation between Euthymos and Heros showed the latter as a black figure dressed in a wolfskin,

---

[17] Plato, *Rep.* 8, 565D (cf. also *Legg.* 782b); Polybius 8.13.7.

[18] Paus. 6.8.2.

[19] Varro (quoted in Aug. *Civ. Dei* 18.17); Pliny *N.H.* 8.22.8.

[20] Quoted in Porph. *de abst.* 2.27. Ps.-Plato *Minos* p. 315 also mentions human sacrifice at the Lykaion, as does Polymnius 8.13.7, who speaks of human sacrificial meat, with no date given.

[21] Eratosthenes *Catast.* 1 (Kallisto).

[22] Paus. 8.38.6.

[23] *Astr.* 2.4.1.

[24] Paus. 6.6.4-11.

[25] Pliny *H. N.* 7.152 from Kall. fr. 98-99 (Pfeiffer).

and gave him the name Lykas. Here, then, we have another wolf figure associated with human sacrifice; we note that here he is also associated with the sea, and with the figure of the husband (Bluebeard).

This story illustrates the way myth was used to make history in the classical period. The symbolism of the wolf as representative of the passage from one realm to another, from inner domesticity to outer ferocity, treated *supra* at the end of Chap. 3, seems to have been employed to restore to society and its values exceptional people who were estranged for political or social reasons in the context of the shortlived democratization of aristocratic athletic values in the period of transition between dictatorship (tyranny) and democracy at the beginning of the Fifth Century, in order to allow the community or *polis* to rehabilitate wayward sons.[26]

The cult on Mt. Lykaion is not the only place an association with the *lyk-* root connects Zeus with human sacrifice. The people of Lyktos on Krete are reported to have sacrificed humans to Zeus,[27] and a Kretan sacrifice of a human being is also attested in the story of Idomeneus of Krete, of the stock of Deukalion, who was said to have sacrificed his son to Zeus.[28] In the classic and Hellenistic periods Zeus was the chief god of Lyktos and it was was one of numerous Kretan cities that claimed the honor of having been Zeus' birthplace.[29] The report of sacrifice of humans there may be related to the notice that the Kuretes of old in Krete used to sacrifice children to Kronos.[30] The existence of human sacrifice on Krete as long ago as Minoan times (c. 1800-1700 B.C.E.) was corroborated in 1979 by the discovery of an ancient sacred precinct bearing clear evidence of human sacrifice, on the north slope of Mt. Yuktas on Krete, at a site called Anemospelia (Cave of the Winds).[31] In the western room of the temple standing in the holy precinct of Anemospelia, destroyed in an earthquake long ago, human victims were sacrificed. There on an altar the bones of a victim, identified as a boy of eighteen, were discovered *in situ*, along with a dagger, whose blade is decorated with a fantastic animal form reminiscent of a wolf.

Mt. Yuktas lies between Ida on the west and Dikte on the east, both famed sites of Zeus worship, and may also belong firmly in the Kretan tradition of the worship of Zeus or Kronos. In the context of the reports of human sacrifice in the worship of Zeus at Lyktos, bearing the wolf-name, and in connection with Idomeneus "of the stock of Deukalion (*sic!*)"[32] the modern name Anemospelia may be not unimportant. It would firmly establish the place of human sacrifice within the wider context of the wolf-name, since the wind is present in the context of the sacrifice and Deukalion too belongs to the context of the wolf-name, as we have seen in our investigation of the appearance of that name in topography.

Thus Zeus Lykaios' connection with death and human sacrifice is clear. Also interesting for us is the werewolf theme connected with his cult. It was thought that one who tasted human innards along with the rest of the sacrificial meat at the holy

---

[26] F. Bohringer, "Cultes d'athlètes en Grèce classique: Propos politiques, discours mythiques," *REA* 81 (1979) 5-18.

[27] Antikleides of Athens, *Nostoi* (*FGrH* 140F7) from Clem. Al. *Protr*. 3.42.5. *V*. Chap. 3 *supra*.

[28] Servius *ad Aen*. 3.121. This is reminiscent of the Canaanite practice of sacrificing children to Baal Hammon.

[29] Faure *op. cit.* (Chap. 3 n. 77 *supra*) 96.

[30] Istros, *Collection of Kretan Sacrifices* (*FGrH* 334F48), from Porphyry *de abst*. 2.56 (cf. Eus. *P. E.* 4.16.7).

[31] By Prof. Ioannis Sakellarakis & Dr Efi Sakellarakis, published in their "'Ανασκαφὲς σ' 'Αρχάνη⸍'Ανεμοσπηλιά," *'Αρχαιολογικὸν Δελτίον* (1979) 331ff.

[32] Cf. the accounts of Lyttos in Chap. 3 p. 33 *supra*.

precinct of Zeus Lykaios on Mt. Lykaion in Arkadia would be turned into a werewolf.[33] The myth that belongs to this theme is found only in Pliny,[34] but must no doubt come from a much earlier time. Pliny quotes it from a Greek author named Euanthes (or Neanthes, according to Jacoby's surmise in *FGrH*), of uncertain date. There were werewolves in ancient society; for we hear of burial rites for murdered wolves at Athens;[35] and murder is a term used only for one man killing another, so that these wolves were surely werewolves. The story told by Euanthes, which we have related *supra*,[36] concerns a certain Lykaon, an illustrious ancestor of the Arkadians. Lykaon's name seems closely related to the cult epithet Lykaios. He is named as the founder of the games of Zeus Lykaios.[37] Mt. Lykaion was the national sanctuary of Arkadia, and the site of some of the oldest athletic contests in Greece.

The modern literature on Zeus Lykaios shows clearly that the werewolf theme has not convinced many scholars that the god had a wolf-connection. That is because, taken by itself in its early form, that found in Plato's *Republic*, it could very well be a superstitious belief surrounding a taboo, a kind of bugbear with no relation to cult practices at all. On the other hand, based on the story told by Pliny from Euanthes, λυκάνθρωπος, "werewolf," has been held to be a name for an outlaw under a nine-year ban, like the nine years of banishment decreed as the punishment for a god who has sworn falsely in Hes. *Th.* 794-804; for "wolf" in the Teutonic linguistic area denoted such a person.[38] There is no justification, however, for limiting discussion of the affinities of the Lykaon story to Teutonic werewolves or to those of any other Indo-European language group for that matter; the Latvian werewolves attested in the document cited in Appendix B seem to be more pertinent to this story than any Teutonic werewolves. Moreover, most scholars who denied that the epithet Lykaios is related to the wolf-name maintained it derived, like Lykeios, from *λύκη, presumed to be a term for "light." This view ought to have fallen by the wayside at once in view of the report that mist was always seen arising at the well of Hagno on Mt. Lykaion, the site of the cult of Zeus Lykaios[39]; for this weather-making site is a sign of a wolf connection at Mt. Lykaion.

Moreover, the nine year ban seems to have a Kretan parallel. In addition to its being the punishment for a god's perjury in Hes. *Th.* 794-804, it is connected[40] with Minos of Knossos' visits to his father Zeus at nine year intervals,[41] and with initiations into the mysteries of Mt. Ida in Krete, like Pythagoras', lasting three times nine days.[42] "Its first year used to recur in the ninth. Many rites in Greece are celebrated with full honors at nine-year intervals." *Primus eius annus nono quoque anno redibat. Multae in Graecia religiones hoc intervallo temporis summa caerimonia coluntur.*[43]

In the context of human sacrifice among the Greeks the cult of Zeus Lykaios has attracted much attention. Today there can be no doubt that human beings were

---

[33] P. 100, n. 20 *supra*.

[34] *N.H.* 8.34 (*FGrH* 3.11 fr. 33, under Neanthes).

[35] Philostephanos (3rd cent. B.C.E.) cited in Chap. 1 n. 48 p. 11 *supra*.

[36] Chap. 4 *supra*.

[37] Pind. *Ol.* 7.83; 9.97; 13.108; *Nem.* 10.48.

[38] Cf. Mary Gerstein, "Warg," in Gerald J. Larson (ed.), *Myth in Indo-European Antiquity* (Berkeley/Los Angeles 1974) 131 ff.

[39] Paus. 8.38.3.

[40] P. Faure, *op. cit.* (Chap. 3 n. 78 *supra*) 113ff.

[41] *Od.* 19.179 with Σ *ad loc.*

[42] Porph. *VP* 17.

[43] Censorinus *De die natali* 18 quoted in P. Faure, *op. cit.* (Chap. 3 n. 78 *supra*) 123 n. 2.

sacrificed in ancient Greece. Our aim is to show that human sacrifice in the Greek cultural area was generally connected with weather and/or agriculture. In the case of the sanctuary on Mt. Lykaion, despite literary testimony to human sacrifice there, no human remains have ever been discovered in the *barathros* during archaeological excavations at the site, although such sacrifices may have taken place somewhere outside the temple precinct. Human sacrifice is better substantiated at other sacred sites in ancient Greece. At the sanctuary of Zeus Laphystios at Halos, one ancient source has it, the eldest surviving descendant of Athamas was sacrificed in a yearly rite.[44] It is hard to take this report literally; for in a short time all Athamas' race would have been annihilated. Still, some sort of human sacrifice, with the victim a surrogate descendant of Athamas, may have indeed been practised.

One hundred years ago the cult of Zeus Laphystios in Halos, where the eldest of the descendants of Athamas was sacrificed, was first interpreted as a weather cult.[45] In fact, the weather connections of the sacrifice in the cult of Zeus Laphystios are clear from one version of the involved myth of Athamas.[46] That version attributes Athamas' attempted sacrifice of his son Phrixus to jealousy between Athamas' second wife Nephele, the mother of Phrixos and Helle, and his first wife, usually named Ino, the daughter of Kadmos and aunt of Dionysos, and takes for granted a human sacrifice, or more particularly the sacrifice of the king's son, as the remedy for drought, or barrenness of the earth.

More pertinent to our investigation is the connection of the sacrifice to Zeus Laphystios (whose name means "the tearer") with the wolf or the werewolf. Athamas himself associates the two themes. He had lost all his children. Taken with madness at the moment his plan to sacrifice his son was revealed as contrary to the will of Zeus, the god of the rain, he snatched up his bow and quiver and began to pursue his remaining sons, the children of Ino, at whom he was enraged as well for having persuaded him to go on with the perverse sacrifice. He is said to have killed Learchos this way, while Ino fled, with the infant Melikertes in her arms, all the way to Athens and beyond, and leapt into the sea from the Skironian rocks on the way from Athens to Megara. Athamas then began to run with a wolf pack, according to one version of the story; in other words, he became a werewolf. What else are we to call a human being who joins a wolf pack and runs with the wolves? Only later did he return to human society.[47]

A further link between Athamas and the wolf can be found in the genealogy of the heroine Atalanta. There are two versions of her story, one from Boiotia and the other from Arkadia, differing essentially only as to the heroine's parentage, though both lineages have wolf-connections. The former has her the daughter of Schoineus the son of Athamas, i. e. Athamas' granddaughter, and in the latter she is the daughter of Iasos, one of the sons of the Arkadian wolf-hero Lykurgos.

A similar syndrome, where initiation of young persons, a weather cult, human

---

[44] Hdt. 8.197.

[45] Eduard Meyer *Geschichte des Alterthums* (Stuttgart, Berlin 1893[2]) p.94.

[46] *V.* under Athamas Chap. 4 p. 80 *supra.*

[47] M.P. Nilsson, *The Mycenaean Origin of Greek Mythology* (New York 1963) p. 134-135, remarks that the kernel of the Athamas myth is a human sacrifice. That sacrifice was not only explained as being occasioned by drought, but, in the common version, if not in Hdt. 7.197, the victim was the son of Nephele, whose name means "the cloud" or "mist," and who is connected by Pausanias 8.38.3 with the rain cloud seen emerging from the well of Hagno on Mount Lykaion.

sacrifice, and the wearing of animal skins are combined, recurs elsewhere in the Greek-speaking area as well. Across the Gulf of Pagasai from Mt. Laphystion near Halos, in Magnesia, thick fleeces were worn in the cult of Zeus Akraios or Aktaios in a ceremony held at dawn at the rising of the dog-star in a cave called Cheironion on the highest peak of Mt. Pelion. The outstanding citizens in the full bloom of their years took part.[48] Our ancient source explains that sheepskins were worn because of the morning cold of the dog-days at the end of the summer, and there is a tradition concerning the philosopher Anaxagoras who wore a sheepskin to the games at Olympia one time, whereupon a rainstorm ensued.[49] This mountain-top ceremony has other resonances as well: it has been compared with one assumed for another cave, that of Zeus Mēlōsios (likely "of the fleece," μηλωτή), on the highest point of the island of Naxos.[50] Zeus is said to have flown there from Krete, where he was born, in the form of an eagle.[51]

It has suggested been that the 'killing and resurrection' of an 'old man,' who wears a black sheep-skin mask, in the modern celebration of Mayday on Mt. Pelion, may be the remnant of an ancient rite of human sacrifice in the cult of Zeus Akraios or Aktaios;[52] for the ceremony on Pelion presents numerous parallels to the cave of Zeus on Ida at Psiloriti in Krete, where initiates wore black boarskins, so that the origins of the mysteries in both mountain caverns would lie with young warrior-brotherhoods clothed in animal skins.[53]

Thus two of the most famous instances of human sacrifice in Greece, that of the cult of Zeus Lykaios and that of the cult of Zeus Laphystios, evince connections with the wolf. The cult of Laphystios also has unimpeachable connections with agriculture and weather, a connection which the well of Hagno on Mt. Lykaion adumbrates as well. We shall shortly have occasion to re-examine human sacrifice in the case of the *pharmakos* at Athens in the rites of the Thargelia in the cult of Apollo; Apollo's epithet Lykeios is much more celebrated than Zeus' epithet Lykaios, but the rites of the Thargelia, the festival of first-fruits, belong rather with the agricultural connections of human sacrifice than with the wolf-epithet directly. Yet the context of the sacrifice to Zeus Laphystios patently and manifestly concerns agriculture, if not weather. Another instance of human sacrifice to Zeus is known to us from a unique source that tells us such sacrifice was performed on Mt. Ithome in Messenia, but gives no clew as to its context.[54] There is other testimony to human sacrifice in connection with the wolf-name in the cult of the god Zeus. in the rites performed in the Kretan city Lyktos, or Lyttos.[55]

Phineus is another figure in Greek myth who is connected with child-murder, and seems to belong in the wider context of the wolf-name as well. He is said to have chosen long life over sight;[56] and he was blinded because he showed Phrixus the way

---

[48] Herakleides ὁ κριτικός, or ὁ Κρητικός 2.8 in Mueller *Geogr. Gr. Min.* 1.107; cf. Däbritz, *s. v.* Herakleides 46 in *PWRE* 8 (Stuttgart 1912) cols. 484-486.

[49] Ael. *NA* 7.8; D. L. *Anaxagoras* 2.6.10; Philostr. *VA* 1.2.

[50] A.B. Cook *Zeus* I 164, and 420 n. 1.

[51] Eratosth. *catast.* 30.

[52] A.J.B. Wace "The Mayday Festival on Pelion," *ABSA* 16 (1909-1910) 244f.

[53] P. Faure, *op. cit.* (Chap. 3 n. 78 *supra*) 118.

[54] Clem. Al. *Protr.* 2.41.

[55] *V.* Chap. 3 p. 55 *supra*. from Clem. Al. *Protr.* 3.42.5, quoting Antikleides of Athens (*FGrH* 140 F7).

[56] Hes. *Cat.* Bk. 3, *fr.* 157 MW.

to Kolchis.[57] He also was said to have sacrificed the children of his first marriage to the wiles of their stepmother, or else blinded them, or let them be blinded;[58] for the stepmother herself perpetrated this crime,[59] if not their own mother.[60] They were cured and their sight restored by Asklepios.[61]

This account presents a number of familiar points: Phineus falling prey to his second wife's plots laid against his children by his first wife corresponds to the same motif in the story of Athamas, whose son Phrixus is associated with Phineus as well. Again, Phineus' familiarity with the length of his life is an example of the gift of prophecy he possessed, and we are told that he was a rival of Apollo himself in prophecy. Moreover the gift of knowing the time of one's own death is given to werewolves as well, according to the testimony of the old Latvian Thies.[62] Finally, Phineus, and his children are associated with the mole, and with Asklepios, the Apollonian mole-god; for not only were his children cured and restored to sight by Asklepios, but Phineus himself was changed into a mole,[63] and his name even recurs in the cult of Asklepios Phinaios of Nicopolis in Epirus.[64] It has been suggested[65] that the name Phineus stands for *σφινεύς, a metathesized form of σιφνεύς, "mole."[66]

Diomedes is another Greek hero of more than passing fame who appears to have been sacrificed, or killed, in a wolf-context. We have noted his history *supra*[67]; here let us recall that there were two or more figures of Greek mythology of this name: aside from Jason, whose original name was Diomedes, there were Diomedes, King of Thrake, son of Ares and Kyrene, the owner of the man-eating mares, who was fed to his horses by Herakles, and Diomedes of Argos, son of Tydeus, the hero of the Trojan War who is perhaps best known for having wounded Aphrodite in battle.[68] This last Diomedes is associated with death and human sacrifice in a wolf-context, in the tale of how he was shipwrecked on the Libyan coast, where it was the practice of the king, Lykos, son of the god Ares, to sacrifice strangers to Ares, his father. Diomedes was saved from this fate by Kallirrhoe Lykos' daughter, who fell in love with him, but he sailed away, whereupon she hanged herself.[69] Diomedes was worshipped as a god, in Metapontum and Thurioi, and nearby, among a wolf-people, the Dauni of Apulia, he was said to have founded Argos Hippion, "Argos of the Horse," and other geographical features are named after him too.[70] He was said to have been killed by King Daunos,[71] whose name means "wolf," and he is also associated with human

---

[57] *Ibid.*, from the *Megalai Ehoiai* .
[58] Apollod. 3.15.3; cf. also *idem* I 9.21.2, Σ Ap. Rhod. 1.211, Σ Soph. *Ant.* 981, and Ovid *Ars Am.* 1.339.
[59] Soph. *Ant.* 981 and Σ *ad loc.*, Σ Ap. Rhod. 1.211, and Soph. *Tympanistai*.
[60] Soph. *Ant.* 978 and 981.
[61] Sext. Emp. *adv. Math.* 1.263; Pind. *Pyth.* 3.96; Phylarchus *fr.* 18 *FGrH.* = Σ Eur. *Alc.* 1 (cf. also Hygin. *Fab.* 14 and Clem. Al. *Strom.* 1.21.105).
[62] Appendix B *infra*.
[63] Oppian *Cyn.* 2.612ff.; Timotheos of Gaza in Constantinus Porphyrogennetos *Excerpta* 421.
[64] Jessen in Roscher *Lex s.v.* Phineus.
[65] Grégoire and Goossens, *op. cit.* (Chap. 2 n. 33 *supra*) 87.
[66] Tzetzes on Lyk. 121.
[67] Chap. 4 p. 80f. *supra*.
[68] *Il.* 5.
[69] Plut. *Parall. Graec. et Rom.* 23 quoting King Juba of Mauretania in his work concerning Libya.
[70] Strabo 6.3.9.
[71] Σ Lyk. 592, [Ar.] *mirab. ausc.* 80.

sacrifice in Cyprus.[72]

It appears, then, that human sacrifice, today corroborated from the excavations at Anemospelia in Krete,[73] was not an uncommon practice in classical antiquity. From the accounts of Christian authors of later antiquity who tell of it in Greece it seems it was often offered for the sake of divination, and hence in an Apollonian wolf-context. Two descriptions of human sacrifice have come down to us from them.[74] Human victims were especially useful in divination because the future is more clearly expressed in human organs than in those of animals.[75] Once, in the reign of Domitian, Apollonios of Tyana was accused of sacrificing a boy at night under a waning moon in order to inspect his entrails for a sign that might encourage Nerva to seize the throne. His defense against the charge was that men, who know that they are going to die, are more likely than animals, who do not, to suffer significant disturbance of their internal organs in consequence.[76] This must not have been an isolated incident; not too many years later the Emperor Hadrian forbade human sacrifice in the Empire,[77] but many years earlier, in 97 B.C.E., there had been a *senatusconsultum* to the same effect,[78] so that Hadrian's edict may have have been no less nugatory in its working.

From these sources it would appear that human sacrifice was most often concerned with predicting the future. If so, it is not far-fetched to imagine that it might have been used in an attempt to shape or influence the future, or agricultural futures, as well; and indeed other instances of human sacrifice in Greek mythology and cultural history are connected with drought, wind, and the fertility of the soil. Molpis was a young man of Elis who volunteered himself as a sacrifice in response to an oracle given in time of drought. The Eleans had built a temple to Zeus Ombrios (Zeus the god of rain) and they set up a statue of Molpis in it.[79] A similar story told of a certain Lophis is also a story of human sacrifice.[80] The River Lophis in Haliartos in Boiotia was supposed to have sprung from his blood. Lophis was a young man whose father had gone to Delphi to find out how to banish a drought from the land. The oracle told him to slay the first to come out to meet him upon his return home to Haliartos. He stabbed his son Lophis, who ran out to meet him, and the blood that fell from him as he ran about dying turned to water as it touched the ground, forming the brook subsequently named after him. Hoplites[81] may be another name for Lophis,[82] and if he is we will be able to identify Lophis with the young man who has finished his term as an ephebe, and like the victim in the sacred precinct of Athena, Diomedes and Agraulos in Salamis on the island of Kypros, where we have noted the practice of human sacrifice,[83] finds his death then and there.

Other stories from Greek mythology tell of a human sacrificed in order to call forth the wind, which can be one way of ending a drought, as well. The most famous of these is the story of the Akhaian fleet immobile at anchor at Aulis because Artemis

---

[72] Chap. 4 p. 81*supra*.

[73] V. n. 31 *supra*.

[74] Socrates *Hist. eccles.* 3.13, Sp. 413 and Eus. *Hist. eccles.* 8.14.5 (IV p.378 Dind.).

[75] Porph. *Abst.* 2.51.

[76] Philostr. *VA* 6.11.20; 8.5.6(12).

[77] Porph. *peri thysiōn* in Eus. *PE* 4.15.6.

[78] Pliny *N.H.* 30.3.

[79] Tzetzes on Lyk. 158ff.

[80] Paus. 9.23.4.

[81] Plut. *Lys.* 29.

[82] Bölte *PWRE* 8 (Stuttgart 1913) cols. 2296-2297.

[83] Chap. 4, p. 82 *supra*.

in her anger held back the wind that could fill its sails and carry it across the sea to sack Troy, until Iphigeneia was sacrificed by her father Agamemnon at the behest of the oracle and the winds began to blow.

Much as Herodotos may disapprove of the act, he takes it for granted that a Greek audience would understand human sacrifice in a case of a prolonged calm holding back ships from a journey; for he tells how Menelaos, in such a plight, was criticized for impiety when he sacrificed two Egyptian boys in order to make the winds blow.[84] A similar story is told of the Greeks, in the story of Sinon at Troy.[85] Referring to the story of Achilles' sacrifice of Polyxena, Vergil tells how the Greeks sacrificed a human when they left Troy, just as they had when they left port at Aulis in Greece, and so Sinon could claim he had been the chosen victim. A certain King Chaon was also said to have thrown a human being overboard when he was caught in a storm at sea.[86] Jonah 1.11-15 teaches us how usual such a procedure was in the ancient world, in an attempt to still a tempest at sea.

The archetype of rites of human sacrifice may be the story of the Thrakian Zamolxis (or Salmoxis).[87] In his account[88] Herodotos describes how the Getai, a Thrakian people, one of whose tribes were the Dacians, demonstrated their belief in immortality:

> They do not believe that they die, but that they go to Salmoxis, their daimōn. Some of them call him Gebeleizis. Every four years they despatch one of their number, chosen by lot, as a messenger to Salmoxis, and they instruct him in whatever they need at that particular time. This is the way they send him off: Some of them stand in a line, each one holding three lances, and others take hold of the one being despatched to Salmoxis by his arms and legs, swing him up high and throw him against the lances.[89] If he is impaled and killed, they believe the god is auspicious, but if he is not killed they put the blame on him, their messenger, and say he must be a wicked person, and, once they have determined that he is at fault, they choose another and despatch him, and tell him what they need while he is still alive. The same Thrakians shoot up arrows at the thunder and the lightning in heaven and threaten the god; for they believe there is no other god than their own. I learned from the Greeks who inhabit the Hellespont and Pontus that this Salmoxis was a man who was a slave in Samos, and that he was a slave of Pythagoras the son of Mnesarchos. Later he was freed and amassed much money, and returned home, but the Thrakians were miserable and quite uncivilized. Now Salmoxis understood the Ionian way of life and that the Greek ways were more profound than the Thrakian; for he had spent time with them, and particularly with one who was not the least of the Greeks, Pythagoras

---

[84] Hdt. 2.119.

[85] Verg. *Aen.* 2.114ff.

[86] Servius-Dan. *ad Verg. Aen.* 3.297, 3.334 and 3.335.

[87] Rhys Carpenter, *Folk Tale, Fiction and Saga in the Homeric Epics* (California 1962), Chap. 6, pp. 112ff.

[88] Hdt. 4.94-96. M. Eliade *op. cit.* (Chap 3 n. 138 *supra*) 21ff. discusses this passage, and comes to a number of useful conclusions, one of which is that Zamolxis and Gebeleizis were never identical.

[89] We may note the similarity of this manner of human sacrifice to the ancient Cypriot yearly ephebic rite celebrated in Salamis in honor of Diomedes, Achilleus, Aglauros and Athena (and possibly Zeus, as well), described in Chap. 4 p. 81 *supra*.

the wise man. Therefore he built a men's house where he entertained the leading citizens and taught them that neither he nor his drinking companions nor their descendants would ever die, but would come to a place where they would live forever and possess all good things. While he was building this structure and telling them these things, he was constructing an underground chamber. When it was done, he disappeared from among the Thrakians; for having gone down into the underground chamber, he spent three years there. They missed him, and mourned for him as if he had died, but in the fourth year he appeared to the Thrakians...

Strabo is more specific about Samolxis' connection to the weather, no doubt combining Herodotos' words to the effect that "the same Thrakians shoot up arrows at the thunder and the lightning in heaven and threaten the god; for they believe there is no other god than their own," with his report of Samolxis' servitude at Samos:[90]

It is told that a certain man of the Getai, Zamolxis by name, was the slave of Pythagoras, and learned part of the science of the skies from him and the rest from the Egyptians (for he had reached Egypt too in his wanderings), and when he returned to his own country he was much admired by the rulers of the country and by his countrymen for his predictions of the state of the skies on the basis of prognostications.

The name of this Thrakian deity was connected in antiquity with the bear,[91] on the basis of a derivation from the Thrakian word *zalmos*, "bearskin," and although this derivation has been revived in modern times[92] it has not generally been accepted. Another modern etymology derives the name Zamolxis from the Skythian (Iranian) *zamar xšiš*, "ruler of earth," and suggests that this was a Thrakian name: "Since the cognate Thracian had the required *l* in the name for Earth, witnessed by Semele, we need not perhaps make Zamolxis a foreigner in Thrace,"[93] but this etymology can not stand if the form Salmoxis is preferred on the basis of the MSS of Herodotos.[94] If the derivation from the Thrakian word *zalmos*, "bearskin," is right, the name Salmoxis-Zamolxis could be a combination like the Skt. *samavṛkaḥ*, or the Gr. αὐτόλυκος, i. e. "the very wolf," and might even stand for something like the Skt. *samarkṣaḥ*, meaning "the very bear," or, if the first element is the Thrakian word for "earth," even "the earth-bear," and we would discover parallelism between the wolf and the bear here.

Any connection with the bear, however, is immaterial to our argument; it is enough to point out that human sacrifice is once again here associated with the storm and the weather, particularly in the form of thunder and lightning. Indeed, one of the most famous harvest festivals in Greece shows a connection with the wolf, and with human sacrifice. Here again we encounter the complex of wind, bringing the growth of grain, and the wolf and death. The Arneis festival at Argos included a sacrifice of dogs, a *hapax* in Greek cult, so far as we know.[95] The etiology of this sacrifice in the Argives' account concerned the life and death of Linos, the son of Apollo and the nymph Psamathē, and the patron of the harvest. According to the tale they told, when

---

[90] 7.3.5.
[91] Porph. *VP* 14.
[92] For a discussion of the etymology cf. Rhys Carpenter *ibid.* (n. 87 *supra*) and M. Eliade *op. cit.* (Chap 3 n. 138 *supra*) 44-46.
[93] A.B. Cook, *Zeus* I (Cambridge 1914) 781, quoting Bartholomae, *Zum Altirischen Wörterbuch* 172-174. For *xšiš*, "ruler" *v.* P. Kretschmer, "Zum Balkanskythischen," *Glotta* 24 (1935) 1-56.
[94] *Ibid.* II (1925) 227 quoting H. Stein's comment on the passage from Herodotos.
[95] Cf. Fontenrose *op. cit.* (Chap. 2 n. 117 *supra*) 104ff.

Linos was still only a small boy he was set upon and killed by dogs,[96] whereupon his mother Psamathē ("woman of the sand") revealed the story of his conception and birth to her father, King Krotōpos of Argos. It seems that when Apollo had come to Krotōpos to be purified of the blood he had shed in achieving his victory over the Python, he had seduced the king's daughter; Psamathē had hidden her pregnancy and given the child to shepherds to rear, out of fear of her father. Her father was incredulous, but made Psamathē pay for her transgression with her life nonetheless, whereupon Apollo sent a hideous monster of a woman, Poinē or Kēr, in his anger, to ravage Argos. She was subsequently killed by the young hero Koroibos and a band of Argive youths. In a parallel to this story a wolf appears in place of Poinē-Kēr; for, as we have noted *supra*,[97] the name Psamathē appears in the story of the sons of Aiakos again, as the name of the mother of Phōkos ("seal-man"), who sent a monstrous wolf against the flocks of Pēleus ("man of the mud")[98] after he, along with his brother Telamon, had murdered Phōkos, their half-brother. This giant wolf was later called off by Psamathē, who appears here as the mistress of the wolf.[99]

Linos is a harvest spirit whose passing is lamented by the reapers in the dirge αἱ λίνον, which they sing for him as they reap, and he is closely connected to Lityerses, a more common Greek harvest spirit.[100] Human sacrifice also figures in Lityerses' story: we are told that he used to feast strangers and make them reap along with him, until, in the end, he beheaded his guests, wound them up in a sheaf, and carried them home with him.[101] Since we have seen that the harvest spirit Linos's mother was the bereft mistress of the wolf in one Greek context, we have here a remarkable parallel to catching and killing the stranger or the Kornwolf in German popular belief as shown in the responses to Mannhardt's questionnaire.

Psamathē, however, is not the only figure of Greek myth who sends a wolf or dog to attack her child, or her child's destroyer. In a parallel story, Aiolos, the guardian of the winds,[102] threw the daughter of his daughter Kanachē (whose name means "barking") and his son Makar, or Makareus, to the wolves when he discovered their incestuous union.[103] It may be that Aiolos' disapproval of the incest between his six sons and his six daughters is a late feature in his story; it seems to go back to Euripides' play *Aiolos*, and is not mentioned in the *Odyssey*. Moreover, the fate of Makar and Kanachē may have been derived from the story of Linos. In another

---

[96] Gerhard Radke, s. v. Psamathe *PWRE* 23.2 (1959) cols. 1301-1302, denies the dogs any role in the original form of this story. By stripping the Argive story of Linos down to its bare essentials and assuming that was its original form, he only demonstrates his great skill at making a précis.

[97] Chap. 5 *supra*, p. 93.

[98] Cf. Σ Lyk. 175, 90; Ovid *Met.* 11.346ff.; and, with no mention of Psamathe, Ant. Lib. 38.

[99] Radke *ibid.* (n. 97 *supra*) introduces Kydon and Miletos here, the Kretan sons of Apollo who were brought up by a bitch and a she-wolf respectively, but only to discredit the evil dogs in Linos' story.

[100] Fontenrose *op. cit.* (Chap. 2 n. 117 *supra*) 112.

[101] Sosith. 2.19f. *Trag. Gr. Fragm.* Nauck² p. 822.

[102] *Od.* 10.

[103] Ovid *Her.* 11 (cf. esp. l. 90). This letter is generally supposed to derive in the main from Euripides' last drama *Aiolos*, and this trait too may be from that source. Canace's exposed child occupies a large part of the letter (ll. 83-84,87, 89-90, 111, 118, 122), and the animals to which it is thrown are first "dogs and birds"(83), as in the first lines of the *Iliad*, but then wolves (90) and finally "tearing, greedy beasts" (111 and 118). Cf. Arthur Palmer's note on *rapidae* in l. 111 in A. Palmer and L.C. Purser *edd.*, Ovid *Heroides* (Oxford 1898). *V.* also Hyginus *Fab.* 238.

version of the story Aiolos sent a sword to Kanachē, here left unnamed, to kill her daughter with, but she committed suicide with it instead.[104] The important thing to notice here, in our context, is that Aiolos, "steward of the winds," could easily be conceived of as master of the wolves, and if the late literary concoction where the child was thrown to the wolves reflects an earlier awareness, then indeed there is more than a trace in Greece of Mannhardt's wind-wolf conception.[105]

Now Zeus was god of the weather, among his other functions. His name seems to be related to the IE word for day, and he is surely to be identified with the Indian *Dyauh*, who is a classic sky-god. In the classic Greek formulation we read ἄλλοκα μὲν Ζεὺς πέλει αἴθριος, ἄλλοκα δ' ὕει, "at one time Zeus shows a clear countenance, at another it rains,"[106] and Zeus had the epithet Ombrios, "of the rain," in Elis, as we have seen, and Hyetios, with the same meaning, in Antimachia on the island of Kos,[107] as well as on Rhodes and in Miletos. At Kallatis on the Black Sea there was a festival called Diombria, which is to say "the festival of Zeus' rain."[108] Zeus Euanemos, "Zeus of the favorable wind," is known to us from Sparta,[109] and Zeus Ourios, "Zeus of the wind from the stern," had a sanctuary on the Bosporus.[110]

The frequent recurrence of themes of human sacrifice in relation to wolf-names on Mt. Lykaion, in the rites that appear to have been performed at Lyktos, and in the juxtaposition of Apollo Lykeios and the rites of the Thargelia at Athens, to be discussed below, comprise a further indication that the wolf-name was associated with the wind and the mist in classical antiquity. So do the rites of Apollo on Mt. Soracte in Italy, where he was worshipped in the form of a god of the dead as "pater Soranus," whose priests were called *hirpi Sorani*, i.e. "wolves of Soranus," no doubt from the Latin name of the shrew, *sorex*.

The variants in the sacrifice of Iphigeneia and the sacrifice of Polyxena, both of which unbound the winds held in check by enraged deities, belong to this complex too, and another possible reminiscence of this connection is Vergil's: *lupi ceu raptores atra in nebula*, "like rapacious wolves in the black mist."[111] Here the wolf and the mist are clearly juxtaposed. Thus death, human sacrifice, fertility of the soil, and the wolf-god and the werewolf, who serves for a given period in the form of a wolf, all are connected in various cults of Zeus.[112]

---

[104] Plut. *par. min.* 28.

[105] In this context it is easy to understand Mircea Eliade's comment on Zeus Lykaios, which must derive from Mannhardt even if it is given unsubstantiated. In *Patterns in Comparative Religion*, tr. Rosemary Sheed (New York, Meridian Books 1963) p. 78, he wrote, "his (i.e. Zeus') animalesque aspect (Zeus Lykaios, as a wolf to whom human sacrifice was offered) can be accounted for by the magic connected with farming (the sacrifice took place in time of drought, storm, and such)." There is no evidence, in fact, that Lykaios was a wolf himself; actually, it is less than likely that he was. The entire statement is only a hypothetical statement of the complex of ideas we are trying to elucidate.

[106] Theoc. 11.

[107] *SIG* 1107=Paton and Hicks, *Inscriptions of Cos* 382.

[108] A.W. Wilhelm, *Anzeiger Akad. Wien* 1922, p.72ff.; *SEG* I 327 col. 14.

[109] Paus. 3.13.8.

[110] *Periplus ponti euxeini* 2(=*Geogr. gr. min.* I p. 402).

[111] *Aen.* 2.355.

[112] Stig Wikander, *Der arische Männerbund* (Lund 1938), has assembled the evidence for human sacrifice in werewolf confraternities from the Indo-European region. He does not, however, try to explain the association of human blood with the fertility of the soil. According to the view of Gahs brought in W. Koppers, "Pferdeopfer und Pferdekult der Indogermanen," *Wiener Beiträge*

Human sacrifice is found in the worship of Apollo, too, in Athens, and elsewhere. We have already noted that Apollo was the patron of the growth of the grain, and that that function of his is represented in cult first and foremost in the festival of the Thargelia, "the first fruits," celebrated at Athens on the same day as is intimated in the Book of Leviticus for the harvest Festival of Pentecost (the sixth day of the third month[113]), allowing for differences in the intercalary month in Athens and in Israel. The festival of the First Fruits in the Athenian calendar fell on the sixth day and its morrow, the seventh, of the eleventh month of the year, the month named Thargelion after the festival (or after the first fruits).[114] On the second day of the festival there were rites connected with the grain, which we have had occasion to examine *supra*, but on the first day of the Thargelia there was a scapegoat rite in which human sacrifice was essential.

On that day a human being called the *pharmakos* was feasted, led around town, beaten with green twigs, and driven out of the city to be put to death by stoning. Accounts of this vary, and according to other reports he may have been thrown into the sea or burnt on a funeral pyre, or there may even have been two *pharmakoi*, one male and the other female. However that may be, there certainly is evidence of human sacrifice here, or of wilfully putting an otherwise innocent person to death in a religious rite associated with bringing in the harvest. The name applied to the victim is the masculine form of the word φάρμακον, "a remedy," and has led to the consensus that the *pharmakos* was a scapegoat. The fact, however, that he was beaten with green twigs suggests rather that the whole rite was sympathetic vegetation magic. We find that the god Pan was beaten with squills.[115] That rite, we are told,[116] was a fertility rite since the god was beaten on his genitals, and his seed was to fertilize the earth. Thus one interpretation of the rite at the Thargelia is that the victim represented the deity, but in fact Apollo is not the god of the foison at the Thargelia; that role belonged to the goddesses honored along with Apollo and Prometheus on the second day of the festival, Demeter and the Hours. The *pharmakos* rite, therefore, is related to Apollo's role in the festival, but is not a re-enactment of the role of the god. Rather it is an adjunct of the role we are trying to understand, the role of the young warrior (ephēbos) in connection with the fertility of the fields.

One famous cult and myth associated with Apollo which shows at the same time his functions as god of death and of the *ephēbeia* is the myth of Hyakinthos and his cult at Amyklai near Sparta, the cult of the young man beloved of Apollo who was killed by the god's discus as they were playing and practising together, and from whose blood sprang the flower hyacinth which bears his name. Hyakinthos was also a sponsor of marriage and of marriage customs. J. Farnell, who believed him to be earlier than Apollo, and originally independent of him, wrote of him: "[h]e was essentially a chthonian power and worshipped with a gloomy ritual, and with *enagismata*, the offerings consecrated to the dead. Now such a character is wholly

---

zur Kulturgeschichte und Linguistik (1935) 279-411, esp. 314ff., human sacrifice in the Indo-European linguistic area, as for example, in the myth of the creation of the world from the body of a (self-sacrificed god like Prajāpati, or of a superman like Puruṣa, is always connected with ceremonies of initiation into secret societies. That is probably an exaggeration.

[113] Lev. 23.15ff.

[114] For this and the other particulars of the Thargelia *v.* V. Gebhard, "Thargelia," *PWRE* 5A2 (1934) col. 1287ff.

[115] Theoc. 3.

[116] Σ *ibid.*

alien to Apollo."[117] Rather, Farnell's verdict is wholly alien to the truth; for, as we shall see, Apollo does not lack connections with death, nor indeed do any of the gods of Greece, and the story of Hyakinthos rather strengthens these connections than weakens them.

One of the best-known of Apollo's connections with death is the story of his service with Admetos as the shepherd of his flocks, in expiation of the blood he had shed in achieving his victory over the Python at Delphi. Admetos, as the Norwegian scholar Sam Wide pointed out long ago, is an epithet of Pluto, god of the underworld, and in this story we have a variant of the tale of the young god or hero ruling over the kingdom of the dead for a given time, like Pryderi king of Dyfed who ruled over Annwfn in the Welsh story from the Mabinogi which bears his name. Another account where Apollo (as well as the wolf) is associated with death, albeit only apparent death and resurrection, is the foundation story of the cult of Apollo Gypaieus from Konon, cited above.[118]

There are various correspondences to the Greek complex of human sacrifice and agricultural functions in India and elsewhere which cast light on the meaning of human sacrifice, or descent into death, in these instances. Here, however, we may say that creation is in itself a function of the dismemberment (and presumably of the secretions also) of the human body (in birth, where two bodies issue from one); and that process is transferred, or extended, to the body of an ancient god, on the one hand, and on the other, the young warrior's ability to restore himself out of death is another reflex of the same act of creation. In this context the sacrifice of the *pharmakos* is a surrogate for the original death of the founder of the grain, who would be Triptolemos, perhaps, in Greece, just as Ikarios' death functions in the creation or the discovery of the vine. The rite of the Thargelia then would parallel the sacrifice of pigs at the Athenian festival of the Thesmophoria.

Other reports of human sacrifice to Apollo occur in a number of contexts.[119] There is a persistent report that humans were sacrificed to Apollo among the Hyperboreans.[120] Elsewhere we find that this people, so closely associated with Apollo, used to throw themselves into the sea in old age.[121] Again, we find a sacrifice of asses to Apollo (in a source that contains the Amphictyonic oath!),[122] and if we introduce here the fact that in early times an ass's head garlanded with vines was set side by side with a human head on the head rests of the *triclinium* at the Roman symposium,[123] we may conjecture that the ass here may substitute for a human victim, especially since there is no other record of this animal being sacrificed to Apollo. Then we have a number of other reports. First, a steep promontory near the end of the peninsula of Leukates at the southernmost end of the island of Leukas, was the site of a temple of Apollo. Here, each year, at a sacrifice for Apollo,[124] someone was thrown

---

[117] L.R. Farnell, *Cults of the Greek States* 4.127.

[118] Chap. 3 n. 17 *supra*.

[119] Strabo 683 and 452; Photios *Lex. s.v.* Λευκάτης; Aelian *N.A.* 118. Cf. L.R. Farnell, *Cults of the Greek States* 4.275.

[120] Pliny *N.H.* 4.26 .90; Paus. 10.32.5; Ant. Lib. 20.

[121] Pliny *N.H.* 4.89 .90; Mela 3.37; Solin. 16.4; Mart. Cap. 6.664; Clem. Al. *Strom.* 131.

[122] *CIG* 1688 1.14.

[123] Prop. 4.8.68f.; Juv. 6.21f., 11.97; Hyginus *Fab.* 274; from R. B. Onians, *The Origin of European Thought about the Body, the Mind, the Soul, the World, Time and Fate* (Cambridge 1951) 226 n. 4.

[124] Ael. *H.A.* 11.8.

into the sea from the rocks, as a scapegoat.[125] This usage is reminiscent of the fate of the *pharmakos* at the festival of the Thargelia, at Athens and elsewhere. Both were scapegoats, as was the περίψημα of a definition in the lexical tradition possibly referring to the ritual at Leukates, who was a young man thrown into the sea to carry pressing tribulations away.[126] Next, the river Lykos is on the south coast of Cyprus to the east of Kurion, an ancient colony of Argos, and both these names are associated with Apollo;[127] to the west of the town there was a sanctuary of Apollo Hylates on a wooded crag in a place called Hylē, where they used to throw anyone who touched the altar of Apollo into the sea.[128] (The epithet Hylates recalls Hylas, Herakles' favorite, who was lost in the land of the Mariandynoi on the voyage of the Argo.) Since holding on to the altar usually meant inviolability for one seeking asylum this is an unusually unmerciful trait. Finally, the name Themisto seems to connect Apollo to human sacrifice as well; for a certain Themisto, the daughter of a king of the Hyperboreans, was a wife of Apollo and the mother of Galeotes in one version of his story,[129] and Themisto also appears as the name of Athamas' wife whose children were lost when their father attempted to sacrifice the boy, Phrixus, in the story as told by Herodotos, and she was the mother of Schoineus, the son of Athamas and Atalanta's father in the Boiotian version of her story. The wolf complex is so pervasive among Apollo's characteristics that there can be no doubt that cases of human sacrifice that belong to it, like Athamas' wolf connections here,[130] the violator of the holy precinct of Apollo Hylates thrown off the cliff not far from the river Lykos in Cyprus, and Euenos' suicide in the river Lykormas, all derive from Apollo's rôle as Lykeios.

From the Germanic belief, evidenced in the replies to Mannhardt's questionnaire,[131] that the "spirit of the corn" was conceived of as a human-like figure caught in the last sheaf of grain harvested and put to death in it, we might have surmised that human sacrifice was part of the complex of ideas connecting the wolf with the wind and with the grain. It is in Greece, however, as we have seen, that we find the clearest indications of human sacrifice in its various forms as part of the wider context of the wolf-name.

The wolf is clearly a powerful symbol of death in other cultures of the Indo-European linguistic area, namely in the Italic tradition, as shown by its use in Italic

---

[125] Str. 10.452; Ampel. *Lib. Memor.* 8; Phot. *Lex. s.v.* Λευκάτης. Strabo tells us the victim was a convicted murderer, and that he was picked up by a boat and conveyed out of the country. Later tradition made of this spot a Lovers' Leap, and told that Kephalos (Phot. *Bibl.* 153a10) and Sappho (according to Menander) had made use of the opportunity it afforded.

[126] Suidas and Photius *s.v.*

[127] Kurion is from κοῦρος, "boy," or κούρη "girl," an official name for the ephebes who are under Apollo's tutelage. The modern name for the river Lykos is Kuris, from the ancient name of the town, and modern Episkopi, closer to the river on a hill to the east of the ancient town site, has usurped the place of Kurion since the middle ages.

[128] Strabo 14.683, who does not mention the sanctuary of Apollo Hylates, known from the royal coins of Kurion (*V.* Jessen in *PWRE* 9.1 (1914) col. 116f.), but speaks of a cliff where they threw people who touched Apollo's altar, τοὺς ἁψαμένους τοῦ βωμοῦ τοῦ Ἀπόλλωνος, into the sea. In a remarkable parallel Paus. 10.32.6 reports that at a place called Hylai near Magnesia on the Meander, where there was a rather large cave of Apollo containing an ancient statue of the god, the priests used to jump from high pine trees in the woods, ἐν ὔλῃ.

[129] Steph. Byz. *s.v. Galeōtai.*

[130] Chap. 4 p. 80 *supra.*

[131] P. 28 *supra.*

grave imagery, in the Keltic tradition, and in Germanic mythology and folklore. We have noted *supra* the Hirpini in Italy in whose territory the wolf-name is associated with death.[132] In Etruscan grave painting, a wolfskin is a permanent feature of the god of the dead, Hades,[133] and in ancient Keltic paintings a wolfskin worn by a prominent human figure, dressed as the god Sucellus, as well as as a staff around which a snake is entwined, parallel these Etruscan portrayals.[134] The wolf's-head helmet or dog's-head helmet imparting invisibility in Greece may be related to this wolf's jaw surrounding a head, especially since the Scandinavian *berserkr* wears such a helmet.[135] It seems warranted to look to the κυνέη Ἄϊδος, a wolf's head, the "cap of Hades," which makes its wearer invisible; for the dead are invisible.[136] These portrayals may owe something to the head in the wolf's jaw found in the story of Dolon.[137] Euripides described Diomedes and Odysseus, the killers of the wolf Dolon, as wolves on horseback slaying the sleeping Thrakians.[138]

We have had occasion *supra*[139] to note the wolves of the Scandinavian tradition, who threaten the sun, the life-giving light of the world: in that tradition the wolf Fenris's release from the chains that bind him to the "western gate," the gate of the sunset, signifies the arrival of *Ragnarøk*, the end of the world and the death of all things. Thus the connection of Fenris and other wolves of the Germanic tradition with death is clear.

The connection of the wolf with the outlaw figure, of one who lives outside society, like the dead banished to another world of eternal exile, is well known in Teutonic mythology and literature. The wolf is associated with hanging and death by strangling in German mythology and literature, where werewolves dig up corpses and eat the dead, and kidnap the living. "Naturally, the predominant factor determining this conception is the strong wind or storm whose psychological effect, that of terror, multiplies the contacts it has with the belief in life after death, as can be seen most clearly in the 'Wild Hunt'.... The names all refer to the attributes of the storm: the

---

[132] Pp. 38 and 98 *supra*.

[133] Roscher *Myth. Lex.* 1.1808, from Orvieto, Tomba Galina, and Corneto-Tarquinia, Tomba dell'orco. P. Ducati, *Pittura etrusca-italo-greca e romana* (1942) Plate 22. For illustrations *v.* F. Poulsen, *Etruscan Tomb Paintings* (1942) illustr. 37, and A.B. Cook, *Zeus* I p.98, figg. 72 and 73.

[134] Keune s. v. Sucellus, *PWRE* IVA1 (Stuttgart 1931) col. 536.

[135] Manfred Lurker, "Hund und Wolf in ihrer Beziehung zum Tode," *Antaios* 10 (1968) 199. This author's hypothesis is that the connection of the wolf and death stems from the conception of "the jaws of death." His argument is weak, because it is only half the story; for he deals only with burial cultures, writing, *Die Bestattung in der Erde erschien dem Menschen von früher wie ein Verschlingen. Der Tote verschwindet im Rachen der Erde und gelangt in den Bauch der Unterwelt; Hades hat auch den Namen 'Allverschlinger.' Die Erde wird selbst zu einem riesigen Daemon, der unersättlich seinen Rachen aufsperrt. Hier ist der psychologische Ansatzpunkt zu einer Gestalt- und Bildwerdung des Todeswesens. Analog dem reißenden Wolfsrachen stellte man sich die Erde vor.* In fact the wolf lives in caverns; he does not only swallow his prey, but he emerges from the earth's maw. Furthermore, Lurker's entire contention pales in the face of our knowledge of initiation and youth confraternities.

[136] Cf. Lamer *s. v.* κυνέη (Hadeskappe) *PWRE* 11.2 (Stuttgart 1922) cols.2519-2527. Cf. also *Hdwb. d. D. Abergl.* 5.1845; Ludolf Malten, *Jahrb.* 29 (1914) p.235; Rudolf Merkelbach, "Die Quellen der griech. Alexanderromans," *Zetemata* 9 (1954) 252f.; and p. 77 *supra*.

[137] *Il.* 10.

[138] Eur. *Rhesus* 783. Cf. L. Gernet, *Anthropologie de la Grèce antique* (Paris Maspero 1968) 154-171.

[139] P. 93ff. *supra*.

'breaker,' the 'injury,' the 'roarer,'or symbolic animal names like 'dog' and 'wolf.'"[140] (Germanic gods entered into wolfskins, just like the "raging army" who appeared in the guise of werewolves. This is a prime example of the rôle that gods—and heroes, par excellence, in Greece, at least—play as eternal forms of human activities.)

Thus there exists a middle term in Germanic tradition (and elsewhere as well) connecting the idea of death with the wolf figure. That term is the "wütender Heer," the "raging army," or the "wilder Jagd," the "wild hunt," a social phenomenon known from all over Northern Europe, and elsewhere, and called in England "the devil and his pack of Yeth-hounds," "the Devil and his Dandy Dogs," or "the Gabriel Ratchets."[141] The Devil's dogs, or the "hounds of Hell," to use the name John Masefield gave his poem on the subject, are none other than wolves or werewolves. "The dog, as a domestic animal, has been confounded with the savage brute which generally represents the monster."[142] There is historical evidence that werewolves did indeed refer to themselves as "hounds."[143] Moreover, no doubt 'Hell' and 'the devil' find their place in the names given to these groups because the participants in the "hunt" represent the dead, and the members of the *wütender Heer* act out the part, or assume the very nature, of spirits of their ancestors who have passed on to the other world.

Now it is sufficiently clear that death and its trappings connote initiation ceremonies, as well as actual physical death.[144] That is because initiation into manhood is considered a rebirth out of death, quite comparable to actual birth. Since birth emerges from death, and in the case of initiation it is obvious that not death but life preceded rebirth into the new state of manhood, death must become part of the ceremony itself, and so, in many cultures all over the world, initiation ceremonies share features with burial, or contain a sham death of some sort. Moreover, inasmuch as young people are the heirs of the elder generation, and hence of the dead who preceded them, in one sense they they make themselves one with their ancestors as they are in the present in the death they experience as they pass from childhood to manhood, and as they become the influential, present, and hence living dead. Thus the procession of the confraternity through the town, which in mediæval and modern Europe took place on the eve of Christmas or of Easter, or of some other numinous day like Allhallows or Ash Wednesday, had the nature of a wild procession of the dead.

Thus in interpreting stories such as that of Molpis, Lophis, and Hoplitēs, and the ephebic sacrifice at Salamis in Cyprus, one must consider always that the deaths told of or perpetrated may have had primarily a symbolic meaning, and that death often has a figurative meaning.

---

[140] Richard M.Meyer, *Altgermanische Religionsgeschichte* (Leipzig 1910) 98: *Die Anschauung wird naturgemäß von dem starken Wind, dem Sturm beherrscht. Sein psychologischer Eindruck, der des Schreckens, vermehrt die Berührungen mit dem Seelenglauben, wie es besonders im 'Wütenden Heer' anschaulich wird.... Die Namen haben durchweg Bezug auf die Sturmesnatur: der 'Brecher,' der 'Schaden,' der 'Brüller' oder symbolische Tiernamen wie Hund und Wolf. Ebenso werden sie in Märchen umschrieben.*

[141] Katharine M. Briggs and Ruth L. Tongue, *Folktales of England* (London, Routledge and Kegan Paul, 1965) Tale 18 'The Hunted Soul.'

[142] A. de Gubernatis, *Zoological Mythology or the Legends of Animals*, (London, Truebner & Co., 1872) reprinted by Singing Tree Press, Detroit, Mich. (1968) 34.

[143] Appendix B *infra*.

[144] Mircea Eliade, *Rites and Symbols of Initiation* (New York 1958); and *idem, Patterns in Comparative Religion* and *Shamanism*.

The subject of confraternities in antiquity, as well as of their wolf-connections, seems to have been broached first by Heinrich Schurtz.[145] Not long after, Gilbert Murray championed the idea that the wolf in Greek mythology stands for such werewolf-confraternities, on the basis of comparative evidence.[146] Martin Nilsson too used comparative evidence to describe ancient Spartan age groups (based on confraternities of young people) and marriage customs.[147] Meanwhile, much comparative evidence was adduced by Bronislaw Malinowski,[148] Lily Weiser,[149] Otto Höfler,[150] and Andreas Alföldi.[151] Many others, including a number of eminent French classical scholars, also examined this aspect of the wider context of the wolf-name in the ancient world. Among the last the most venerable is Louis Gernet,[152] who blazed the trail for several other prominent francophone scholars in this field, including Henri Jeanmaire[153] and Paul Faure.[154] For us this facet of our problem is of no little importance; for Gernet has shown that Dolon in *Il.* 10 is the representative of a werewolf-like confraternity, so that the *Iliad* depicts a werewolf-like group as nocturnal warriors busy with killing and death, and Thēseus' adventures at the bottom of the sea,[155] in the labyrinth with the slaying of the Minotaur, and his carrying off of Ariadne, as well, were set in the context of ancient Greek initiatory practices by Jeanmaire, as was another ancient Greek initiatory confraternity, the Spartan *krypteia*, in which he perceived a number of essentially lycanthropic traits. Clear involvement of confraternities in human sacrifice is evidenced only from India, and the limitation of werewolf activity in Europe to one or two nights a year in Christian Europe is a severe stricture, under the rule of the Church, put upon an ancient pagan institution, found throughout the Eurasian continent.

Entire peoples, like the Dacians, the Hyrcanians,[156] the Hirpini, the Dauni along with their Anglo-Saxon counterparts, the Deanas, and the Lucanians of Southern Italy, and the Iranian *Sakā haumavargā* of the Darius reliefs, share the name of the wolf[157] (as noted *supra* in Chaps. 3 and 4). They assumed the name taken by their groups of young men (and women) who dressed in wolfskins for the purpose of their initiation into adulthood, the adolescents of the group that formed the confraternity of their agemates, and often settled where the landscape offered them features that belong to

---

[145] *Altersklassen und Männerbünde* (Berlin 1902).

[146] "Anthropology in the Greek Epic Tradition outside Homer," pp. 72ff. in *Anthropology and the Classics*, ed. Robert Marett (Oxford 1908) 66-92.

[147] "Grundlagen des spartanischen Lebens," (first published *JRS* 12 [1912]) *Opuscula Selecta* 2 (Lund 1952) 826ff.

[148] *Myth in Primitive Psychology* (London 1926).

[149] *Altgermanische Jünglingsweihen und Männerbünde* [=*Bausteine zur Volkskunde*, Heft 1] (Baden, Bühl, 1927).

[150] *Kultische Geheimbünde der Germanen* I (Frankfurt, Diesterweg, 1934).

[151] *Die Struktur des voretruskischen Römerstaates* (Heidelberg, Winter, 1974).

[152] "Dolon le loup," i.e. "Dolon and the wolves," *Annuaire de l'Institut de Philologie et d'Histoire orientales et slaves* 4 (Brussels 1936=*Mélanges Franz Cumont*) 189-208 (reprinted in Louis Gernet, *Anthropologie de la Grèce antique* [Paris, Maspéro 1968] 154-171).

[153] *Couroi et Courètes. Essai sur l'éducation spartiate et sur les rites d'adolescence dans l'antiquité hellénique* (Lille 1939) esp. p. 540ff.

[154] *Op. cit.* (Chap. 3 n. 78 *supra*) 81-198.

[155] Chap. 5 p. 87 *supra*.

[156] This name is from Iran. *Vehrkāna*, "wolf-land," on which *v.* Chap. 3 p. 54 *supra*.

[157] M. Eliade, "Les Daces et les Loups," *Numen* 5-6 (1956) 15-31, esp. p. 20ff. This article appears in English as Chap. 1 of M. Eliade, *Zalmoxis, the Vanishing God* tr. W.R. Trask (Chicago 1972) 1-20.

the wider context of the wolf-name. Still, most peoples evince characteristics of wolf-confraternities without bearing the wolf-name. In fact, many common European beliefs and stories concerning the wolf really relate to werewolves. Thus we have noted the punishment for murdering a wolf in ancient Athens, and in Sicily it is believed a wolf's head adds courage to one who puts it on.[158] Baronius wrote that in the year 617 a number of wolves came to a monastery and tore to bits those among the monks who held heretical beliefs. "[W]olves sent by God tore the sacrilegious thieves of the army of Francesco Maria, Duke of Urbino, who had come to sack the treasure of the holy house of Loreto. A wolf guarded and defended from wild beasts the head of St. Edmund the Martyr, King of England."[159]

Stories of the frightening procession of the Devil and his Yeth-hounds are legion from all over Europe, and much of the material is collected in Otto Höfler's epoch-making book on the confraternities and the werewolf complex.[160] Here we may quote one French source which, though not much over a hundred-fifty years old, yet must go back to great antiquity.[161] It deals with *loups-garous* or werewolves. "Werewolves are people like us, but they have made a pact with the devil, and so are compelled to change into beasts one Sabbath a year and run all night long; and yet there is a way to cure them. Their blood drawn once they have left human form, they resume it forever."

It remains for us to relate the werewolf confraternities, with their hellish, deathly nature, to the realm of agriculture and of the weather that contributes to the growth and maturity of the crops. With that we will have come full circle in our argument in delineating the wider context of the wolf-name, and Zeus Lykaios' two salient attributes, his wolf connections and his mist (weather) cult will be seen to form one coherent whole, rather than being merely two disparate, unrelated features. Therewith we will have unmasked the ideology that allowed the many Eurasian (and even North American) confraternities, and nations as well, that have borne the wolf-name or some other closely related name, like "the Phōkians," the nation of the seal (in Greece), to maintain a transcendent and elitist ideology, and to insist on their divinely beneficent rôle in the world despite the rapine they practiced. In Athens, moreover, Apollo's agricultural rôle at the Thargelia can now be seen as integrally related to the death inflicted on the *pharmakos*, for one thing, and for another, Hyakinthos and his sepulchral cult will not appear so foreign any longer to Apollo's divine nature.

---

[158] de Gubernatis *op. cit.* (n. 142 *supra*) p.146.

[159] *Ibid.* p.145-146. "Wolves sent by God" is a name applied to the werewolves in the testimony of old Thies in Appendix B *infra*, as well.

[160] *Op. cit.* (n. 150 *supra*).

[161] Bladé, *Contes et Proverbes Populaires recueillis en Armagnac* (Paris 1867) 51, quoted in de Gubernatis *ibid.* p.147:

> Lous loups garous soun gens coumo nous autes; mès an heyt un countrat dab lou diable, e cado soun fourçatz de se cambia en bestios per ana au sabbat e courre touto la neyt. Y a per aço un mouyén de lous goari. Lous cau tira sang pendent qu'an perdut la forme de l'home, e asta leu reprengon per toutjour.

CHAPTER VII
WEREWOLF-CONFRATERNITIES AND WIND EVIDENCE

There is a document that establishes a direct connection between a werewolf confraternity and the agricultural sphere to which the wind belongs. It is unique among the reports of such confraternities for another reason too. It seems to be the only testimony ever given by a defendant who actually was, and admitted to being, a werewolf, speaking in his own defense in a court of law in late seventeenth century Latvia. The Baltic countries were the last to be converted to Christianity in Europe, and his testimony was given at a time when the old beliefs were still very much alive and werewolf groups had not yet gone underground, as they had in the rest of Christian Europe. The document is the record of the cross-examination of a certain octogenarian, named Thies, deposed at his trial, held in Jürgensburg in Livonia (in present-day Latvia) in 1691. The transcript of the trial was published by von Bruiningk about sixty-five years ago,[1] and the classical parallels to Thies's testimony were collected some years after.[2] Old Thies's loyalty to his werewolf group, as it is revealed in this document, is remarkable, as is his conviction that the only way out of the confraternity was to transfer membership to a new recruit.

Many aspects of the wider context of the wolf-name are tied together for us in this remarkable piece of evidence. Despite patent contradictions in Thies's testimony, and the possibility he may have added details to impress his German examiners, his testimony as to the association of the werewolves with the fertility of the soil, and with game and fishing, stands fast. For example, when the werewolves throw the grain stolen from the sorcerers up into the air, to be wafted about by the wind as a blessing for the harvest, the wolf and the wind act in concert.[3] Also clear from the testimony, despite Thies's retraction, is the fact that the werewolves here, as everywhere, do not turn into wolves, but rather dress in wolfskins to effect their transformation. The girls or women appear here as flying pucks or dragons, so that we encounter the dragon here again as well, and the Hell-hole cave makes explicit the werewolves' association with the passage to and from the other world.

There is more, too, in Thies's deposition, about the werewolves' importance for the growth of the grain, and for the rest of the harvest, of fish and game as well as of plants, and Apollo's rôle at the Thargelia, and his other agricultural functions, are elucidated herewith in the context of his epithet Lykeios. The wider function of the Hell-hole cave, to ensure the success of fisheries and fruit orchards, as well as of the fields of grain, furnishes a northern parallel to Apollo's agricultural association expressed in the Apollo cult at Dēlos, the sanctuary of the god second only to Delphi in Greece. The first fruits of the grain were brought to Dēlos each year, and we have already encountered Anios, the island's local hero, son of Apollo or of Zarex the son

---

[1] H. von Bruiningk, *Mitteilungen aus der livländischen Geschichte*, Vol. 22 (Riga 1924-1928) p. 163ff. A translation of the German and Latin of Thies' cross-examination, from the appendix of Otto Höfler, *op. cit.* (Chap. 6 n. 150 *supra*), is found in Appendix B *infra*.

[2] K. Meuli, "Maske und Maskereien," *Hdwb. d. dtsch. Aberglauben* 5.1744-1852; p. 1848 deals with the classical parallels.

[3] The seeds of the grain falling from the air are also reminiscent of the "seeds of all plants" that fell from the World-tree when the Senmurw settled into its nest on that tree in Iranian myth. *V.* Chap. 3 p. 62 *supra*.

of Karystos.[4] We may recall here that he was the first king of Delos and first priest of Apollo there, taught prophecy by Apollo himself and given divine honors as a daimōn. He was the father of the Oinotropoi, or "wine-growers," whose names were Oinō, Spermō, and Elais, after οἶνος "wine," σπέρμα "seed" or "grain," and ἔλαιον "olive-oil," the three staples of ancient Mediterranean agriculture, and his name too probably reflects the agricultural sphere; for it seems to be from the verb ἀνύω "to bring to maturity, to speed, fulfill." We have also seen Aristaios surrounded by fishes as well as livestock[5]; so here too fishing, hunting, and agriculture go together, as they do also in the traditions of the cave of Zeus at Mt. Ida on Psiloriti.[6]

The warrior-function, common in the wolf-syndrome, as we have seen it, is not entirely absent here either. The ceaseless confrontation between the sorcerers of the Devil's entourage and the Yeth-hounds,[7] or the hounds of God, leads virtually to open battle in this Latvian version, and the stage is set for warrior's valor. Perhaps characteristically, the wolves' victory here is one of cunning, rather than combat; but then, discretion is the better part of valor, and the truest strategy is to avoid battle.[8] More to the point in the context of so much werewolf literature, is the status of Thies as an outcast from society; the secret rites of recruitment to the ranks of the werewolves here guarantee the existence of a separate group within society, and the functions the werewolf assumes show his opposition to society, even as he "helps" it. These are the functions of the true criminal outlaw and outcast, like Robin Hood. We may conjecture that Thies ascribed the more unpleasant features of werewolf practice to the sorcerers in his testimony before the judges; for the 'Īsawīya, a werewolf confraternity of Morocco who eat meat from animals not ritually slaughtered, claim they do so because they have an ancient dispensation to eat toads and snakes and other vermin (sic!),[9] the food attributed to the sorcerers in the Livonian court record. Thus here too the phrase "dead horses' heads, toads, snakes and other vermin" probably means stolen meat killed on the run, and cooked and eaten as Thies describes it, so that the sorcerers will have eaten the same food as the other werewolves.

Thus the werewolf, as a figure in human society, has more than social or agricultural significance, just like his namesake the wolf in its symbolism. The slice of reality bands of werewolves purported to represent cuts through more than one area of meaning, like any other mythological concept. It stands for a force penetrating the body and the world, first and foremost connecting the outside with the inside. Because it penetrates the boundary between the limited world of activity and the unlimited source of strength and power it possesses all the potential for good and for evil: for

[4] V. Chap. 2 p. 24 and Chap. 4 p. 82 supra.
[5] In a tomb painting from Kyrene. V. Chap. 4 p. 80 supra.
[6] Cf. P. Faure op. cit. (Chap. 3 n. 78 supra) 124ff.
[7] Briggs and Tongue op cit. (Chap. 6 n. 141 supra) tells of a soul in the form of a little white rabbit saved from "the Devil and his pack of Yeth-hounds," by an old goodbody on her donkey. The phrase in quotation marks is a parallel to the werewolves of the Latvian evidence who are also involved with the Devil; but the English story includes the motif of the dead riding along with the werewolves. "The Devil and his pack of Yeth-hounds" is an English name for the Wild Hunt (motif E50 in Stith Thompson, Motif-Index of Folk Literature), to which parallels in the ancient Greek cult of Zeus at Delphi have been pointed out by Weniger (Chap. 6 n. 11 supra). Cf. John Masefield's poem "The Hounds of Hell."
[8] V. Epilogue n. 5 infra.
[9] I have this in a personal communication from Cyril Glasse. For the 'Īsawīya v. Robert Eisler, Man into Wolf: An Anthropological Interpretation of Sadism, Masochism, and Lycanthropy (London, n.d. [1951 paperback]).

battle and death or for a warrior society on the one hand, and for fertility and continued life, even after death, on the other. Thus the bands of werewolves could promise the natural world and society in general, as well as the soul of the warrior, his internal organs, and his social groupings, benefits, while in reality they represented a bane for the larger world of general society with their rapine and their elitist ideology.

Moreover, the female element belongs to this syndrome as well, understandably, as it is connected with fertility; indeed from Old Thies's werewolf testimony we learn that women too were werewolves. In ancient Greece, if Apollo was Lykeios, and Zeus, too, in his connections with death, Artemis had the epithet Lykeia as well in her temple founded by Hippolytos at Troizen near the theater[10]; and Artemis is associated with sudden death coming to women, whether in childbirth or otherwise.[11] When Penelope, full of worry and care, prays for death, she turns first to Artemis to kill her with an arrow,[12] and then says, "or else I would a storm (θύελλα) might snatch me up/ And sweep me hence a-down the murky ways, /And cast me forth, into the out-goings / Of backward-flowing Ocean"(Marris). Here, little to our surprise, the wind, who we have seen may appear as the wolf, is a lethal agent.

In the same passage Penelope goes on to give an example of girls who were snatched away by the storm-wind, namely the daughters of Pandareos. Orphaned at an early age they were tended by goddesses: Aphrodite, their chief guardian, fed them with cheese, sweet honey, and pleasant wine; Hera bestowed upon them beauty and wisdom; Artemis gave them stature and height; and Athena taught them handicrafts. But when Aphrodite absented herself to go to Olympos to consult with Zeus about marriages for them, the whirlwinds (Harpyies) snatched them away and gave them as servingmaids to the Erinyes. Aēdōn was also a daughter of Pandareos, or of Pandion, and she became a bird, the nightingale, after she had inadvertently murdered her son Itylos when she proceeded with malice against her nephew with whom he had been sleeping in the same bed. In a rationalistic explanation of the story of Pandareos' daughters[13] we find that the girls were afflicted with a disease called κύων, "dog." This disease was cynanthropy or lycanthropy; the girls became werewolves.[14] We may note that the name Pandareos is identical to Pandaros, who appears in the *Iliad* as a son of Lykaon.[15]

It comes as little or no surprise to discover that Artemis seems to have been connected with the Greek form of the Wild Hunt.[16] A remarkable ancient folksong in epic dialect whose motifs recall this syndrome belongs to her.[17] This popular song is

---

[10] Paus. 2.31.4.

[11] *Od.* 15.409-410.

[12] *Od.* 20.56ff.

[13] Σ *Od.* BQ 20.66.

[14] W.H. Roscher, pp. 3ff. and 62ff. of his work *Kynanthropie* on lycanthropy in the *Abhandlungen der Sächsischen Gesellschaft der Wissenschaften* 18.3, as well as in *RhM* 53.189ff., and *Myth. Lex.* 3.1500ff., in connection with his treatment of the fragment on the same subject preserved from the work of Marcellus of Side, a famous physician of the age of the Antonines. Cf. also Frazer *Pausanias* 5.381ff., on Paus. 10.30.2. A "female werewolf" is a *contradictio in terminis* in English and in German, but certainly not in Greek where the word for a werewolf is λυκάνθρωπος and not *λυκάνηρ.

[15] Carl Robert, *Die Griechische Heldensage* (Weidmann, Berlin, 1966⁵) 1.380.

[16] Athamas' story (Chap. 4 p. 80f. *supra*) demonstrates beyond any doubt that werewolves in ancient Greek society were fugitives from society, anti-social beings associated with murder and death.

[17] Hippolytos *adv. haer.* p.72 Miller.

of uncertain date, although its language would make it early, and it runs:

νερτερίη χθονίη τε καὶ οὐρανίη μολὲ Βομβώ,
εἰνοδίη,τριοδῖτι,φαέσφορε,νυκτεροφοῖτι,
ἐχθρη μὲν φωτός,νυκτὸς δὲ φιλοῦσα,
χαίρουσα σκυλακῶν ὑλακῷ τε καὶ αἵματι φούνῳ
ἐν νέκυσιν στείχουσα κατ' ἠρία τεθνεωτῶν.

The Artemis-Hekatē to whom this song is sung is "of the underworld, chthonic and heavenly at once," and named Bombō. She is bidden to "come, goddess of the road, of the parting of the ways, luminous night wanderer, enemy of the light and delighting in the night and friendly towards it, who rejoices in the barking of dogs and in [their?] gory blood, and walks among the corpses and the barrows of the dead." This goddess seems more like Hekatē than Artemis, and her name Bombō probably derives from the verb βομβῶ "to buzz." Nevertheless she is indeed Artemis,[18] and her appearance here makes it virtually certain there were women werewolves in ancient Greek-speaking areas. The presence of women among werewolves is attested from the not far distant past in the Yugoslav cultural area as well. A female werewolf from Slovenia or Croatia who ravaged a herd of sheep effected her transformation into a wolf and back again by passing through a *Purgelbaum*, most likely a castor-oil plant.[19] In the early part of the twentieth century there seem to have been female werewolves in France, Belgium, Germany, Austria-Hungary, Norway, Sweden, Iceland, Finland, Lappland, and many other countries.[20] On the other hand, the religion of Mithras in the Roman Empire in the early centuries of the Common Era seems to have had its origin in an adolescent confraternity that excluded women from the ranks of its initiates. Likewise Manichaeism, which shares with Mithraism a common Iranian origin, forbade marriage and procreation to its higher ranks of holiness.[21]

The agrarian connection of the werewolf confraternity, evidenced in the transcript of the Livonian court proceedings, and the presence of women among the werewolves in Greece, Croatia, Latvia, and elsewhere, make it clear that the transformation of human into beast, specifically into a wolf, does not have solely, or even primarily, to do with hunting, or killing, or shedding of blood.[22] The world of the neolithic age, the world of incipient agriculture from which Greek mythology and Northern European practice for the most part ultimately derive, was not a world in which "hunting [was] the master behavior pattern of the human species"[23]; for in that world the wolf, in particular, meant much more than simply the rapacious hunter. The Teutonic context, where the sole function of the wolf-warrior, like Sinfjötli of the *Volsungasaga*, is to do deeds of valor, and to stand up to a great number of his enemies, seems a later

---

[18] *V.* W. Dilthey, "Die Artemis der Apelles und die wilde Jagd," *RhM* 25 (1870) 321ff.

[19] Friedrich S. Krauss, *Slawische Volkforschungen* (W. Heims, Leipzig 1908) 139. No doubt she changed into and out of her wolfskin as she hid behind the large leaves of the plant.

[20] Elliott O'Donnell, *Werwolves* (New York 1972², first edition c. 1913), who tells stories of werewolves from many countries and is careful to stipulate whether they were of both sexes in any given area.

[21] F. Decret, *Mani et la tradition manichéenne* (Paris, Seuil 1974) 106ff.

[22] The contrary thesis, that these are its main associations, has been maintained by W. Burkert, *Homo Necans, Interpretationen altgriechischer Opferriten und Mythen (Religionsgeschichtliche Versuche und Vorarbeiten*, vol. 32 Berlin, New York: De Gruyter 1972) 12-235, 58f., as it had been before him by Eisler, *op. cit.* (n. 8 *supra*). These scholars, especially Burkert, also deny that women participated in these rituals despite our clear evidence that they did.

[23] W.S. Laughlin (1968) quoted in Matt Cartmill, "Four Legs Good, Two Legs Bad," *Natural History* 92 (1983) No. 11, p.75.

development. The Latvian werewolf seems closer to the wolf-complex as it has revealed itself in the Greek context, where the werewolf (Lykaon and the cult of Lykaios) functions in connection with weather, fertility, and the agrarian scene, although he appears there in the world of death in another facet of his personality. The Greek context is no doubt the earlier, and it may be compared to the bull-roarer of Australian aboriginal initiatory ceremonies, which "is the symbol of a divinity who bestows not only death but also life, sexuality, and fertility."[24] The key to the conjunction of death and life, sexuality, and fertility is the necessity of passing through a barrier between two realms, one hidden and the other manifest, a barrier through which wind and the wolf can find a passageway and penetrate.

We have noted more than once above the neolithic paintings of flying wolves on what are the remains of the Indo-European invasion of Europe through southern Russia, according to Marija Gimbutas.[25] The same context, according to our surmise, appears in the story told by Jacques de Guyne, a Flemish monk of the late Middle Ages, who wrote the annals of the town of Tongeren (Tongres) in Belgian Limburg. Here the wolf is again a wind-creature, as well as a warrior. Jacques de Guyne told that 1100 years before Julius Caesar the town had been besieged by the Phrygian prince Bavo the Wolf. Bavo condensed the atmosphere such that his troops rose up into the air holding their bows and arrows, whereupon the people of Tongeren surrendered the town to them. Here the Wolf is capable of making people rise up on the wings of the wind, by working an otherworldly sort of magic that compacts the air.

It is remarkable that also in the neighborhood of Tongeren (Tongres), an apparently unrelated ancient rite involving the procession of Yeth-hounds and werewolves continues today, in the guise of a church festival: In the yearly festival of St. Evermarus, his death at the hands of a robber knight named Hacco is mimed. Hacco and his twenty-two wild henchmen on horseback fall upon Evermarus and a group of pilgrims, whereupon the youngest pilgrim makes off into the woods in flight, pursued by the horsemen. Hacco shoots after the fugitive twice, in vain, but another hits him with an arrow from his bow, loads him across, "like a sack," in front of his saddle, while the other pilgrims are stabbed with daggers. Then all pick themselves up and go off to have a drink.[26] In this ceremony the priest's two vergers carry clubs and are decorated with ivy like wild men. In connection with the antagonism between the Devil, his sorcerers, and the Devil's guards, on the one hand, and werewolves, on the other, in the testimony of Old Thies, Hacco has been identified with Hache, the father of Eckhart, one of the figures of the German Yeth-hound bands.[27] Altogether, the motif found in this performance belongs to the larger category of the pursuit of a demon or demons by Yeth-hound bands, the one pursued often being female.

The pursuit here is of a scapegoat, a motif we have already seen in connection with Apollo and his agricultural function, in the *pharmakos* at the Thargēlia from Athens.[28] In the ideology behind such performances evil is demarcated and expelled or annihilated.

In the Greek-speaking world, again, in ancient Krete, we find a very different outcome in a reflex of such a dyadic relationship. Such a relationship held between

---

[24] M. Eliade, *op. cit.* (Chap. 4. n. 120 *supra*) 14.

[25] Chap. 2, pp. 25-26 *supra*.

[26] O. Höfler, *op. cit.* (Chap. 6 n. 150 *supra*) 280 from Bovy, *Promenades historiques dans le pays de Liège* (Liège 1838).

[27] *Ibid.* 281.

[28] Chap. 2 p. 24 *supra*.

Kuretes and Daktyls in the cult of Zeus at the cave on Mt. Ida (Psiloriti) in Krete.[29] In Krete, where the civilizing influences of the Daktyls and the Kuretes were emphasized, the Idaean Daktyls, who may have been identified with the Mother Goddess or Lady of the Mountain of the cave of Ida, the mother of Zeus, and the Kuretes, associated with Zeus himself,[30] live in peace and mutual co-operation, unlike the sorcerers and the werewolf representatives of the ancient warrior confraternities in the Northern European cultural area.[31] The Kuretes, armed dancers who protected the baby Zeus from the onslaughts of his father Kronos in the common myth, were magicians who could revive the dead, like Polyïdos, or seers, like Epimenides, who could foretell the future after a long sleep. The Daktyls were said to have been the earliest inhabitants of Krete, the ancestors of the Kuretes, and the inventors of metal-working, many traces of which are found round the entrance to the cave of Zeus on Psiloriti dating back to antiquity, as well as the founders of the Mysteries and the Olympic games.[32] They are named Kelmis, Damnameneus, and Akmōn,[33] or else their names are Herakles, Paionaios, Epimedes, Iasios, and Akesidas,[34] the last four of which refer to healing (properly Apollo's purview, or Asklepios's).

The realms between which the ancient wolf, or the werewolf, mediates are not the realm of settled life and agriculture, on the one hand, and the wild trackless bush and bracken where the hunter roams on the other, but rather, as we have seen, two more inclusive and comprehensive realms: that of the hidden powers, be they inside the body or outside the visible universe, with which the werewolf-warrior confraternities claimed to be in contact, and the world of known, visible phenomena. This is one source of the Greek ἄδηλον, "the unmanifest," concerning which the Greeks were fond of employing the saying attributed to Anaxagoras, ὄψις τῶν ἀδήλων τὰ φαινόμενα, "phenomena are the surface of the hidden."[35]

Wolf-confraternities, of the sort that have given their names to those peoples whose name means "wolf-people" in the Indo-European area (and outside of it as well, as in the case of the Pawnee Indians of the Great Plains and of the Yawelamni nation of the Yokut Indians of California whose territory was the southern part of the San Joaquin Valley), probably have their origin in ceremonies of initiation, where the

---

[29] P. Faure op. cit. (Chap. 3 n.78 supra) 110ff.

[30] Ibid. 118.

[31] The peace that prevails between the warlike representatives of the wolf who promote agricultural prosperity and the female element, or the element that must be expelled, like the scapegoat, in Krete, where initiations based on warrior confraternities' rituals and traditions are found, may be due to the peculiar development of religion on that island, described by Faure ibid. 127f. He writes: les mystères de l'Ida suivaient une évolution tout à fait différente des autres grandes cultes de Grèce. Tandis que ceux-ci s'épanouissaient en manifestations sportives, théâtrales, artistiques ou en spéculations philosophiques, à Olympie, Delphes, Délos, Athènes ou Eleusis, l'originalité du clergé de Zeus s'est exercée dans quatre directions...: The four areas he lists in which the religious innovators of the cave of Zeus at Ida were active are meticulous techniques of purification, descriptions of the world to come, the construction of a cosmogony, and a unified Kretan political order. These ideas are found conjoined in such a syndrome nowhere else in the Greek-speaking area, except in the traditions ascribed to Orpheus, which are Thrakian traditions perhaps influenced by Persian ideas. May we see in Krete an innovative surmounting of the divisive tendencies of the wolf-name similar to that found in Zarathustra's revolution in thought in early Iran?

[32] D. S. 5.64.

[33] Phoronis (Σ A.R. 1.1129, and Strabo 10.473).

[34] Paus. 5.7.6-7, 5.14.7, 6.23.2.

[35] S.E. M. 1.140.

young are helped to pass from one state to another. That passage is where the wolf is at home, as he is in the realm of death, which also signifies passage from one state to another.

Greek myth and cult show a connection between sacrifice and fertility, particularly ploughing. The child in front of the plough appears in the story of the ruse employed by the Atreidai and Palamēdēs to foil Odysseus' feigned madness in his attempt to shirk his vow to go to Agamemnon's aid if Helen was stolen away from him and had to be retrieved, and hence his obligation to go to Troy, when, in order to feign madness, he yoked oxen and horses together in front of the plough and was sowing salt. He desisted when Palamēdēs put the baby Telemachos in the furrow he was ploughing.[36] The tale of the meeting of Theiodamas, king of the Dryopians, and Herakles, a ploughing scene involving Herakles' hungry child Hyllos, and his double, Theiodamas' son Hylas who was carried off by Herakles,[37] is reminiscent of the same setting. We may add here the myth of Hera suckling the infant Herakles found lying on the earth, and without doubt the story of Erichthonios, born of Earth, and adopted by Athena,[38] belongs here too. All these tales show a child as it were born directly from the earth, or appearing in the vicinity of the plough. The goddess Gē or Earth, moreover, is one of the goddesses responsible for rearing children to adulthood and supporting them.[39] Furthermore, ploughing is a well-known ancient metaphor for sexual intercourse, so much so that in Hellenistic Greek thought we find a persistent current of thought opposing agriculture in general because to puncture the surface of the earth with a ploughshare is to wound the Mother of all things.[40] From these conceptions it follows, in the context of ancient thought, that agriculture, or giving life to plants, is a species of propagation, just like begetting children, or giving life to humans. Granted this, if the world is constructed according to correspondences, it follows that just as human life is dependent on the life of the grain, the grain as it grows must be dependent on human life. Hence human sacrifice (in the form of a scapegoat) at the festival of the First Fruits at Athens, the Thargelia, and in the cult of Apollo at Leukates on Leukas, and of Apollo Hylates near Kurion on Cyprus, is probably related to werewolf myth and cult and will have had its origin in agricultural magic. This is much more probable than for it to have originated in an attempt to accustom innocent people to the shedding of blood in hunting rituals, as Eisler and Burkert[41] would have it. That effort would be otiose; for we do not know of any

---

[36] The story appears in Hyginus *Fab.* 95, Σ Lyk. 815, and Servius *ad Aen.* 2.81, and was depicted in antiquity in paintings of Euphranor (Pliny. *N. H.* 35.129) and Parrhasios (Plut. *de aud. poet.* 3, p.18A).

[37] For Theiodamas as father of Hylas cf. Hyginus *Fab.* 14, Ap. Rhod. 1.1212, and Apollod. 1.117. The story of Herakles devouring the ploughing steer, and the subsequent outbreak of hostilities, seems to derive from Kall. *Aetia* I Fr. 24 and 25 in *Callimachus*, ed. R. Pfeiffer (Oxford 1949) 1 pp. 33 and 34; cf. also Apollod. 2.7.7.1, and 2.5.11.8. The names Hylas and Hyllos must surely be connected with Apollo Hylates of Cyprus, whose cult involving human sacrifice we have noted above (cf. Chap. 6 p. 114 *supra*).

[38] Cf. the author of the *Danais* fr. 2, and Pindar fr. 253; also Eur. fr. 917, Eratosth. *catast.* 13, *et. al.* Erichthonios was tended by the nymphs Drosos, Herse, and Aglauros, whose names mean "dew" and "bivouac," so that they too belong to the ephebic sphere.

[39] Aesch. *Seven* 16ff.

[40] Cf. A.G. Drachmann *s. v.* Pflug, *PWRE* 38 (1938) cols 1471-1472: *Bei den verschiedensten Völkern finden die Ethnologen denselben Gedanken, daß die Erde durch das Pflügen fruchtbar gemacht wird; der Pflug spielt dabei die Rolle eines Phallos.*

[41] *V.* n. 22 *supra*. The hypothesis is unlikely in view of the fact that human sacrifice in two of

human society that is free from murder. The development, in the Teutonic linguistic area, and elsewhere perhaps,[42] of the wolf-name of the ancient Indo-European werewolf confraternity into a name for a murderer must be a later phenomenon. There death and killing do indeed become the earmark of the nature of the *vargr*, for "Bears and wolves (*ulfr*) are outlawed everywhere,"[43] and likewise:[44]

> Brother shall be brother's bane,
> sisters' sons shall slay each other.
> There will be evil times, an age of whoredom,
> of sharp sword play and cloven shields,
> a wind-age, a wolf (*warg-*) age,
> till the world is made to fall.
> No man shall spare another.

In this description of the end of the world it is not clear whether the wolf-age is the wind-age, or rather the age of the murderers. We are back once again to ambiguity, or to poetry, concerning death and the wind, and we may recall here the alternately beneficent and maleficent nature of Apollo Lykeios, the wolf-Apollo.

The connection of confraternities with the wolf complex thus includes the same sort of weather aspects that belong to Apollo Smintheus, patron of the field-mouse, with, as we have noted, the field-mouse's double function of creating a blessing and holding it back to repress fertility. Now, in the oldest testimony to werewolf-confraternities, in Vedic literature, they are associated with weather-phenomena; for the names of the Indian divinities, the companions of Rudra, the Maruts, as well as of the *mairya* of the Zoroastrian sources, who are called "two-footed wolves, worse than the four-footed kind," as well as sorcerers and eaters of carrion, and of the Roman god Mars as well, derive from the Indo-European root **marjo*, "member of a cultic confraternity,"[45] and the Maruts are tornado-divinities and the prototype of the Indo-European confraternity. The Maruts are connected with Apollo Smintheus,[46] and so by extrapolation with Apollo Lykeios. They also personify the wandering souls of the dead.[47] Hence the Yeth-hounds, who ride with the souls of the dead, and the werewolves belong to one and the same complex. In Greece, the Homeric word λύσσα seems to mean "wolfish rage."[48] When *lyssa* has taken hold of Hektor he is described as having no regard for gods or for men.[49] The word is applied directly to wolves in Theoc. 4.11 where it presumably refers to the wolf-like behavior of the rabid canine, and Σ on that passage says that the proper meaning of the word is "rabies in dogs." This word, as it appears in Homer, is one of the earmarks of the wolf-confraternity, which has left its name in the name of so many peoples.[50] The meaning

---

these cases consists in pitching people off cliffs, in any case.

[42] Cf the Hittite Code 2.30, *sarnikzil NU-GAL zik-wa UR-BAR-RA kisat* "There is no compensation possible. 'You' the sentence is, 'are become a wolf,'" which has been taken to mean that wolf here too is a name for an outlaw or murderer.

[43] *Gulaþinglov* 94.

[44] *Voluspá* 39.

[45] Stig Wikander, *op. cit.* (Chap. 6. n.112 *supra*) 75ff.

[46] Grégoire and Goossens, *op. cit.* (Chap. 2 p. 30 n. 33 *supra*).

[47] Wikander, *ibid.* n. 40 *supra*.

[48] Bruce Lincoln, "Homeric ΛΥΣΣΑ: Wolfish Rage," *Indogermanische Forschungen* 80 (1975) 98-105 Cf. also Andreas Alföldi, *Die Struktur des voretruskischen Römerstaates* (Heidelberg 1974) 33f.

[49] *Il.* 9.237ff.

[50] Lincoln, *Ibid.*

of the word *lyssa* is parallel, in that case, to the Latin "animus," so close to the Greek ἄνεμος, "Wind," as well as to the Greek term θυμός, "high spirits," cognate with the Latin "fumus," "smoke." It has been compared to the Germanic "Wut" of the "berserkr," literally the one who wears the clothing of the bear,[51] and to the Celtic Ferg in the story of CúChulaind. At any rate, as far as we can tell, Lyssa was personified for the first time, in Greek literature, in Aeschylus.[52] When she appears again in the *Heracles* of Euripides,[53] on the heels of the chorus' invocation of Apollo as Paian, or Healer, in order to execute the wishes of King Lykos (Wolf) come to slay the children of Herakles, she is compared to a gust of wind: "a storm (θύελλα) shakes the house, the roof falls in."[54] Thus the wind, with its manifold symbolism lies at the heart of the madness of the bands of adolescents and adults who constituted the confraternities and conceived that they, like the wind, could pass over barriers of all sorts.

Despite the correspondences of ancient Greek terminology, and of the practice and ideology of Indian cultic confraternities and Teutonic Männerbünde, to Apollo's attributes, the Wild Hunt *per se* in Greece is not associated with him, so far as we know, but rather with Artemis,[55] and most especially with Zeus, whose rites involving human sacrifice often include wearing animal skins, like the initiates in the cave of Zeus on Mt. Ida in Krete, dressed in boars' skins, and those on Mt. Pelion in Magnesia, clad in sheepskins, or the wolfskin clad figures around Mt. Lykaion in Arkadia, and initiatory rites for the young involving symbolic death.[56] We have seen that the Daktyls of the cult of Zeus of this nature on Krete are given the names Herakles, Paionaios, Epimedes, Iasios, and Akesidas,[57] the last four of which refer to healing, which is properly Apollo's purview, or Asklepios', and the ritual of the Apaturia at Athens, also a festival of Apollo, was essentially an initiatory rite.[58] Apollo Lykeios himself is nowhere associated with the confraternities of the young, so that we have come to the end of our investigation of Apollo the Wolf-god, and we hope we have succeeded somewhat in illuminating the wider context of the wolf-name, as well.

---

[51] *Ynglingasaga* Chap. 6.
[52] *Xantriai* fr. 169N.
[53] *Her.* 822f.
[54] *Ibid.* 905.
[55] P. 120-121 *supra*.
[56] P. Faure *op. cit.* (Chap. 3 n.78 *supra*) 110ff.
[57] V. n. 33 *supra*.
[58] V. P. Vidal-Naquet *op. cit.* (Chap. 4 n. 125 p. 83 *supra*).

EPILOGUE

Apollo's name has been derived most plausibly from the Indo-European *apelo-*, *aplo-*, common to Greek (εὐηπελής), Illyrian, and Germanic (ON *afl*, "strength") and meaning "strength," or "power." The god was known as Apollōn in Athens, as Apellōn in Sparta and the other Dorian settlements, and as Aplun in Thessaly. All these names can easily be derived from the Indo-European root. Hence, Apollōn Lykeios was "the powerful master of the dragon-wolf," which last figure we have come to know.

The figure of a master of the wolf is known to us from a peculiar conception found in Croatia and Slovenia. There, there was thought to be a *vucovij pastir*, or herdsman of the wolf, who cared for wolves just as human shepherds care for their flocks.[1] The epithet Lykeios belongs with Apollo's many other cult titles, and we have examined the unexpected connection it has to many others of these through the wind and agriculture. Still, it is most closely related to Pythios; for both epithets refer directly to Apollo's role as a monster-slayer. We have seen the wolf as a complex of active forces in the world; their subjection to Apollo, the chief representative of the strength of the Olympian gods, was seen as a battle that had actually taken place between the god and a monster dragon figure in history (actually mythology, or pagan *Heilsgeschichte*). The description of that battle as it concerned the wolf figure Lykos is not extant; but from the fact that the grave of Lykos is found at Delphi, the site of Apollo's greatest battle with and victory over a monster, it can be surmised that it once did exist. The many accounts of Apollo's battle with Python, or Delphyne, may perhaps allow us to reconstruct the outlines of a conflict with Lykos as well. For an attempt to treat the entire subject the reader is well-advised to consult Joseph Fontenrose's great work *Python*.[2]

Apollo's real name, then, is not known to us, for his name Apollo is a descriptive epithet. Like the wolf or the bear in many localities, his name must have been forgotten; for the Indo-European word for the bear, extant in Lat. *ursus*, Gr. ἄρκτος, and Skt. *ŗkaḥ*, has been supplanted in English by the word, "bear," which originally referred to the animal's brown color, and in Russian with the word медведь, which refers to his predilection for honey, in order not to call him inadvertently by pronouncing his true name, and have to face him.[3] So Apollo's power made the Greeks loath to speak out his true name, and it fell into oblivion. Like Baal, "the Master," Apollo was simply "the Lord."

Apollo, too, may be like Baal in that he may be conceived of as finding his place between a father-god, whose surrogate he becomes in many respects, and a mother-goddess. These seem to be Zeus, to whom Apollo's subordination is well-known from texts like Aeschylus' *Choephoroe*, and Demeter, the goddess of the Thargelia along with Apollo, a goddess whose role in the Apollo-complex we have noticed above.[4]

---

[1] Friedrich S. Krauss, *op. cit.* (Chap. 7 n. 19 *supra*).

[2] For further thoughts on Lykos and Lykeios, with a consideration of their place in a Dumézilian scheme of things, *v.* Appendix C *infra*.

[3] Richard von Kienle *op. cit.* (Chap. 2 n. 16 *supra*) 14 .

[4] Another connection between Demeter and Apollo Lykeios may be perceived in the story of the death of the great warrior Pyrrhos of Epeiros at Argos in 262, as told by Phylarchus (Plut. *Pyrrhus* 31ff.). In that account Pyrrhos dreamed he would die when he saw a bull and a wolf battling. Subsequently, in the course of his foray into Argos, he came upon the statue of the wolf and the bull at the temple of Apollo Lykeios, in fulfillment of the evil omen, as it were, and the

Of what, however, is Apollo the Lord? Is it the wind he controls as master of the wolf, or is it something more? The answer to these questions is the answer to the nature of the wolf in Greek thought, and it leads us directly to the heart of the question as to Apollo's true nature. To understand Apollo's mastery over the wolf we must put it in the context of the rest of Apollo's myth and cult. Apollo displays fundamentally only one function in all his manifold roles. When he overcomes Marsyas, the satyr-like, flute-playing attendant of the great mother goddess Kybele, he rehearses his mastery of the wolf, as he does over and over again. Another example of the same mastery is his dragon-slaying, the feat for which he was best known, under the name Pythios, in antiquity. His retirement to the land of the Hyperboreans again seems part of the same complex; for he retires in the month of Pyanopsion, whose name ("Bean-roasting time") denotes the onset of winter not by reference to the weather outside, but emphasizing the family, or the social group, gathered indoors, sheltered from the cold, and roasting beans about the fire. Winter, the time of Dionysos at Delphi, saw public activity cease, as indoor activities, and darkness, prevailed. At this time Apollo was off to the land of perpetual light, the land of the Hyperboreans, where the people sacrificed asses, the animal of Dionysos, *par excellence*, to their god Apollo. The same Hyperboreans brought the first-fruits of the grain to Delos, the island of Apollo that contains the best clues to his nature, and to his pertinence to the wider context of the wolf-name.

The nature of Apollo the wolf-god, as we have seen, is, like the wolf, to be the messenger, the fearsome being that passes the boundary between the known and the unknown, between the manifest and the hidden. The story of Marsyas, the slaying of the Python, the yearly journey to the Hyperboreans, all also deal with the subjugation of the Dionysiac, the hidden, dark side of existence, to the bright realm of Phoibos, the shining, open deity who is Apollo. The wolf represents the realm of the hidden; for unlike man, but like the raven and the dolphin, he has licence to enter the realm beyond the boundary, and pass into the land of the unseen and return to the light once again from there. In this context the wolf's association with death and with initiation becomes comprehensible; for death is the passage from the manifest to the hidden world, and initiation ceremonies use the symbolism of death as the prototype of the passage from the childhood to adulthood that they signify.

The name of the island Delos means "the manifest," and it sets the stage for Apollo's career, and is itself the symbol of the myth of emergence from obscurity. Apollo was born at the foot of a mountain on the island called Kynthos, from the Greek root *keuth-*, or *kyth-*, which signifies "to hide," or "to be hidden." The epithet Kynthios, which belongs to Zeus and to Athena (Kynthia, or Cynthia), as well as to Apollo (and to Artemis), signifies "master of the hidden," just as Lykeios signifies "master of the wolf." Thus the epithets Lykeios and Kynthios must be very close in meaning. The same signification, namely "master of," of the epithets in *-ios*, can be seen in the epithet Pythios, as well. When that epithet is understood as from the root *pyth-* of the verb *pynthanomai*, it will denote "master of the known," or "discovered," although Apollo as the oracular deity primarily bears the epithet Loxias, which is an epithet referring to animal behavior in the light, as we have noted *supra*, and not to the crossing of frontiers implied in the epithets Delios, Kynthios, Lykeios and Pythios. Still Loxias too signifies revelation, if in riddles, athwart, and not straightforwardly.

---

old woman who felled him with a roof-tile (after he was wounded by her son, and was about to slay him) was identified with the goddess Demeter.

In Dumézilian terms Apollo, as the patron of ephebic confraternities, is the great second-function god of Greece, but he is not the god of the wild warriors who belong to Ares, but rather of their opposite numbers.[5] It is he who overcomes the uncontrolled outbursts of adolescence, and guides its unearthly energy into open, profitable channels. From such manifestations as the "E" at Delphi, he appears to be the god of present time in Greece, and the preponderance of his temples and shrines points to the same thing, as do his prophetic functions, as well. As Lykeios, surely, his sphere is first and foremost the life of the ephebe, the young Greek warrior who grew up into the pillar of Greek society and the defender of its values; for Lykeios is the patron of the martial spirit exemplified by the Iranian *haomavarga*.

Thus Apollo must remain the placid god Nietzsche[6] and Rohde[7] found him to be, the symbol of the ideal, calm, thoughtful Greeek warrior.

There can be no doubt that Dumézil's categories lead to the same fundamental understanding of the wolf-figure in Greek mythology; for the two aspects of the second function are precisely those of the warrior. Insofar as the warrior functions within society he is reasoned and sane, but toward his enemies he must be wild and ferocious. However, Apollo's connection to representatives of the third function, in Dumézilian terms, creates an ambivalent relationship. He shares the festival of the Thargelia with Demeter, and their partnership is paralleled and corroborated by the report we have adduced in Appendix B of the Latvian werewolf confraternity whose task it was to guarantee a plentiful harvest; in these things, as in the stories of the she-wolf who suckled the exposed twins, we find cooperation between representatives of the second and third functions. Furthermore, the story of Amphiōn and Zēthos, and their defense of their persecuted mother Antiopē against the force of Lykos, and especially Dirkē, is one of a series of tales concerning the divine twins and their endangered female companion, their sister, mother or bride (of one of them), who are representatives of the Indo-European third function, comparable to the Iranian Armaiti with Hauretat and Ameretat. The ambivalent relationship is exemplified in Antiopē, who is the daughter of a Lykos, or Lykurgos, and the victim of another Lykos.

In the realm of the wild warrior in the wider Indo-European linguistic area, those heroes who represent the second function, that of Apollo, are, like him, masters of baneful exhalations that must be channeled into the right paths, but they practice rites unheard of in Greece. So CúChulaind, in Irish myth, can suck one eye far into his head and protrude the other out while blowing it up (v. *The Death of Aife's Only Son*). In the Scandinavian lands the warriors are closer to the Dionysiac rites of inner madness and enthuisasm in the guise of Berserkir (those dressed in bearskins). In the ancient Iranian regions to the north and east of the Caspian Sea the same is true. There, in the land of the *haomavargā*, a word that probably means "the wolves created by the *haoma* drink," the great hero Franghrasyan (Afrasiab) is a foreigner, one of the Tura

---

[5] For the two aspects of the warrior function cf. Udo Strutynski, "The Three Functions of Indo-European Tradition in the *Eumenides* of Aeschylus," in *Myth and Law among the Indo-Europeans*, ed. Jaan Puhvel (U. of Cal., Berkeley 1970) 211-228; Idem, "Ares: A Reflex of the Indo-European War-god," *Arethusa* 13 (1980) 217-231; and Joel H. Grisward, *L'Archéologie de l'Épopée Médiévale* (Paris, Payot 1981) 211-228.

[6] Friedrich Nietzsche, *The Birth of Tragedy out of the Spirit of Music* (1872) tr. Walter Kaufmann (New York1967) 35 *et passim*.

[7] Erwin Rohde, *Psyche: the cult of souls and belief in immortality among the Greeks* [first published 1920] (New York 1972).

people, the traditional enemies of Iran with their own variant of Scythian religion.[8] Thus, like the ephebes of ancient Athens, who were sent out of the polis to guard the borders in solitude, and support themselves from their unarmed hunting, the young men of Iran may have been apprehended as foreign to the society whence they sprung and which they were one day to defend with their life's blood. But they drink the famous *soma* or *haoma*, the likes of which is unknown in Greece, although we may have found an echo of it in the ergot (Kornmutterkorn) of the German peasants, and perhaps elsewhere as well. These ancient Indo-European confraternities were of a predominantly martial nature, and that is the way they have been mostly apprehended in the modern literature. In this connection the great Indo-European god from whom Apollo arose must have been a powerful god and a priestly one, but one who controls, par excellence, the springs of martial behavior. Here he approximates his father, the almost otiose sky-god in the Indo-European pantheon, who held his own as Zeus in the Greek world and also took on the role of dragon-slayer in some areas (Kilikia). Yet Apollo's agrarian connections are clear. In the previous chapters we have examined the agricultural side of the activity of the Baltic werewolves which connects the wolf with agriculture through the agency of the confraternity, and not only, as in Greece, through the concatenation of Apollo's epithet Lykeios and Apollo's connection with agriculture in the Athenian festival of the Thargelia and the Dorian festival of the Karneia. In the Athenian festival of the Oschophoria, celebrated in the month of Pyanopsion, October-November, we again find a combination of agrarian and military traits.

These agrarian and military traits are one in the perspective of safe passage of boundaries that the association both share with the wolf presupposes. Moreover, the Thargelia and the Karneia clearly stem from the agricultural context of the neolithic period, as do the flying wolves of Petreni and Schipenitz, and the werewolves of the Latvian werewolf document. The oldest wolf concerned with passing boundaries, not necessarily in safety, is the one for whom emissions of ground gases are named. We can trace him back to the palaeolithic hunters[9] who settled near ground-fires, gaseous emissions, and empty sinkholes, and in many cases he has given his name to tribes and peoples of the ancient world. Both men and women of the palaeolithic world, hunters and provisioners alike, needed the assurance the wolf-name provided that passage could be successfully accomplished and crises overcome.[10]

---

[8] H.S. Nyberg, *Die Religionen des alten Iran* (tr. H.H. Schaeder Leipzig 1938) 250ff.

[9] W. Burkert *op.cit.* (Chap. 7 n. 20 *supra*) esp. 12-25, 58f., holds that the nature of religion in general and Greek religion in particular has been dictated by the experience of palaeolithic hunters; but his treatment leaves out of consideration any experiences they may have had, *qua* human beings, aside from the kill in the hunt.

[10] Victor Turner, *The Forest of Symbols: aspects of Ndembu ritual* (New York 1967) 29-32 defines the dominant symbols in ritual as multivocalic, having various referents arranged about two semantic poles: the orectic, or physiological, and the social pole. The wider context of the wolf-name encompasses these two poles, in its reference to flatulence and to youth confraternities, but it also has referents outside the human domain, in creatures that represent safe passage in the animal and plant world, and in natural phenomena in the earth, sky, and sea. *V.* on this Chap. 6 *supra* as well.

Appendix A

THE STOIC EXPLANATION OF THE EPITHET LYKEIOS

The Stoic theory that Lykeios means "light god," if we may call it that, has had substantial echoes in the modern age. Among its most eminent defenders was Hermann Usener[1] whose most telling argument was the juxtaposition of the names Nykteus (from νύξ "night") and Lykos in Greek mythology, which would dispose of the objection that the wolf-name *per se* never refers to light, should it stand up. (Cf. Chap. 4 p. 71 *infra*.)

Among the earliest of the modern supporters of the light theory was F.G. Welcker,[2] who refers to G.F. Creuzer,[3] and K.O. Müller,[4] for support of his view that the wolf is a light and sun animal. Müller, in fact, stops short of the conclusion that would make of the wolf a symbol of the sun, although he explains the epithet Lykeios as deriving from the root of Lat. *lux*, and so admits a light connection. Wilamowitz wrote[5] "Otfried Müller denied Apollo was the sun." Müller himself found it "difficult to discover what analogy even the lively imagination of the Greeks could have found between the wolf and light."

It is an indisputable fact that a root *lyk-* meaning "light," and related to Gr. λευκόν "white," Skt. *lokam*, "world," *lokayāmi*, "look," and Eng. "look," exists in Greek. Hesychius' glossary, for example, has no fewer than four entries where it appears in words or phrases referring to light: (1) λυκοειδής, (2) λυκοειδέος ἀοῦς, (3) λυκοειδές, (all really the same adjective referring to the dawn twilight), and (4) λυκοπόδες, "the Alkmaionids, according to one explanation, because their feet were white; because they always wore shoes." Of these the adjective λυκοειδές seems genuine. Herakleitos *Quaestiones Homericae* 6 also derives one of Apollo's wolf-epithets from the dawn-light in his interpretation of the epithet Lykēgenēs, but the opposite tendency is in evidence too. For example, the *Et. Magnum* explains the word λυκόφως, "dawn twilight," by reference to wolves' hair, which is white at its roots and black at its tips. This explanation is popular in the lexical literature. It shows there was a school of thought in antiquity that saw a wolf in all occurrences of the root *lyk-*.

The Greek word λύκος, "wolf," is a common Indo-European word for. the wolf, and the reconstructed form of the word in Proto-I.-E. is $^u lq^u os$,[6] whereas λύκη in ἀμφιλύκη is separate and rather related to Lat. *lux*, Gr. λευκόν "white," Skt. *lokam*, "world," *lokayāmi*, "look," and Eng. "look," and also to the name of the lynx, famed for its acute vision.[7] There is no substance to ancient attempts to connect them.

From the ancient discussions, then, we see that the tentative distinction implied

---

[1] *Götternamen Versuch einer Lehre von der religiösen Begriffsbildung* (Schulte Bulmke, Frankf./Main 1896) 199ff.

[2] *Griechische Gotterlehre* (Göttingen 1857).

[3] *Symbolik und Mythologie der alten Völker*[3] (Leipzig, Darmstadt 1836-1842) 2.532-535.

[4] *Religion and Mythology of the Dorians*[2] (tr. Henry Tufnell and George C. Lewis, London 1839) 313-317.

[5] U. v. Wilamowitz-Moellendorff, *Greek Historical Writing and Apollo* (Oxford, 1908) 28.

[6] Julius Pokorny, *Indogermanisches Etymologisches Wörterbuch* (Bern, München 1959) 1178f. Cf. also Hjalmar Frisk, *Griechisches Etymologisches Wörterbuch* (Heidelberg 1961) 2.143.

[7] From an original Proto-I.-E. *leuk-; cf. Pokorny *op. cit.* 687f.

by Schirmer,[8] namely, that ancient poets identify the epithets Lykeios, Lykios, etc., with the wolf, while prose writers support the identification with the light and the sun, really reflects a distinction in time rather than in genre, a much more fundamental distinction, actually. Poetry is much older than prose. Indeed only at the middle of the fifth Century in Athens do we find prose first being written in Greece, the "Old Oligarch" being generally considered to be the first prose writer there, while poetry begins with Homer and its tradition is even older. This confirms the late Stoic origin of the speculations which make of Lykeios, etc., light-epithets. There is no escaping the fact that the oldest interpretations hold these epithets to be wolf-epithets. Their earliest frame of reference must have been to the wolf and the wider context of the wolf-name.

Because so much of the history of modern mythological research is that of the naturalistic school of interpreters of myth of the nineteenth century, it is no surprise to find that modern theories of the meaning of Apollo's wolf-epithets were so long dominated by their identification with the sun. One hundred years ago, however, the sides were already chosen and the battle joined. Jane Ellen Harrison, *Mythology and Monuments of Ancient Athens* (London 1890) 219, referred to A. Lang, *Myth, Ritual, and Religion,* (second edition, London 1906) 2.199,[9] and to A.M. Verrall, ed., *The Seven Against Thebes*, p. 13, for support of her identification of the epithets from the *lyk-* root with the wolf. Since 1909, when L.R. Farnell completed publication of his great work, *The Cults of the Greek States* 1-5 (Oxford 1896-1909), hardly a voice has been raised to claim that Apollo is a light-god.[10]

Farnell based his argument on what he thought were the laws of adjective-formation in Greek. In vol 1 p. 113 he wrote:

> The... theory that derives the word from an assumed form λύκη = "light," which appears in ἀμφιλύκη and λυκάβας, is etymologically unsound. Serious error has arisen both among the older and younger school of mythological inquirers,by ignoring the well-attested law of adjectival formationn by which noun-stems in *o* [*e*] give rise to adjectival forms in *eios* [*ios*] and stems in *a* to forms in aios.

Thus Farnell considers Apollo Lykeios to be a wolf-god, and Zeus Lykaios a light-god,[11] but his conclusion in its turn is "etymologically unsound" as far as Zeus Lykaios is concerned, since Schwyzer has shown that the adjectival ending *-aios* is indeed applied to second declension nouns (stems in *o* [*e*]) outside Attica.[12]

---

[8] In Roscher *Lex.* 2.2175.

[9] Andrew Lang was the standard-bearer of the attack on naturalistic interpretation of mythological data, and his controversy with Max Müller, the outstanding proponent of the solar hypothesis, on this point was once well-known. Lang believed that animals were totems of social groups, and not symbols of natural phenomena. Totemism as a theory is dead today, thanks, by and large, to the structuralist approach of Claude Lévi-Strauss (Chap. 1 n. 92 *supra*) and to Georges Dumézil, but social interpretations are very much alive today.

[10] One exception is Th. Hopfner, *Offenbarungszauber* (Prague 1921) 99, who maintains the old etymology from ἀμφιλύκη and holds to the sun-god theory.

[11] He gives credit for this discovery to W. Robertson Smith in his article "Sacrifice" in the *Encyclopedia Britannica* (ninth edition).

[12] E. Schwyzer, *Griechische Grammatik* (Munich 1939) 1.467: "Auch zu o-Stämmen kann *aios* treten: ion. ὀδαῖος (Od.) zu ὀδός f.; ἰσαῖος σκοταῖος (wie κνεφαῖος) u.a. lak. συρμαία; anders -aios in (Kose)Namen: Ἀγκαῖος Ἀλδαίη, Εὐφραῖος, Ὀρθαῖος, Πτολεμαῖος" and he refers to Jacobsohn, *Zeitschrift für vergleichende Sprachforschung auf dem Gebiete der Indogermanischen Sprachen* 42.264ff., and to Bechtel *Dial.* 2,82 and 3.104. Indeed, Plut.

Nevertheless, as far as Apollo Lykeios is concerned, Farnell's argument is sound; for the ending *-eios* is not applied to *a* stems in Greek, and so Lykeios can not by any means be a light-epithet. There is no doubt that the epithets of Apollo from the root *lyk-* are derived from the name of the wolf, and not from a root meaning "light."[13] .

Quaest. Rom. 280c uses the term Λύκαια as a translation of the Latin *Lupercalia* with the meaning "wolf-festival."

[13] This view was propounded with certainty by M.W. Nilsson, *Gesch. d. gr. Rel.*[2] (München 1961) 536ff. Nevertheless, the controversy concerning the derivation of Lykeios, whether from the roor meaning "wolf," or from that meaning "light," persisted well into this century on regard to the Homeric word λύσσα, "wolfish rage," according to the literature on the word collected in Bruce Lincoln, *op. cit.* (Chap. 7 n. 47 *supra*) 80. He cites Wilhelm Havers, "Geister und Dämonenglaube," *Die Sprache* 4 (1958) as the most recent proponent of the theory that this word, found in *Il.* 9.239, 9.305, and 21.542, is from the root of the word λευκός, "white." Lincoln shows conclusively that it is derived from λύκος "wolf."

Appendix B

THE TRIAL OF OLD THIES, 1691

[p.203] In the matter of lycanthropy and other forbidden and obscene deeds. Judges present: Mr. Assessor Bengt Johan Ackerstaff; as substitute assizes judge Mr. Assessor Gabriel Berger.

When Peter, the innkeeper of Kaltenbrunn, smiled at the conclusion of his testimony, he was asked why he did so.

His answer: Because he saw his tenant, old Thies, would be called on to take the oath as well.

Question: Why should he not be just as willing as you to be put to the proof of the oath concerning his testimony in the matter of the theft from the church?

Answer: Well, everyone knew that he had dealings with the Devil, and was a werewolf. How then could he swear, since he could not deny these things, and he had been such for many long years?

Hence when Thies was called to the stand to give his testimony in the affair, after the other witnesses had been heard, these charges were put to him, and he quite freely admitted that he had been a werewolf previously, but had given it up in the course of time, that is some ten years before. He further informed the judges that he had once before appeared in court at Nitau, when Baron Crohnstern and Messrs. Rosenthal and Caulich were still the judges, at which time Skeistan, a farmer of Lemburg, no longer alive, had split his nose in two with a blow because the witness had removed ears of grain which Skeistan had swept into a cave to keep from sprouting. The judges at that time, named above, however, took no measures against him, but rather laughed and set him free, because Skeistan did not put in an appearance.

At this inquiry was made, before further questioning, as to whether Thies had always been of sane and healthy mind, and not at some time or at present crazy in his head, whereupon, in addition to the other people present who knew Thies well, the substitute assizes judge Mr. Bengt Johan Ackerstaff, at whose estate he had lived and served for a number of years some time ago, declared that he had never been lacking in healthy understanding; he had never denied his conduct and had been freer in his actions after nothing had been done to him on that account by the former judges, and was idolized by the farmers.

He was questioned about these things: At what spot had Skeistan given him the blow and with what instrument?

Answer: In the cave, with a broomstick to which a lot of horses' tails were tied. — The chief judge deposed that Thies's nose had been injured on that occasion.

Question: How had the witness come to the cave, and where was it located?

Answer: The werewolves went there on foot in the shape of wolves. The location was at the end of the lake called Puer Esser, in the bog below Lemburg, about half a mile from Klingenberg, the estate of the substitute assizes judge; there were wonderful chambers there and appointed doorkeepers who repulsed any who wished again to carry off the sprouted grain that had been brought there by the sorcerers, and the unsprouted grain. The sprouted grain was kept in one special store and the unsprouted grain in another.

Question: What shape did they assume when they changed into wolves?

Answer: They had a wolfskin that they put on, and he had been brought one by a farmer of Marienburg who had come from Riga, but had given it over to a farmer from

Alla some years before. When questioned he would not give either of their names, and when a more special inquiry was made he changed his tale and asserted that they simply went off into the woods, took off their usual clothing, and became wolves at once. Then they ran around as wolves and tore any horses or livestock they met with to pieces. The witness however had not torn any kine to bits, but only lambs, kids, pigs, and such, though there had been a fellow in the neighborhood of Segewold, no longer alive, from Tirummen's place, a fine fellow and the witness had nothing against him—after all one person was given more strength by the Devil than another—, who used to carry off any large cattle he came upon, and fatted porkers as well, bring them to the servants' quarters, and eat them up with his mates, since often twenty or thirty of them would go around together and eat a whole lot; they would have their meal on the road and roast it.

Question: Where did they get fire and utensils for that?

Answer: They took fire from the servants' quarters, and made spits of wood. Pots they took from the servants' quarters, and they singed away the hairs and ate nothing raw.

Question: Had the witness often taken part in such meals and feasts?

Answer: Yes. How could it be otherwise?

Question: What happened to the smaller livestock he had taken?

Answer: They had eaten them up too.

Question: If they were transformed into wolves, why had they not eaten the meat raw, like wolves?

Answer: That wasn't their way; instead they ate it like human beings, roasted.

Question: How could they manage it if they had wolves' heads and feet, as he had said they did, and could not hold a knife or prepare a spit or do the rest of the work needed?

Answer: They didn't need any knives for it, because they tore the meat with their teeth and stuck the pieces on whatever sticks they found with their feet, and when they ate it they were like people once again, except that they did not use bread; they took salt with them from the servants' quarters when they went out.

Question: Did they fill themselves up on it, and did the Devil eat with them? Answer: He said yes to the former and no to the latter. But the sorcerers ate with the Devil in the Hell-hole cave; the werewolves were not allowed to join but rushed in from time to time, snatched something, and ran out again with it, as if running away. If caught, the Devil's guards stationed there would beat them off furiously with a long iron whip which they called the switch and drive them out like dogs, because the Devil, in the Lettish language "Ne eretz," could not bear them. Question: If the Devil could not bear them, why did they become werewolves and run to the Hell-hole cave?

Answer: They did this so that they might be able to carry what the sorcerers had brought in by way of livestock, grain, and other growing things off out of the Hell-hole cave; for, last year, he came late along with the others and did not arrive at the Hell-hole cave in time, so that they could not carry off the sprouts and the grain brought there by the sorcerers while as the gates were still open, and we had a bad year for grain. This year, though, he and the others had arrived in time and had done their duty; the witness himself had carried off as much barley, oats, and rye as he could, out of the Hell-hole cave, so that we should have plenty of all kinds of grain this year, though more oats than barley.

Question: When did all this take place?

Answer: The eve of St. Lucy's before Christmas.

Question: How many times in the year did they come together in the cave?

Answer: Ordinarily three times: Whitsunday eve, the eve of St. John's day, and St. Lucy's eve; as far as the first two are concerned, it was not always the same night, but when the grain was in its prime and at the time of sowing the sorcerers carried off the gift of blessing and brought it to the Hell-hole cave while the werewolves got ready to bring it out once again.

Question: Who was with him in the company last Lucy's eve?

Answer: They had assembled out of many places, from the regions of Rodenpei and of Sunßel, and who knew them all and asked their names? There were different bands, and Skeistan Rein, the son of the Skeistan mentioned before, had belonged to his band before, but he had not seen him recently and did not know how it turned out. When he was asked about the people from Jürgensburg he said that the people from Jürgensburg must belong to another band, since none of them were in his.

Question: How could the witness say that they had already carried the blessing out of the Hell-hole cave, where it was brought by the sorcerers, last Lucy's eve, before the time of sowing or the time the grain is ready for reaping, so that nothing of the sort could have been accomplished?

Answer: The sorcerers had their special time and the Devil had done his sowing long ago. That was where the sorcerers got some and brought it into the Hell-hole cave, and that was the blessed gift the werewolves carried away with them out of the Hell-hole cave, and in consequence the success of our sowing would ensue, as well as of fruit-trees, of which there were many in the Hell-hole cave too, and of fisheries. At Christmas all sorts of grain were already full-grown in the Hell-hole cave, and trees too were growing there. Since for the most part they had carried off the fish the sorcerers had brought there last Lucy's eve as well, this year there were hopes of a better year for fishing. Still the sorcerers would take grain that had not yet sprouted, and bring it to the Hell-hole cave, but they could not do so much with it as with seed sown and grown in the Hell-hole cave.

Question: Was that sort of cultivation always in the Hell-hole cave, the other times they came there too, and was it there all the time? He said yes.

Question: How come other people who lived in the neighborhood could not see it too?

Answer: It was not on the ground but underneath it, and the entrance was guarded by a gate no one could find unless he belonged there.

Question: Were there not women and girls among the werewolves too, and Germans too among them?

Answer: There were indeed women among the werewolves, but girls were not taken in, but used as flying pucks or dragons, and so sent away to carry off the gift of divine favor for the milk and the butter. The Germans did not participate in their community, but had a different Hell-hole of their own.

Question: Where did the werewolves go after they died?

Answer: They were buried like other people, and their souls went to heaven, but the Devil took the sorcerers' souls to himself.

Question: Did the witness support the church diligently, listen to God's word with attention, pray diligently and support the holy Mass? He said, "No, he did neither the one nor the other."

Question: How then could his soul come to God, if he neither served God, but rather the Devil, nor went to church, much less partook of confession or Mass, as the witness himself confirmed?

Answer: The werewolves did not serve the Devil, but rather carried off what the sorcerers brought him. This was the reason the Devil was so hostile towards them that he could not bear them, but had them driven out with iron whips like dogs; for they were the hounds of God, but the sorcerers served the Devil and followed his will in all things, so that their souls belonged to him as well. Everything the werewolves did was for the benefit of mankind; for if they were not there to rob or steal the stolen blessing back again, all blessings would be gone from the world. He affirmed this under oath, adding that last year the Russian werewolves had come first and carried off their country's blessing, which is why they had a good harvest in their country, something we lacked in this country because on this side they came too late, as we said. But this year they got there before the Russians and it would be a good year, for flax too. Why then shouldn't God take his soul even though he did not go to church or partake of Mass? He had never been taken or taught to go when he was a child, but otherwise he had not done anything wrong either.

He was swiftly and diligently reproved, and edified: —

Question: Was it not evildoing not only for him to have stolen his neighbors' livestock, as he himself had confessed, but most particularly for him to have changed and corrupted the image of God in which he was created from that of a man into a wolf, as he imagined, and thus, forgetting God, to have broken the vow he made to Christ, his redeemer, in holy baptism, when he renounced the Devil and his nature and all his works; to have persisted so in committing such extremely heinous sins to the disgust and irritation of other people; not to have betaken himself to the house of God where he might have acquired knowledge and come to serve God through the sermon and the Christian doctrine, but rather to have gone running off to the Hell-hole cave, while the Pastor went round to the servants' quarters and exhorted people to come pray and to go to church and let themselves be instructed diligently?

Answer: He had done little harm to livestock; others had done much more. It was true the Pastor went round to the servants' quarters, taught them and prayed with them, and the witness had indeed repeated the prayers the Pastor had dictated to him, but since he was so set in his ways he could no longer free himself of them nor could he begin to learn this sort of thing for the first time at his age.

Question: How old was he and where was he born?

Answer: When the Swedes took Riga (1621, seventy years before) he already knew how to hoe and plow. He was a Courlander by birth.

Question: If he was at the Hell-hole cave last Lucy's eve with all the rest, why did he allege before that he had given his wolf's costume to a farmer from Alla long ago?

Answer: In that particular he had not been speaking the truth, but now he wished to change his ways, because he no longer had any strength; he was old.

Question: What advantage had he derived from being a werewolf, since to all appearances he was a beggar and completely destitute?

Answer: None. A scoundrel from Marienburg had brought it on him by drinking a toast to him, and from that time onward he had had to conduct himself just like any other werewolf.

Question: Did they receive no sign from the Devil, by which he might know them?

Answer: He said no. But he marked the sorcerers and treated them to dead horses' heads, toads, snakes, and similar vermin, with which he fed them.

Question: Since he was so old and weak that he might expect to die any day, did he wish to die a werewolf?

Answer: No, he wished to initiate someone else before he died, anyone he could.[1]

Question: How was he going to initiate someone else?

---

[1] By finding a replacement for himself, he might free himself from the obligations of being a werewolf.

138

Answer: He would do what had been done to him. He need only drink one toast to someone, breathe into the mug three times and say: "You will be like me." Then, if the other fellow took the mug from him he would receive it and the witness would be free of it.

Question: Didn't he think that was a sin too, and a false phantasm of the Devil? He could not initiate anyone unless the other fellow, like him, was ignorant of God and did it willingly.

Answer: Truly he could not initiate anyone unless he agreed and showed a desire for it, like all the people who had already approached him to ask if he would leave it to them, since he was old and destitute.

Question: Who were those people who had spoken to him about it?

Answer: They were far away, some on the Judge's estate and others below Sunßel, and he did not know their names.

Question: When the witness and others had turned into that sort of wolf, and were in the shape of wolves, weren't they ever attacked by dogs or shot at by guards, especially since the witness said there were large, ferocious hounds at the gate of the Hell-hole cave?

Answer: They could easily get away from the hounds, but they were liable to be shot by the guards, if they could hit them; the hounds of the Hell-hole cave did not harm them.

Question: According to the story he told, that fellow of Segewold, from Tirummen's place, even used to go into farmyards, and carry off fatted porkers; but all the farmyards had dogs. Wasn't he ever attacked or even bitten?

Answer: The dogs were really always aware of them, but even when the dogs were alerted they could not catch the werewolves. They ran much too fast for them. But Tirummen['s man][2] was a really bad fellow, and had done people much harm. That was why God had let him die young. When asked where his soul was now, he said he did not know if someone like him had been taken by God or by the Devil.

Question: Where did they leave the grain and tree saplings and the other things they took from the Devil, and what did they do with them?

Answer: They threw them up into the air, and the blessing rained down over the whole country out of the air again for both rich and poor.

At this they spoke to him with emotion, and it was put to him that all this was nothing but devilish delusion and trickery, which he could tell, among other things, from the fact that people who lost livestock and fatted porkers this way never failed to track them down and find the traces of fatted porkers, especially, and where they had been roasted and eaten.

Answer: They did not steal in the neighborhood, but only far away; and who could track them down?

Question: How was it possible that one of them could carry off fatted porkers and great horned livestock, like a wolf, and in wolf's shape, from twenty, thirty miles or more away through bush and bracken, and in fact all the way from Estonia, and bring them here, as the witness asserted? All the more reason to conclude it all was nothing but imagination, false trickery and delusion.

Answer: He stuck to his story. It really happened that way and Tirummen's man often spent a week at a time out of doors, and then the witness and his band would wait for him, as they had agreed, in the bushes, and if he brought a fatted porker or so would eat it with him. Meanwhile they would live on hares and other wild animals in

[2] This is the true reading for "Tirummen."

the bush. Now the witness was no longer strong enough to run so far and catch or fetch anything, but he still could get as much fish as he wanted, and even when others came home emptyhanded he was exceptionally successful in his fishing.

Question: Did he not intend to turn to God before he died and agree, of his own free will, to be taught to put away this devilish monstrosity, to repent his sins, and so to save his soul from eternal damnation and the pain of Hell?

To this he refused to answer at once but asked, "Who knows where my soul will go?" He was old. "How can I understand these things now?"

Finally, after he had been admonished harshly many times, he stated he was willing to give it all up and turn to God.

Appendix C

LYKOS AND LYKEIOS: NOTES TOWARD A THEORY OF THE FORMS OF ANCIENT INDO-EUROPEAN RELIGIOSITY

If Lykeios is Apollo, first and foremost, we should now be able to understand the relationship between him and the figure of Lykos, whom we have seen identified with Dionysos in Delphi. We have seen in Chap. 4 *supra* that divine twins are associated with the wolf complex; the story of Romulus and Remus brought up by the she-wolf is typical of this group. Now we may be able to distinguish between the official adoption of certain aspects of wolf-ideology in the Apollo-cult of the ephebes at Athens and the underground survival of other aspects among the werewolves of ancient Athens, and elsewhere in Greece. Even at this stage we can see clearly that the werewolves were never received back into society fully, at least during their lifetime. They may have maintained to the end an ideology abandoned in the official forms that bore a variant of the wolf-name.

What is the relation between Lykeios and Lykos? Divine twins can appear in each of the three functions documented for ancient Indo-European society by Dumézil. For example, Ward[1] writes that according to Wikander[2] one of the twins belongs to the third function (this he infers from the attributes of Zēthos, the herdsman and, later, the supplier of stones for his brother's construction effort, *inter alia*) while the other belongs to the warrior, i.e. second, function. On the other hand the twins bear clear first function roles too; "the first function of the Indo-European tripartite system consists, according to Dumézil, of a dual structure, and is ruled by a closely associated pair of gods"[3] and so we find twin kingship in Sparta as well as among the Germanic deities Oðinn and Týr, of whom the latter is *le dieu manchot*, i. e. one-armed, like the Spartan Lykurgos. Of the two first function Indo-European divinities, one is the magical lord of the world, whose attributes include heavenly signs and omens, as well as the other appurtenances of prophecy, while the other is concerned with law and order in the world. Most important for us, as we have seen in the Epilogue *supra* (esp. n. 5), there are two aspects of the warrior function as well; perhaps the two warriors may be viewed as twins as well.

We have seen that like the divine twins, so too the wind, or spirit, part of the wider context of the wolf-name, can appear in each of the three functions documented for ancient Indo-European society by Dumézil; for wind associated with the prophetic spirit, as in the Greek fable about the Pythia inhaling vapors from the earth, belongs to the first function, whereas wind associated with the martial spirit, and with the wolf-name, as in the case of the Iranian Sakā Haomavargā, and of many other peoples bearing wolf-names who settled near sinkholes or sources of gaseous emissions from the earth, to the second, while the wind that brings the rain belongs to the third function, as most likely do sinkholes and sources of gaseous emissions from the earth as well. This wind comes from beneath the earth like the mouse and the wolf, has the power to coax

---

[1] Donald Ward, *The Divine Twins: An Indoeuropean Myth in Germanic Tradition* (Folklore Studies 19, University of California Press: Berkeley and Los Angeles 1968) 21.

[2] Stig Wikander, "Nakula et Sahadeva," *Orientalia Suecana* 6 (1957) 66-96, esp. p. 81.

[3] Ward *op. cit.* (n. 1 *supra*) 31.

forth the grain out of the earth, and can be recognized as the impregnating wind of the Semites according to William Robertson Smith.[4]

Where exactly then are we to locate this complex that seems to encompass all of ancient Indo-European society in terms of the ancient ideology Dumézil speaks of, in order to achieve a final comprehensive view of the wider context of the wolf-name? *In the Dumézilian schema the task of embracing the first two functions as their synthesis is traditionally relegated to the third function.*[5] No doubt that is the reason Mannhardt found the ancient wind-wolf's chief and latest trace in the agricultural sphere in the Teutonic and Romance linguistic areas. Yet Apollo seems first and foremost to have been the god of the ephebes, the young warriors, in classical antiquity, despite the fact that he is the god of prophecy, a first function role, and has third function agricultural functions as well. Thus he is anchored in the second function; and, indeed, his troubles with Admetus (a father figure) with Hyakinthos (a friend) and with Daphne (his beloved), show he conforms to Dumézil's typical second function hero-type,[6] and yet his influence permeates all the functions. Such a set-up may well reflect the primacy of the warrior in the Indo-European society of the ancient conquerors of the peoples of Old Europe who dwelt in Greece, the forefathers of the Hellenes; it may go far to explain why wolf-names are so common as tribal appellations in and around Greece.

The killing of the monster provides another key to the relation between the three trifunctional complexes of wind, wolf, and twins, and casts further light on the figure of Apollo. Ward[7] contends that the Teutonic dragon-slayer Wolfdieterich, named for the wolf, was originally a twin, i. e. a Dioscuric figure.[8] Part of the myth of the Dioscuri, Kastor and Polydeukes, is that the twins ride on the wind on their horses, and so fly through the air, a feature we have seen belongs to the wider context of the wolf-name. Monster-killing also pertains to all three Dumézilian functions; it is the prerogative of the paragon, (1) the king, the one blessed with divine aid and knowledge (Perseus) who is also (2) a warrior, and its direct result is often (3) the opening of the blocked up passages, a work attributed to the wolf endowed with the power of enhancing agricultural prosperity.

From such indications we are led to inquire whether Dionysos and Apollo might not also be viewed as Dioscuric figures. We have noted *supra* the parallel between the figures of Lykeios (Apollo) and Lykos (Dionysos); for, granted that Apollo is primarily the ephebic god, the Lykeios-name in Greece must have been as much associated with agriculture as *Wolf* is in the Germanic linguistic area. Apollo, on the other hand, is also the divinity who guides the young ephebes even after they marry and become hoplites, i. e. enter the ranks of the third function, when they become those who have Lykos, the dead Dionysos, god of wild abandon and enthusiasm, buried within their hearts, ready to burst forth renascent at the

---

[4] *The Religion of the Semites: The Fundamental Institutions* (New York: Meridian Books 1956) cf. 135: "mephitic vapours...potent spiritual influences."

[5] This is a paraphrase of G. Freibergs, C.S. Littleton, and Udo Strutynski, "Indo-European Tripartition and the Ara Pacis Augustae: An Excursus in Ideological Archaeology" *Numen* 32 (1986), 29.

[6] Georges Dumézil, *The Destiny of the Warrior* (Chicago 1970) 53-107.

[7] Ward *op. cit.* (n. 1 *supra*) 74.

[8] He adduces this from Karl Müllenhoff "Excurse zur deutschen Heldensage," *Zeitschrift für deutsches Altertum* 12 (1865) 346-354.

appropriate time in battle. Here we have another example and a further corroboration of the surmise that the third function traditionally embraced the first two functions as their synthesis.

In the motif of the identity of the attacker and the attacked we rediscover the attempt to merge a dualistic conception of society and the world in a monistic one;[9] an important facet of the warrior function is the appearance of the same figure as the pursued and the pursuer at once, the coexistence of the active and the passive. So we find in Greece that the goddess Artemis, who we have seen as the goddess of the Wild Hunt in Greece, and who, we must not forget, also bears the epithet Lykeia, is at once the persecuting deity who takes the lives of women who die in childbirth, and at the same time, the Hanged Goddess in the person of Artemis ἀπαγχομένη.[10] She is identified with her human victims in the case of Iphigeneia; for Artemis Iphigeneia was worshipped at Brauron in Attika, as a goddess who helps and saves women in childbirth.[11] The same relation holds between Poseidon and Erechtheus, and between Perseus and Dionysos. Poseidon was identified with Erechtheus, who even received sacrifice at Athens on the altar of Poseidon in the Erechtheion;[12] but the myth tells how Erechtheus was slain by Poseidon in revenge for his having killed a son of the sea-god.[13] In the case of Perseus and Dionysos, the same reversal of rôle is found: Perseus the monster-killer pursues Dionysos, who appears as the monster also in the Delphic context, as we have noted, and in the Orphic tradition as Dionysos Zagreus torn to bits in the *sparagmos*, but Perseus also appears as the one who emerges from the sea, like Dionysos himself, when Akrisios locked him and his mother Danae into a chest (λάρναξ), and set them afloat upon the sea (in a Dionysiac context); and this is the context in which we can understand the Orphic paradox of the vegetarian hunter.[14]

The same relation holds in the story of Atalanta who killed the Kalydonian boar sent by Artemis,[15] although Atalanta was a priestess of that goddess.[16] She had been suckled by a she-bear sent by Artemis when she was exposed as a baby, and when she was thirsty in the waterless region of Kyphata, Artemis caused water to gush forth for her out of the ground. The same rôle reappears in the personage of Orestes in the Anthesteria festival at Athens. There he is the criminal welcomed back into society by the rite of drinking wine together at the festival.[17] Hence in numerous places on Greek myth we find an ambivalent attitude between the patron and his client whether animal or human; they are antagonists at times, and at other times they function in unison.[18] In the confusion of the attacker and the attacked a

---

[9] On the attempt v. Chap. 7 n. 31 p.124 *supra*, on innovative surmounting of the divisive tendencies of the wolf-name, and n. 19 *infra*.

[10] Artemis Kondyleatis, Paus. 8.23.6.

[11] John Papadimitriou, "The Sanctuary of Artemis at Brauron," *Scientific American* (June 1963) 110-120, esp. 112-113 and 116.

[12] Paus. 1.26.5; *IG* 1.387 and 3.805.

[13] Poseidon destroys all Erechtheus' house: Apollod. 2.204. Erechtheus was said to have killed Eumolpos son of Poseidon (V. Escher *s.v. Erechtheus* PWRE 6.1 (Stuttgart 1907) cols. 404-411).

[14] Propounded so beautifully by Karl Kerényi, *Pythagoras und Orpheus* (Berlin 1938).

[15] Paus. 8.45.2 *et al.*

[16] Σ Aesch. *Seven* 532.

[17] Cf. Aesch. *Eum.* 727-728 and 754-777.

[18] The case of Asklepios (on whom v. Chap. 2 p. 30ff. *supra*) belongs here too. It parallels

dualistic conception of society and the world is merged in a monistic one, just as the third function can be a synthesis of the characteristics of the other two.[19]

Philostephanos of Kyrene bears witness to the existence of werewolves in Athens, a fact unknown to other sources. He writes of murdering werewolves, and of their burial, things that point to their equivocal legal status. The end of Athamas' story, too, shows werewolves as fugitives from society, anti-social beings. On the other hand, ephebes were sent out of Athenian society to undergo difficult trials on the frontier, only to be received back again as adult members of society. This is another example of a dualistic conception being merged in a monistic one; the werewolves maintained the dualistic conception, and the original hostility to the rules of organized society, to the end, inasmuch as they could never be received back into society fully, as were the ephebes. From the comparative evidence we have marshalled in Chap. 6 *supra* we can be sure that the werewolves lived off the rapine of peaceful citizens, and probably believed they benefitted society thereby.

The two variations of the wolf-name designated two separate strands in Greece: one, the official wolf-confraternities surviving in the official ephebic training of the youths of Athens, for example, and the other some criminal elements reflecting different ideologies. The difference between them may be seen also in mythology, in the history of the god Dionysus who appears also as Lykos. Lykos' fate is to die, like a criminal werewolf, whereas his killer Lykeios, who is Apollo, is able ultimately to overcome the symbolic death of adolescent initiation and enter the adult world of production. Here we may see in action the ideal correspondence between social function and myth.

Long ago Usener pointed out that the relationships between Melanthos and Xanthos, Hippōtēs and Karnos, and Achilles and Tennes, are reflexes of one tale.[20] For him this tale was the alternation of light and darkness in nature; Pierre Vidal-Naquet has shown rather, at least for the first of these alternations that it involves the struggle between age-classes and the initiation of young warriors into the ranks of adult warriors. The wind-wolf is involved in this confrontation as well, because the myth that pictures Apollo, the god of the mature and reasoned warrior, subjugating and controlling the high spirits and ravenous appetites of the young, represented by Dionysos, is present in the relationship of Apollo and Lykos, at Delphi, where the grave of Lykos is found in the precinct of Apollo. This may be the prototype of the alternation of the victorious warrior and his unfortunate mate, his victim, so that we may perhaps add Apollo and Hyakinthos and Achilles and Telephos to Usener's list as well.

Artemis ἀπαγχομένη; for his death by lightning is recorded in Philod. περὶ εὐσεβ. p. 52 Gomp., as well as in Apollod. 3.10.3 and S.E. *M.* 1.260, while he is said to have resurrected the dead in Pind. *Pyth.* 3.96 and Aesch. *Ag.* 1022 *inter al.* He is therefore the wounded healer, to borrow a term from Christian pastoral psychology (Cf. H.J. Nouwen, *The Wounded Healer* [1972]) and in the study of Asiatic shamanism in anthropology (Cf. the publication with the same name: Halifax 1982).

[19] On the attempt to merge a dualistic conception of society and the world in a monistic one, cf. P. Duchesne-Guillemin, *The Western Response to Zoroaster*, Ratanbei Katrek Lectures 1956 (Oxford, Clarendon Press 1958), quoted in Mary Douglas, *Natural Symbols* (New York 1973) 71-72, and esp. Helmut Waldmann, *Heilsgeschichtlich verfaßte Theologie und Männerbünde* (2 vols., Thesis Tübingen 1983).

[20] Hermann Usener, *Sintfluthsagen* (Bonn 1899) 95. Cf. on this also the end of Chap. 4 *supra*.

Subject Index

Index of Authors

Greek Index

..

156

ACKNOWLEDGEMENTS

I first undertook this study upon the prompting of Anne Thomas, and it is to her that I am indebted for the original insight upon which the rest is built. Of the others who have aided me in the research presented here I wish especially to express my thanks to Professors Otto von Sadovszky, Helen Bacon, Gerson D. Cohen, Marija Gimbutas, Atsuhiko Yoshida, Jacqueline de Romilly, Jaan Puhvel, Julia W. Loomis, Michael Moerman, Udo Strutynski, and Pierre Vidal-Naquet, to Drs. Helmut Waldmann, Rodney T. Cox and Chana B. Cox, and to Cyril Glasse and Robert L. Flye. I also wish to acknowledge my indebtedness to my colleagues in the Department of Classical Studies at Tel-Aviv University, most especially to Professors John Glucker and Israel Roll, among to the many others whose suggestions and aid have stood me in good stead over the years.

I have dedicated this study to my wife Hanna, whose patience and encouragement have allowed me to bring this study to completion; I also wish to thank my children, Rachel, Navah, David, and Jane (Haggith) for bearing with me so long.

Abbreviations

CPG: Leutsch-Schneidewin, *Corpus Paroemiographorum Graecorum*.

FGrH Jacoby *Fragmente der griechischen Historiker*.

M.-W.: Merkelbach and West, *Hesiodi Fragmenta*.

PWRE: Pauly, Wissowa and Kroll, edd., *Realenzylopädie der klassischen Altertumswissenschaft* (Stuttgart).

Σ: Scholiast to (i.e. ancient or medieval notes written in the margin of a manuscript).

The names of ancient authors and works are abbreviated as in the *Greek-English Dictionary* of Liddell, Scott and Jones, and of modern journals in the field of classical studies as in *L'Année Philologique*.

Note on Transliteration

I have used the following system of transliteration for Greek names, except in a few cases where common English names are given:

α = a	φ = ph
β = b	χ = ch
γ = g	ψ = ps
δ = d	ω = ō and
ε = e	ου = u
ζ = z	
η = ē	
θ = th	
ι = i	
κ = k	
λ = l	
μ = m	
ν = n	
ξ = x	
ο = o	
π = p	
ρ = r	
σ, ς = s	
τ = t	
υ = y	